W9-BZY-903

What Happened *to* Paula

What Happened *to* Paula

On the Death of an American Girl

Katherine Dykstra

W. W. NORTON & COMPANY

Independent Publishers Since 1923

For information about permission to reproduce selections from this book,
write to Permissions, W. W. Norton & Company, Inc.,
500 Fifth Avenue, New York, NY 10110

For information about special discounts for bulk purchases, please contact
W. W. Norton Special Sales at specialsales@wwnorton.com or 800-233-4830

Manufacturing by Lake Book Manufacturing
Book design by Lisa Buckley Design
Production manager: Lauren Abbate

Library of Congress Cataloging-in-Publication Data

Names: Dykstra, Katherine, author.
Title: What happened to Paula : on the death of an American girl /
    Katherine Dykstra.
Description: First edition. | New York : W. W. Norton & Company, [2021] |
    Includes bibliographical references.
Identifiers: LCCN 2020053663 | ISBN 9780393651980 (hardcover) |
    ISBN 9780393651997 (epub)
Subjects: LCSH: Oberbroeckling, Paula, –1970. | Murder—Iowa—Cedar
    Rapids—Case studies. | Cold cases (Criminal investigation)—Iowa—
    Cedar Rapids—Case studies. | Young women—Iowa—Cedar Rapids—
    Social conditions—20th century. | Pregnant teenagers—Iowa—Cedar
    Rapids—Social conditions—20th century.
Classification: LCC HV6534.C315 D95 2021 | DDC
    363.25/95230977762—dc23
LC record available at https://lccn.loc.gov/2020053663

W. W. Norton & Company, Inc., 500 Fifth Avenue, New York, N.Y. 10110
www.wwnorton.com

W. W. Norton & Company Ltd., 15 Carlisle Street, London W1D 3BS

1 2 3 4 5 6 7 8 9 0

For my children. For the Paulas.

If no one is guilty, then everyone's to blame.

—*Susan Taylor Chehak*

Contents

Preface   xi

Chapter 1 • The Crime   1

Chapter 2 • An Inheritance   15

Chapter 3 • The Girl   29

Chapter 4 • Her Birthright   47

Chapter 5 • Her Coming of Age   63

Chapter 6 • The Black Boyfriend   79

Chapter 7 • The Detective   96

Chapter 8 • The City   116

Chapter 9 • The White Boyfriend   125

Chapter 10 • The Timeline   142

Chapter 11 • The Flood   154

Chapter 12 • The Double Bind   169

Chapter 13 • Her Options   185

Chapter 14 • The Phone Call   205

Chapter 15 • The True Crime   225

Chapter 16 • The Paulas   244

Afterword   255

Acknowledgments   267

Notes   271

Selected Readings   287

Preface

UNDER A WASHED-OUT WINTER SKY, I STEERED A rented car away from downtown Cedar Rapids, Iowa. My travel companion was my mother-in-law, the fiction writer Susan Taylor Chehak. Our destination: a slip of land that spooned the Cedar River. The area was just outside the city proper but felt otherworldly—barren, desolate, removed. Heading south on Otis Road, the river lazed flat and gray on our right, the Chicago & North Western railroad tracks ran silver on our left. Beyond them, Van Vechten Park's wooded darkness stretched up a steep hill. We passed a giant smoking factory, a cold freight train heavy on its track, and a handful of Canadian geese who'd never made it south for the winter.

When Susan indicated, I pulled off onto Miller Lane, a narrow gravel drive that jutted up from Otis, thus far the byway's only interruption. I stepped out of the car into the bitter air and followed Susan through the snow, which came up over my shoes. After intersecting with the railroad tracks, the drive continued under a gate and up through private property until it dead-ended in a horse farm on the hill. "Private Drive" and "No Trespassing" signs were nailed to trees and staked into the ground before it. We turned right at the tracks, trudging over the ties for about twenty paces until Susan stopped abruptly, turning toward the river. "Here," she said.

Across the Cedar lay Mount Trashmore, the city's landfill. The puffing stacks of the Cargill cereal plant loomed in the distance. At my feet, I found a rocky crevice that sloped back down toward Otis. And there, sticking out amid a cascade of steel-gray rocks, was the culvert. A culvert is a pipe that diverts rainwater under railroad tracks in order to prevent their flooding; I had gone my whole life and had never encountered the word, but now it was everywhere. That's where Paula Jean Oberbroeckling's body had been found, just beyond the mouth of this culvert.

Paula was eighteen years old when she disappeared in the summer of 1970. It's been fifty years, and her killing has never been solved.

In the summer of 2008, seven years before I looked down into that culvert, I tagged along with my then boyfriend and his family to Cedar Rapids, where the goal was to shoot footage for a documentary film about Paula. Susan, my boyfriend's mother, had attended the same high school as Paula. The two never overlapped, missing each other by a year, but in adulthood Susan had become fixated on Paula's story, filled as it was with conflicting narratives and unreliable narrators, with hearsay and speculation. Paula's was the story of a small city and small-city police, of disappointment and squandered potential, of race and class and sex. A story that became more complex the deeper one dug. A story all the more compelling for the fact that it had been mostly forgotten even though the case still yawned wide open. Susan was haunted by its lack of resolution.

The documentary was a family affair—my boyfriend, who

at the time had just gotten a foothold in the film world, was the producer; his father, a longtime television showrunner, was the executive producer; and his brother, an art photographer, handled sound. They enlisted a director they'd worked with in the past, and the director brought on a cinematographer. The entire endeavor was spearheaded by Susan.

She secured interviews with Paula's family—her mother, her sister, one of her three brothers—with her friends, with a number of the detectives who worked on Paula's case. She scheduled meetings with Paula's boyfriends. She made maps of the routes taken by key players on the night of Paula's disappearance, and lists of relevant landmarks.

During the lead-up to the trip, Susan asked if I was interested in helping out with the film. As a journalist, I was equipped to conduct interviews or brainstorm lines of inquiry. But I had no interest in considering the grisly death of a young woman. It frightened me.

I was thirty-one in 2008 and in a stretch of my life I now think of as "before," by which I mean before marriage, before children, and before everything that comes tethered to being responsible for the lives of others. Basically, I was in a time of my life that was easy—I was in love, and I had a raft of writing and editing jobs that kept me afloat and afforded me the lease on my small Brooklyn apartment. But even more, I had the extreme privilege of not *having* to complicate that ease with the sticky web of real life.

It wouldn't be until "after"—marriage, children—that my life, specifically my life as a woman, would kaleidoscope, appearing so differently that not only would I agree to involve myself in the story of this young woman's death but I'd find myself unable not to, convinced as I was that I owed her.

That decision would lead me down a long and circuitous

path that began with the arrogant certainty that I could solve Paula's death when others had not and evolved into a different goal. For, over the course of the years I spent researching and writing Paula's story, it dawned on me that what I wanted to say about her death was less true crime and more sociological study. Meaning, though a girl had been killed, and though the details of her disappearance and death are important and will be included in the pages of this book, this is not about a murderer. I do not know who killed Paula Oberbroeckling. What I do know is that the onus of her death extends well beyond whoever dumped her body down that hill.

This is the story of the grave injustice served one girl and all the factors that conspired to allow, even ensure, that injustice. It is about the reasons it was easier for the authorities in Cedar Rapids to forget what happened to Paula than to face it. It is about the ways in which women are the same and how we are different—and the role society played then and plays now in our choices and in our opportunities or lack thereof. It's about legacy and the things that are handed down between women over generations. It's about the women in Paula's family and the women in my own. It's about women who lived in Cedar Rapids in the 1960s and women who also lost mothers, sisters, daughters to violence.

It is infuriating, but maybe it is also hopeful. *My* hope is that by giving Paula voice, by interrogating the generally accepted story of her life and death, by searching for nuance, I might pay my debt not only to her—for showing me that my womanhood is important and powerful and comes with responsibility—but to the long continuum of women before me and to come. To the women who shaped me—my mother, my grandmother, Susan, my friends and mentors—to women I don't even know, and to the one little girl, one day a woman, who, when I began this quest, had yet to be born.

What Happened
to
Paula

Chapter 1

The Crime

THIS IS WHAT IS KNOWN. ON FRIDAY, JULY 10, 1970, AT 9 p.m., Paula Oberbroeckling, fresh out of high school, clocked out of her job in the Misses Sports section of Younkers department store, a regional chain, in Cedar Rapids, Iowa. Stepping out of the fluorescent lighting and into Lindale Plaza's open air, Paula found Lonnie Bell waiting for her. He was leaning against his red 1960 Porsche coupe. Dusk was falling.

Paula, eighteen, slender, and blonde, was easily as tall as Lonnie. Lonnie had sun-kissed skin and slick blond hair that fell to his shoulders. He tended toward tight shirts and faded bell-bottom jeans; he was built like a tongue depressor. Lonnie was twenty-one and had graduated high school a few years before Paula. He was unemployed and lived with his mother and stepfather in a small house on the northeast side of Cedar Rapids. Paula and Lonnie had met a couple of summers before at Henry's Hamburgers, a local drive-in on 1st Avenue where high schoolers hung out on hot afternoons or took pit stops while cruising after dark. But they had been dating only since May after being reintroduced by mutual friends.

Their relationship had started while Paula's on-again, off-again boyfriend, Robert Williams, was out of town. Paula and Lonnie had gone out a handful of times as school wound down. When Robert returned, Paula briefly rekindled with him. Around this time, there was an altercation between the two boys. Fists were thrown, but Robert was unable to convince Paula to stay with him. Paula responded to the fight by vowing to Lonnie that she would leave Robert for good.

As the summer began, Paula and Lonnie spent most nights together. The two hung out and drank Ripple wine or went to dive bars and bought rounds of Budweiser. Paula drank Schlitz or Bacardi rum and Coke. They smoked Marlboros and occasionally Kools. They cruised Cedar Rapids looking for something to do, somewhere to go, someone with whom to hang out.

Waiting with Lonnie outside Lindale Plaza that night was Billy Ben Carroll, a friend of Paula's from high school who went by Ben. Paula and Ben had known each other since freshman year when they attended Regis Catholic High School together. Both later transferred to Washington High, the public school. That night, the three of them, Ben, Lonnie, and Paula, planned to go to the Nowhere Lounge to listen to live music performed by a local band that Ben liked. The evening had been Paula's idea.

In the parking lot, the three briefly discussed logistics. Then Paula folded her long legs into Lonnie's Porsche, and with Ben following in his black-over-bronze Mustang convertible, the party made its way from Lindale Plaza east to the Nowhere. There, Austin & Garf, a band whose music was in the vein of the Byrds and other folk-rock groups of the late 1960s but who never progressed past gigging small stages like the Nowhere,* performed to a dark room of shadowy people.

Lonnie and Ben played pool. Paula chatted with some friends from work. They each had a few beers. Around 11:30 p.m., Paula asked Lonnie and Ben to drive her home. The three got into Ben's car, leaving Lonnie's at the Nowhere, and headed into the darkness. Ben told police later that Lonnie had been "having problems" with his Porsche. He also said that he'd sensed Paula and Lonnie had been fighting.

Paula lived on the white, working-class, northwest side of Cedar Rapids at 116 10th Street in a $10-a-week boardinghouse. She'd been there barely a month, having just moved out of an apartment around the corner from Robert's house after officially breaking things off. On 10th Street, she lived with two other girls, one of whom was Debbie Kellogg, the friend who'd agreed to look for an apartment with Paula when she suddenly needed a place to stay. Debbie was short and boxy with mousy brown hair and wild eyes. She was known mostly for being trouble.

Debbie told police that Paula had seemed upset when she got home that night. She said that she, having just gotten off work herself, had found Paula crying in the den while hanging Simon and Garfunkel posters on the wall. Paula had been listening to the Intruders, a soul group, which Debbie said Paula put on "when she is sad and wants to think about Robert."

Robert had been the reason Paula moved out of her childhood home at eighteen in the first place. The two met at Washington High School. Robert, a star on the basketball team, was handsome, outgoing, and gaga for Paula. He was also Black, a

---

* Austin & Garf recorded a record in 1970, but didn't cut it until 2016. It's called *Mississippi Woman, My Own*.

fact unacceptable to Paula's mother, Carol. Rather than suffer the tension, Paula packed her belongings and left.

That night in July, Debbie chatted with Paula for a little while and then headed to bed. Around 1 a.m., Paula woke Debbie and asked if she could borrow her car, a black 1962 Chevy Nova, promising to put gas in it and that she would only be gone a short time. Debbie agreed. Paula left the house wearing a baby-blue empire-waist dress, which the police file repeatedly refers to as a "nightgown." She wore matching underwear. She wasn't wearing shoes.

Where Paula could have been going dressed in this manner is confounding. Yes, the night was hot; it reached 88 degrees that day. Midwestern summers stifle, the humidity hanging in the air like gauze. And Lynn, Paula's older sister, swore that the girls spent whole summers running around without shoes, that what the police called a nightgown was for sure a dress, a dress Lynn had borrowed and worn herself. One of Paula's friends upheld this, claiming he hung out with Paula once while she was wearing said dress. But something rings false. It was 1 a.m. Either Paula was going directly to someone's house, or she planned on being gone only for a minute, or she left in a big hurry.

Between 9 and 9:30 the following morning, Ben Carroll, who was also employed at Lindale Plaza, left to pick Paula up for work, an arrangement they'd agreed on the night before. En route to her house, he saw and stopped for Robert Williams and two other boys who were hitchhiking home on 1st Avenue after an all-night party at Charles "Butch" Hudson's house. Ben told police he dropped the boys off downtown.

When Ben pulled up to Paula's house on 10th Street, Debbie, in her housecoat, was in a panic. Paula still wasn't home. Debbie considered Paula a responsible friend. Debbie had to get to work herself. She needed her car, and Paula knew this. Something was wrong.

Ben called Paula's mother to ask if Paula was at her house. Carol Oberbroeckling told Ben she hadn't seen her. Next, Paula's manager at Younkers called Carol wondering after Paula. Paula was fastidious about her job. She would call to let her manager know if she was going to be fifteen minutes late. There was no way she'd forgotten she had to work that day. Carol told Paula's manager the same thing she'd told Ben. Then she woke Lynn, who had recently moved back home, and asked her to call Lonnie. Lonnie, who had just arrived home from the night before, drove over to the Oberbroecklings'. Not knowing what else to do, Carol dialed the police. The officer she spoke with was unconcerned. Paula had likely run away, he said. Girls her age were prone to unpredictability. Paula was probably "at one of those rock concerts like Woodstock."

Frustrated, the Oberbroecklings initiated their own search. One of the neighbor boys worked at Ford Town in the auto body shop, and his family had a truck-washing business that took them all over town on the weekends. Figuring they knew the area well and would be good at recognizing cars, Carol reached out to ask if they were available to help. She stayed at home to listen for the phone.

Cedar Rapids, the second-largest city in Iowa, is divided into four quadrants. Bisected by the Cedar River, which runs from northwest to southeast, and by 1st Avenue running from northeast to southwest, aerially the city appears like the four triangles of an X. Damaged in the flood of 2008, the city hall was relocated to the eastern bank of the Cedar River, but in

1970, when Paula was alive, it lived on May's Island in the middle of the water, the Cedar flowing around it.

The oldest neighborhoods fill much of the southeast quadrant, which is stuffed with grand homes built in the 1920s on sprawling lots adjacent to wide, twisting, tree-lined streets. The families who lived there, and who live there today, have spent generations in Cedar Rapids. This is where the post office, Washington High School, and Mercy Hospital all resided. The southeast side also contains the Oak Hill and Jackson neighborhoods, where the highest percentage of African American families lived in 1970 when Cedar Rapids was still mostly segregated. Robert lived in Oak Hill with his grandmother and his mother. Paula had lived in Oak Hill briefly that spring. The Cedar River provides the neighborhood's southern border. Eighth Avenue and Mt. Vernon Road acted as the border to the north.

It was there, just off Mt. Vernon Road, that the Oberbroecklings' neighbors found Debbie's abandoned Chevy. The car had been left on the street outside the Eagle Food Center parking lot in a tow-away zone. It was unlocked and empty— no keys, no purse. The right rear window was rolled down.

When she arrived at Eagle with Debbie, Lynn, and Lonnie that Saturday afternoon, Carol was overcome with fear. She was terrified to open the trunk. Lynn said, "That's what I thought . . . They raped her, and then they strangled her, and they threw her in the trunk and left the car. I was almost dead positive she was going to be in that trunk. But she wasn't."

Upon finding the trunk empty, Carol called the police from a pay phone near Eagle. Two officers were dispatched. The policemen didn't take any forensic evidence from the car. They didn't dust for fingerprints or take any photographs.

Instead, they told Debbie that she would need to move the car; it was in a no-parking zone, and it would be impounded if she didn't. Then they left the scene.*

Carol was unsure where to turn next. She was friendly with Joe Hladky, who worked at the *Cedar Rapids Gazette* (in 1980 he would become its publisher). She phoned him to see if she could buy space in the paper on which to publish a photograph of Paula and a bulletin alerting the *Gazette*'s readership to her disappearance; maybe someone would come forward with information. Hladky told her that they didn't put "stuff like that" in the paper. The best he could do was pitch the idea to the features team to see if anyone wanted to write a story about Paula. When he circled back, he said that the writers had declined, telling Carol, "There's no interest." She tried the local news station as well. The editors there told her that the police would have to request a spot if they determined it necessary to help with the case. The police did no such thing. The response from everyone was the same: shrug. This was what teenage girls do. They disappear. There was no story.

Realizing that they were on their own for the time being, Lynn and Lonnie printed flyers with Paula's photograph over the word "Missing". They posted the signs at gas stations, 7-Eleven, wherever they could find a corkboard.

It took four days for an investigating officer to conduct the first inquiry into Paula's disappearance. On July 15, Offi-

---

* In Paula's file not only is there no record of the police dusting for fingerprints or collecting forensic evidence, there is no record of their trip to Eagle on July 11, 1970, until December 9, *five months* after the fact. When police got around to writing the report on the discovery of Debbie's car, the officers noted that they didn't find any keys in the Nova and didn't "notice" any personal belongings. It ends: "At this time we talked to the owner of the 1962 Chevrolet who was also with Mrs. Oberbroeckling and she stated they would see if they could find another set of keys for the car and get it out of the 'no parking' zone."

cer C. Smith went to Paula's childhood home to speak with Carol. Lonnie was present. It was then that Carol revealed what would become the most talked-about detail of Paula's disappearance—Paula believed herself to be a month and a half pregnant. Indeed, this was the statement that opened the police file. It was literally the first thing recorded after Carol's home address and the fact of Paula's disappearance.

Carol also told the officer that she'd received a call from an acquaintance who claimed to have seen Paula stalled at the side of the road in the darkest hours of Saturday morning—a man had stopped to help her with her car. This story would eventually bear out. Months later, a merchant policeman—basically an officer-for-hire commissioned for jobs like security work—came forward to say that he remembered stopping to help Paula put the gears on the Nova back in place that night. The gears had a tendency to slip—a common problem in cars of that era. Fixing them required two people, one under the hood and the other inside the car depressing the clutch. A carful of girls who'd been cruising 1st Avenue around the same time confirmed the policeman's story, saying they'd seen him in front of the post office helping Paula just after 1 a.m. They even confirmed his description of Paula's outfit—sheer blue nightie. One said she was "quite sure" the girl she'd seen had been barefoot. After some thought, the carful of kids circled the block to see if the girl needed help, but by the time they turned back onto 1st Street, the car, the girl, and the merchant policeman were gone.

Knowing that Paula had been paid at Younkers the night before, Carol estimated that she had about $70 in cash on her person. She would have had that money in what Carol called a "squaw" bag, a slouchy rough leather purse hemmed in fringe with a long strap, which she'd handed down to Paula. The bag was never found. Carol also mentioned that Paula had few

friends notwithstanding Lonnie and the girls she lived with—
by which she must have meant Debbie Kellogg, as Paula barely
knew her other roommate. Aside from that, Carol said she
could offer no other information. What she did know was that
it wasn't possible that Paula had run away; she'd left her clothing, her makeup, and her curlers, and as anyone who knew
Paula could tell you, she wouldn't go anywhere without those.

In the weeks that followed, Carol sent her three boys, the
youngest in the family, to stay with a friend. Caring for them
felt impossible. Paula's father, Jim, who lived across the country with his new wife, kept in touch from there. Debbie Kellogg moved out of the house on the northwest side and back
in with her mother, claiming she was afraid for her own life.
She then mostly stayed away from the Oberbroeckling house.
Lonnie Bell, though, came over almost every day.

The home telephone rang incessantly. There were calls
from concerned friends and relatives, prank calls, people
breathing. Some claimed to know where Paula was. The Oberbroecklings followed up on every lead, driving around town
asking questions and banging on doors. Sometimes they found
people on the other side. Sometimes the addresses didn't even
exist. None of these calls proved fruitful, but Carol found herself afraid to leave the house lest she miss one.

The police followed various tips and dropped others. A
friend of the family said she saw Paula riding shotgun in a
green Plymouth. The Plymouth ended up being owned by a
blonde girl who was the spitting image of Paula. Two local
girls told police that one of their boyfriends had said that
Paula had been raped. When the police contacted the boyfriend, he said he'd heard the rumor from a group of girls at

the Tastee-Freez. An officer in nearby Marion, Iowa, alerted Cedar Rapids police to a break-in at a trailer park. He pointed out that the owners were the parents of one of Paula's friends and that a neighbor had said she'd seen two girls coming and going, one of whom she thought went by the name of Paula. The police showed the neighbor Paula's photograph, and she told them that Paula was not the girl she had seen.

In the beginning of the investigation, the police file showed that there were reports made each day, often with multiple entries made from multiple sections of Cedar Rapids. This lasted through much of July. In August, there was only one report. There were none in September. In October, a woman phoned the police department to say she'd overheard a conversation in a bar about a Paula "Ober"-something (she didn't know the rest of the last name) speculating that Paula had gone to Florida to have her baby or to get an abortion. After this, the file went dark. Days turned into weeks, weeks into months, the summer into fall. The police had stopped looking.

When the Oberbroecklings inquired about what was happening with the case, they said the police reminded them that Paula was eighteen. She was "of age." In fact, the age of majority in Iowa in 1970 was twenty-one years old.* So she was still a child, still the responsibility of her parents. Regardless, the police said that young girls did things like this; meaning they are impulsive, they run away, they go in search of themselves. But Carol was certain this wasn't the type of thing her Paula would do. Paula was conscientious. She wouldn't fail to show up for work. She wouldn't just disappear. When Carol's Sep-

---

* In 1972 the Iowa state legislature changed the age of majority to nineteen, and in 1973 it was dropped to eighteen.

tember birthday came and went without a greeting card or any word from Paula, she knew: Paula was gone.

"The first time I heard it rain . . ." Carol said, "I thought, it's raining on my baby."

On November 29, four months after Paula disappeared, after the encroaching cold had stripped the trees of their leaves and the undergrowth had died back revealing all that was hidden by summer's lush green, two young brothers happened upon a set of human remains while hiking. The bones were half buried in the brush on a steep incline adjacent to Otis Road just beyond the mouth of a culvert. The wrists and ankles were bound with nylon rope. The arms, forced behind the back. The body was horseshoed around a steel guy-wire anchor as if it had been flushed out of the pipe and gotten caught. A blue dress, matted with mud, was bunched up around the neck. There were no shoes.

That evening, a detective called the Oberbroeckling house. Lynn answered the phone and told him, yes, she and her mother were home. Yes, he could come by. The man said he would be bringing along another officer. It was the Sunday after Thanksgiving. When Lynn told Carol that two policemen were on their way over to the house, Carol said, "Oh, that's bad. When they come in twos like that, that's bad."

The police had recovered two rings on the ground around the mouth of the culvert. When Carol answered the door, the officers told her about the body and presented her with the rings. One was a gold band with silver trim, the other was yellow gold with a black pearl. At the sight of the rings, Lynn began to sob. Carol moved to comfort her daughter. Paula had purchased the one with the black pearl from Siegel's Jewelry where her grandmother, Vera Oberbroeckling, was employed. She wore it on the ring finger of her left hand where she might have worn a wedding band. Lynn had bought the gold ring from the Spartan Department Store, but at some point Paula had co-opted it and began wearing it herself. There was a third ring Paula wore, silver with a cluster of tiny stones in the shape of a hazelnut. It would never be recovered.

Word of the body's discovery blazed through Cedar Rapids. Lonnie showed up at the Oberbroeckling house before Carol could reach out to him. Carol chose not to tell Lonnie that the police had been to their home. She didn't know whether or not she should trust him. He had been at the Oberbroeckling house nearly every day in the immediate wake of Paula's disappearance. Then he attended a two-day rock concert in Minneapolis the weekend of July 18, eight days after Paula disappeared. And by July's end, he had stopped coming by altogether. Carol had barely heard from him in the three months since.

That evening on the news, Carol and Lynn watched footage of two EMTs loading a box filled with the bones found off Otis Road into the back of an ambulance. "They just put her bones in a bunch of cardboard boxes and piled them in," said Lynn. "That was horrible."

Within days, dental records confirmed what the Oberbroecklings had feared: the body was Paula's. But lying there as it had been—alone in the grass, exposed to both heat and cold, wind and rain for four long months—it was in such an advanced state of decomposition that the cause of death could not be determined. Carol noted, though, that the skeleton had beautifully done long nails, which she recognized. And alongside her devastation she felt a strange relief. At least she knew now where her daughter was.

Paula's police file shows that in the weeks that followed, detectives brought Lonnie, Debbie, Robert, and Ben separately into the station to give statements. The merchant policeman who had helped Paula with her car came in voluntarily. One girl told police she might have seen Paula and Lonnie together at Lake McBride *after* Paula had gone missing. Carol was suspicious of Lonnie for spending so much time at her house. "He wants to know what we know," she said to Lynn at the time. The police who interviewed Lonnie called him hazy, evasive, and "not very communicative."

Lynn heard that Paula had been left dead in a basement. She was confident that Debbie Kellogg knew more than she was letting on. The police agreed with Lynn's assessment. One kid said he'd heard Paula left for a hippie commune in Colorado. Many came forward to say they'd seen odd cars, odd people in the vicinity of the culvert at odd times. While waiting for the police to arrive at the scene of an accident on Otis Road the night Paula disappeared, a man saw a car drive by carrying three "colored males" and a "white blonde female." Another source said he'd heard around his plant that "the Black boyfriend" had lured Paula out of the house on the night of the 11th and then had two friends intercept and kill her because she was pregnant. More than one person came forward to say they heard Paula had gone for an abortion.

———

The investigation into Paula's death* lasted less than a year and a half. The police file ends abruptly on March 4, 1972, with no explanation for why it went quiet without a resolution.

---

* I want to call what happened to Paula murder. She was found in a ditch with her limbs bound, after all. And murder is the word the police used in their file. But because no one knows how Paula died, murder becomes a tricky word. In Iowa murder is defined as killing someone with "malice aforethought," and I believe there are plausible scenarios that do not include this premeditation, so I have opted to use the words killing, homicide, death.

Chapter 2

An Inheritance

IN THE SUMMER OF 1993, WHEN I WAS SIXTEEN, A GIRL from my neighborhood was brutally murdered. Stephanie Schmidt and I overlapped for one year in high school—me a freshman to her senior—and she'd even looked after my brother and me a handful of times when we were younger. The man who killed Stephanie washed dishes at the restaurant where they both worked in her college town of Pittsburg, Kansas. He had been released from prison not long before he was hired, having served half of a twenty-year sentence for rape. But Stephanie didn't know that when, out celebrating her twentieth birthday a few days early, she accepted a ride home from him one night in July.

I also worked in a restaurant at the time. I waited tables Sunday mornings and weekdays after school at a family establishment in Overland Park, Kansas, an overwhelmingly white, upper-middle-class suburb of Kansas City. My parents had relocated there from Omaha, Nebraska (New Orleans and Hartford, Connecticut, before that) so my father could accept a job directing the microbiology department at a local hospital. They chose our suburb over neighborhoods just across the state line in Missouri where we might have been able to afford "more house" because the school system in Johnson County was purported to be that much better.

At the restaurant I delivered shepherd's pie, chicken fried steak, and squares of cornbread as big as bricks to little blue-haired ladies or to families swarming with kids. We didn't serve alcohol, and almost everyone ordered pie. The staff was a sort of family. The owner and managers acted as parents and advisers to us, the waitresses, the hostesses, and to our "brothers," the guys who worked in the back, the line cooks and, yes, the dishwashers. I liked all of these men, if only because they were different from everyone else I'd met so far in the tiny bubble in which I was raised. The owner's son-in-law, easily twice my age, called me Demi, because he said I looked like Demi Moore. The line cooks would tease me during lulls in service. Never having been popular with the boys at school, I loved this dynamic. I looked forward to having to come off the floor and into the kitchen. I found it exciting, playful, and fun. I found it self-affirming. Their interest made me feel like I might actually *be* interesting.

But Stephanie's murder shook me with its warning: I could never be certain of a man's motives. Of course, I knew that all men weren't rapists and killers, but when a woman is raped and killed it is nearly always by a man. This idea and its implication of weakness conflicted with the post-feminist world promised to me—one in which I was both powerful and in control of my life's direction. I didn't want to walk through my days wary of every man I encountered. I wanted to flirt with the line cooks, and I wanted to feel safe doing so. When I considered it, Stephanie Schmidt's murder made me feel helpless and afraid, so I chose not to. Instead, I filed her death away in a place far from my everyday life.

When Susan approached me about helping out with the documentary film on Paula, I didn't have to consider it. The answer was no. I was averse to stories that involved violent crime of any kind, but especially ones that depicted violence inflicted on women. I avoided movies that revolved around the abductions of women. I didn't read detective novels or true-crime stories. I didn't follow Nancy Grace–style news coverage of lost girls. I'd never watched an episode of *Law & Order: SVU*. A good friend covered crime for the daily newspaper where we were both employed in our mid-twenties. The stories fascinated her, but they terrified me.

Just like Stephanie's story, what happened to Paula reminded me of the vulnerability inherent in being a woman, and thus risked the confidence I had built in myself, confidence that, as a single adult woman living in New York City, allowed me to go wherever I pleased, whenever I pleased, to talk to or to not talk to whomever I pleased. So I hung back while my then boyfriend and his mother did their reporting. From across the dinner table at the tiny lake house Susan had rented, I half-listened to accounts of their days. They reenacted highlights from their interviews, tense moments, ones of revelation. But even then, when I was barely paying attention, the detail of Paula's potential pregnancy stuck firmly in my mind: Paula had died three years before the passage of *Roe v. Wade*.

I knew two girls from high school who'd gotten pregnant in the early '90s. They gradually swelled and then disappeared and that was the last I heard of them. I also had a friend in college who became pregnant. She dropped out of school and moved home. I attended her baby shower and then I don't remember ever seeing her again. I heard that at some point, when the baby was older, she went to nursing school, but by then I had graduated and was living in New York working on a career and a life of my own.

Around the time I moved to New York, a good friend found out she was pregnant. She was a couple years into building her career and had no desire to embark on a relationship with the man who'd impregnated her, a man who didn't even live in New York. Nor did she want a baby. I escorted her to Planned Parenthood to procure an abortion. My accompanying her hadn't registered for me as a momentous event in our long friendship, only something that had happened, something to be gotten through. But years later, after she and I drifted apart, and after I became pregnant myself, she told me that my walking her into Planned Parenthood that day, holding her hand and waiting while she underwent the procedure, and then checking in on her in the days that followed, was the single most important act of friendship she had known. She had been very, very scared. And she had felt very, very alone.

I chose to get pregnant when I did because I was ready to have a baby. I was in my mid-thirties, married to a man willing to help with the cooking, the cleaning, with childcare, a man who wanted to build a loving relationship with his child, who supported my career decisions, who worked full-time making enough money to allow me to stay home with my son when he was newborn—none of my three jobs allowed me paid maternity leave. I had the emotional support of a community of parents and of my family, albeit from a distance. And I *wanted* a child. Then I gave birth to my son and nothing looked the same.

I'd anticipated that my husband and I would split the additional work of parenting fifty-fifty or at least sixty-forty. That I'd be back at my desk, if a touch tired, in twelve weeks. I'd seen other women do this. One of my closest friends wrote a cookbook in the weeks after having her daughter. As it turns out, I was not my friend. In reality, the daily tasks and round-the-clock care—feeding, diapering, soothing, bathing, in addition to cooking, cleaning, laundry, managing doctors' appointments, and stocking up on wipes and onesies—fell almost exclusively to me. The toll that pregnancy, labor, delivery, nursing, lifting, and carrying took on my body was devastating. The responsibilities my husband, because he was a man, could not share—gestating, birthing, nursing—were manifold. Our son ate with me, rocked with me, slept with me. At night I was so in tune with him that I woke when he sighed or rolled over. He had a tender stomach but was constantly hungry, so we were in a continual cycle of crying, nursing, spitting up, and then cleaning up—this all day long and then through the night. I barely slept for months. I became an extension of my son, existing only to assist in his need of the moment. My husband was changed by parenthood, for sure, but I was completely remade. The me who had become pregnant nine months before simply no longer existed.

When, from inside the fog of new motherhood, I considered returning to work, I found my priorities had changed. I'd look at my son—downy head, petal skin—and find myself overwhelmed by my feelings for him. The love was beautiful and burdensome equally. The guilt I felt when I was away from him was incapacitating. My time became precious. My reporting gig, covering real estate for a tabloid newspaper, didn't pay enough to cover childcare with any worthwhile net for me. And my jobs teaching creative writing to continuing-education students and editing nonfiction pro bono for a literary magazine—jobs that exercised my creativity but paid little or nothing at all—suddenly felt like luxuries. Within the first six months of my son's life, I quit all three.

Though this choice made practical sense, I was unsettled to find myself sacrificing my career for motherhood. This was something I had promised myself I would never do. Not long after my parents divorced when I was twelve, I came home from school to find my mother sobbing on her bed. When I sat down beside her, she turned to me, gripped my arm, and said, "*This* is why you have to have a job. We would not be able to keep this house if I didn't have a job. You must never become dependent on a man." When I heard it, I swore I would only ever rely on myself. Now here I was staying at home with my child, allowing my husband to support us all. Who was I if I wasn't making money?

This unmooring had me reconsidering my womanhood, a fact I had spent much of my life thinking was inconsequential. When I admit this to women today, women just a little bit older or a little bit younger, they usually furrow their eyebrows: How could I have been so naive? And I feel naive. But the overall message of my youth was that I could do whatever I set my mind to; my gender was of no import. It was a message I'd received from both my parents, one I believed and that my experience bore out. I played basketball in high school rather than try out for drill team, and I enrolled in honors classes. I was no star athlete nor was I valedictorian, but I felt I was as successful as anyone else. I had the same positive experience in journalism school and then again as I entered the workforce, first, perhaps predictably, at a women's magazine, but also later at the tabloid newspaper. So when my mother told me stories of being one of only two women in her company on the senior executive team, of having to fight for privileges that had been handed to her male counterparts, of having to rebuff advances, I didn't internalize them. And I shrugged off the argument I had in the early 2000s with another female MFA candidate who informed me that I was deluded if I thought I'd be given the same publishing opportunities as the men in our class. More than not believing her was the fact that I didn't want to. Entering my career convinced I'd be overlooked because I was a woman seemed a waste of energy. What was I to do? I am a woman.

On the night of my bridal shower, Susan and I had an argument about whether or not my generation of women had dropped the ball after all the progress her generation of women had made with regard to women's rights. In that moment I was incensed; how did *she* know what I did or didn't do for the cause? But now, from the vantage point of my marriage with a child and the abandonment of my career, I began to see that in my refusal to even consider my gender, I was exactly what Susan had accused me of, a woman who had taken her own privilege and what she was gifted by the hard work of others and had run, never thinking about how she could further that work nor appreciating the sacrifices that had been made for her. Because it wasn't until I watched my own life change— the greater share of childcare and housework, the tax on my body, the inevitability of scaling back work—that I began to sense that womanhood was indeed a strike against me.

Simultaneously, there was outrage in the air. In the year and a half after my son was born, Ray Rice, a running back who played for the Baltimore Ravens, beat his fiancée unconscious in an elevator; female bloggers were threatened with their lives or with rape by hordes of anonymous men online; more than fifty women, one by one, accused comedian and actor Bill Cosby of sexual assault;* states across the country instituted laws that forced women to go to further and further extremes to exercise their legal right to an abortion. I became outraged myself. Outraged that society placed the onus on young women to protect themselves from violence. Outraged that women were expected to walk through their lives instilled with fear. Outraged that the mechanic in-taking my car could look from me to my six-week-old son in my arms and, when I asked where he wanted me—that is, where I should park—felt it was acceptable to say, "Oh, please don't say it like that," and then mimic going weak in the knees.

When I relayed this experience to my husband—a man who thinks female leadership would go a long way toward fixing the problems of this country, a man who works almost exclusively with women and who supports this very book— he was perplexed by why I was making such a big deal about what he viewed as a harmless, if eye-rolling, comment (for the record, all I'd done was tell him about it). I tried to describe for him the discomfort I experienced during the exchange, how I'd felt disempowered, put in my place. If that was the case, my husband said, then why hadn't I told the mechanic to fuck off, gotten into my car, and driven away?

I tried to convey the stark reality of the situation— me, alone, with my baby in my arms, standing under the Brooklyn-Queens Expressway just inside a barbed-wire fence that obstructed the view from the street, an arm's-length away from a man I did not know, who'd just admitted, more or less, that he was attracted to me. Frankly, I told my husband, I had been afraid. At this my husband became annoyed. "Not all men are out to hurt women," he said.

---

* By summer 2016, this number rose to more than sixty.

"Of course not," I said, knowing he was offended by the implication and how it might extend to him. "But how are we to know who is and who isn't?"

At which point, he threw up his hands.

It was then, as I was struggling to equalize the balance between my role as a mother and my ambition to work, trying to understand my anger at all the injustice I saw around me, that Paula came to me again. Six years after that initial trip to Cedar Rapids, Susan reapproached me.

Susan had been trying for years to find a way into Paula's story. When Paula disappeared in 1970, Susan was nineteen and living across the country in San Francisco with her boyfriend. Leading up to that, she'd spent a year in college and, before that, a couple years at boarding school, by which I mean Susan had been away from Cedar Rapids for a long time, but *still* she knew Paula Oberbroeckling. She knew Paula because people talked about her. They pointed her out. Paula was so cool, so beautiful, something out of another world—ethereal. "She was legend," Susan said.

But as an adult, when Susan tried to look into Paula's death, there was nothing to find. During the entire investigation, the *Gazette* published only four stories, one of which was her obituary.

Susan got a court order to obtain a copy of the investigation file from the Cedar Rapids Police Department (CRPD). She read the entire thing on the flight home to Los Angeles. By the time the wheels touched down she was hooked. For her, the story was the quintessential midwestern gothic, the flat landscape and pristine surfaces masking dark underbellies, the veneer of calm and tidy, beauty and success, rolling golf courses with clear edges over a labyrinth of complex emotion, cops who didn't do their jobs, corrupt officials, a beautiful young woman with a complicated story. It was the mess of life and family, and it had all transpired right there in Cedar Rapids where Susan had grown up, a place she knew intimately and loved. But despite her commitment—including her work with me, she put in nearly twenty years—she could never seem to pin down the story, straighten the narrative. The biggest problem: there was no ending. When she tried to tell people about Paula, they shrugged: Who cared about a decades-old homicide?

When she came to me, she hadn't given up on Paula's story, but she was no longer convinced that it lent itself best to a documentary film. She thought it could function well as an essay, maybe a book. As a writer who dealt in fiction, Susan didn't feel capable of accurately rendering the story, but it seemed perfect for a journalist, someone who wrote essays, someone like me.

Susan had maintained a website where she uploaded all the research she'd compiled on Paula's case: the police file, the witness statements, the interviews she'd conducted with the family, the boyfriends, the friends. The newspaper clippings she'd unearthed, the photographs she'd been given or had dug up. She'd built the site in an attempt to crowd-source any information that remained at large. She encouraged me to scroll through it. "Just take a peek," she'd said.

It took one morning—me in a local coffee shop, my son at home with a sitter—spent clicking through the black pages, white text swimming before my eyes, for my interest to be piqued. What sparked was not the mystery of who killed Paula or a morbid fascination, nor was it an attraction to the story's midwestern gothic elements like Susan, but a connection instead. A connection I tumbled to when I got to Carol's quote about the rain.

When I read that Carol knew for certain Paula was gone when she didn't receive a birthday card from her, and that now when it rained, she knew it was "raining on her baby," I stopped still. I had felt so many things as I read through Susan's website—fury at the police, at the editors of the newspaper, and at the local news affiliate, mystification over the circumstances of Paula's disappearance, astonishment at how little support Paula had had living on her own at such a young age. And then, reading that quote, I knew I should feel sadness.

Carol's conviction was heartrending; she was contemplating the death of her child, the possibility that her baby's body—a body that she had built inside her own and then had raised from infancy through toddlerhood, childhood, and teenage, a body she had watched take first steps, utter first words, a body she had fed, clothed, and sheltered—had been abandoned somewhere, exposed to the wind and rain and snow, defenseless and alone. And she was confronting the bleak reality that she was powerless to help, to do the one thing a mother was supposed to do: protect her child. But my eyes remained dry. I thought briefly about what it would be like to lose my son, but it was too horrific to contemplate.

The thing was, sitting there alone, for the first time lost in the world of Cedar Rapids circa 1970, Carol wasn't the person I found myself relating to even though I was a mother. No, I wasn't Carol. At least not yet. As I sat and read about first love and newfound independence, controlling parents and flighty friends, I was Paula. Me at eighteen. Young, willful, curious, dizzy with excitement, on the brink of life, standing with everything, every possibility and every person before me. Me, overflowing with the confidence and bravado of youth, with the arrogance of ignorance. Me, not knowing enough to be wary of the world around me.

Our situations were so different, Paula's and mine, and yet they were bound. I too grew up in the Midwest with a single mother. And I remember those years—sixteen, seventeen, eighteen. No longer an adolescent; not yet a woman. Those first tastes of freedom that came from driving, from working, from being able to move outside the strict gaze of my mother. The dawning realization of my sexuality and its power coupled with the complete lack of understanding for how to use it. My confusion over my body, the ache I felt for certain boys, the way I couldn't concentrate for thinking of them—much more important than good grades, which had always come easily to me. The feeling of being on the cusp of everything but having no clue what everything could possibly entail.

On top of all this was the limitless anger toward my parents—for having divorced, for being consumed with work, for not understanding me. The anger exacerbating the desire to shake off what had shaped me, to free me from my family. Giving me license to behave however I pleased, to sneak out at night and drink wine coolers in parks, to smoke cigarettes and pot, to listen to my music loud, to drive fast, sometimes drunk, to tease and play and make everything into a game, to be with one boy and then to be with another. And the risk of it all, the glorious feeling of being off the rails yet outside of consequences, because consequences didn't exist. I believed, as many eighteen-year-old girls do, that I was invincible. Maybe Paula felt this way too. And, I thought, didn't we deserve to?

Paula's story consumed me in a way I hadn't realized I wanted to be consumed, filtering into every facet of my life. I thought about Paula while doing the laundry, while strolling my son around the neighborhood, during the long hours of the night while I was up rocking and nursing. It was the complexity of the case, the intricacy of her experience, the time period, so different and simultaneously so similar to the time in which I lived. It was the outrage I felt on her behalf. I was outraged by the way the police department dropped her case, by the media's failure to cover it. Outraged that her death had gone unrecognized, unremarked upon, unresolved, effectively equaling a second disappearance—the disappearance of Paula even after her body had been found. I was outraged at the inequality she faced in the late 1960s, outraged at the privileges she lacked.

Paula had a high school education with no immediate plans for college. She had a $70-a-week job in the Misses Sports department at the mall. She had two men in her life, both of whom lived with their parents and neither of whom had a job or any real professional prospects. Having fled her childhood home, Paula lived with two roommates, one of whom she barely knew, in a cheap boardinghouse on the "wrong" side of town. Her father was living across the country. She was on the outs with her mother, and even if their relationship hadn't been strained, her mother, newly divorced, was on welfare and struggling to stay afloat herself. Paula had few friends. She didn't have a car. Ultimately, she had little personal support, little financial support, no social or state or federal support. She was eighteen and all on her own. If Paula was pregnant when she died, then she faced potential motherhood with *none* of the support I had. On the cusp of adulthood, she'd been trapped with her future already mapped out for her.

For a while I worried that, with all my privilege, my life of safety, and everything I'd been given, I didn't have the right to consider what happened to this young woman who had so little and who had met with such horror. "How dare I?" I said to a trusted friend. "Maybe," she responded. "Or, how dare you not?"

It was in that moment that I decided that I owed Paula, that she was a woman and that our lives had intersected across time and through space, and the least I could do was to not turn my back. I didn't know where my investigation would take me, but I would commit to taking the next step. I would read the case file. I would start to make my way through Susan's research.

It never occurred to me to wonder why Susan had been so possessed by Paula's case, why, before handing it off to me, she had invested so much time researching the story and sifting through the facts. But I would learn that Susan and Paula had something that bound them together beyond Paula's death. "Thank God, she's yours now also," she once said to me. "It is such a relief not to have to care for her alone."

Chapter 3

The Girl

IN A PORTRAIT PHOTOGRAPH OF PAULA, HER BLONDE hair falls just below her shoulders. It is parted on the left and has the slightest bit of height near the crown—not the bouffant of her mother's day, but the subtle mod lift of the late 1960s. The dark crewneck she chose to wear makes her hair that much blonder, so blonde in fact that it appears her hair didn't reflect light so much as emanate it. She smiles unabashedly, looking up and past the camera as if the photographer has just said something untoward and, rather than answer with the blush and lowered eyes of the time, she is responding with a dare: a dare to continue that line. If he did, she might engage, perhaps flirt back, but she could just as easily stand up and walk out, or retort with a word that cuts.

This photograph of Paula was what transfixed me; it was the artifact that became the cornerstone of my reconstruction of her.

Susan had been trying to tell Paula's story for years, from the documentary she started in 2008 to a fictionalized novel version to a television series, and each time the complexity of the story—the twists and turns and contradictions—derailed the narrative. I had no intention of sinking ten years into a story that might be untellable. I'd been home with my son for a little over a year. Labor Day was in just under two months. If I couldn't find a road into Paula's story by then, I told Susan, I planned to walk away, to go back to reporting at the paper, to teaching.

She seemed not to register the parameter I'd laid down and instead responded with aplomb. "I knew it," she said, vindicated. "You're hooked. No one can hear about this case and not become obsessed. I'm going to overnight you my files."

In addition to the 150-plus-page police file and witness statements, Susan emailed me a Zipped folder of photographs that spanned Paula's life. There was Paula as a ringlet-crowned toddler, as a gawky adolescent—an egret, all arms and legs. There she was as a bridesmaid in her sister's wedding, as a hippie in elephant-leg pants with shining blonde hair. I knew that there was no way I could understand what happened to Paula without understanding who she had been. And so, my nose inches from my computer screen, I clicked through the photos in an attempt to conjure the girl.

In one picture a toddler-aged Paula is standing in the grass swinging an Easter basket. The hem of her starched white dress stops over her chubby thighs. She wears Mary Janes, a tiny bonnet secured beneath her chin with a bow. Her face is scrunched and she has her hand between the ribbon and her chin as if it is bothering her. In another, she's older, thinned out, ten maybe, and standing in front of a brick-sided house looking ethereal, the sun having washed her out almost completely. In still another an adolescent Paula sits for her school portrait donning a Catholic school uniform and looking academic.

These were the photographs of my parents' generation, the baby boomers—from the pictures' tones (rendered in sepia or black-and-white) and their poor quality (alternately grainy or soft or overexposed or cast in yellow) to the clothes they depicted (bobby socks and poplin skirts, jumpers and Peter Pan collars) and the context they revealed (department-store photo studios and carpeted basements with giant black-and-white televisions on faux-wood TV stands hovering in the background). My mother and Paula were born only two years apart, and I'd seen versions of all these pictures in my mother's photo albums. Perhaps because of this I found the photos impenetrable. They read as visual clichés, as the experiences of every middle-class white family during the early 1950s and '60s, when the postwar economy made mortgages affordable and brought convenience by way of kitchen appliances into the home.

It wasn't until I opened the portrait of Paula with her glowing hair and defiant look that an idea took hold. It was that look of confidence and security, that cheek, that "don't fuck with me" that I recognized. She seemed like every girl who had to sit and be looked at, every girl who had been told to smile, that "she'd be prettier if she did." She seemed like every girl who at eighteen had to sort out alone how to behave in the world, how to both invite interest and fend it off, how to have fun without getting into trouble, how to direct attention between her body and her mind.

When I considered the potential psychologies for a young woman, the qualities I intuited in Paula seemed to be good ones to aspire to: confidence with humility, obliviousness of or disinterest in the opinions of others, comfort with one's sexuality without dependence on it. When I thought about them, they represented my own goals in my thirties. And certainly they were the goals I would have for a daughter, if I had one. They struck me as healthy, as well-adjusted, as a recipe for a woman capable of self-realization.

Later, on one of several reporting trips I would take to Cedar Rapids (alternately ill-fated and illuminating), one of Paula's friends from high school verified what I saw in the picture. At a restaurant in Cedar Rapids, Larry Martin described Paula as someone who had always seemed a spirit freer than the rest, more open to joking around about sex, more confident in her own skin while at the same time holding no airs and never conveying the impression that she thought she was "any cuter than anyone else." But Larry Martin's assessment would be the most nuanced portrait of Paula I got. I learned quickly that to talk about Paula was to mention her appearance, and that everyone did: her friends, her roommate, the boys who attended her school, her sister Lynn, and even her own mother, herself a former high school homecoming queen.

"Paula was absolutely gorgeous. . . . I mean, you couldn't make a girl that pretty. Model gorgeous."—George Steinke, a freckled redhead who was in the same class as Paula and now runs a bar in Cedar Rapids.

"Paula was a very attractive young lady."—Rick Williams, the star of the high school basketball team and aces around: attractive, popular, smart.

"I have a very close friend, we grew up together, and he always said that [Paula] looked like she belonged to the 'horsey set.' She looked like she had a million dollars."—Paula's mother, Carol Oberbroeckling.

I understood that impulse. Paula's appearance was the first thing anyone knew about her. It was the first thing I had noticed too. But it was as if Paula's beauty wasn't subjective, wasn't a matter of opinion or taste, but a fact inherent to the person she was. Her beauty had nothing to do with perspective or desire. Said another way, one might not be attracted to her, but he or she couldn't deny that she was beautiful.

Beyond her blonde hair and long legs, most people didn't have much to say about the person she was. An old boyfriend talked about her kindness, the way she cared for him while he was housebound in a full-leg cast thanks to a motorcycle injury. Her mother said that "for quite a while" Paula spent time teaching children who struggled with learning disabilities how to read. She said that Paula had loved lingerie and linens, pretty towels, lotions and powders, that she was a "girly girl." Her sister Lynn called her smart and creative, said she liked to draw and had beautiful penmanship. She even said that Paula wrote poetry, that she had it published in a magazine. But none of this was anchored in specific detail. Why did Paula choose to spend her weekends working with children who had learning disabilities? What were her poems about? Lynn said she doesn't remember, that she didn't care about that type of stuff at the time, only that "[Paula's poetry] wasn't deep." None of this told me what motivated Paula.

In fact, the mythos of Paula told me more about the people who knew her (their reconstructions based on their own judgments and experiences), more about the time in which she was living (the late 1960s, when women were often reduced to their appearances), than it did about the person she was.

It concerned me that I might never be able to understand Paula. We were from different times and had different circumstances. I was born six years after she died. I had so many questions. What did she want? What occupied her thoughts? What made her laugh or cry? What did she fear? Who did she love? I knew that my reconstruction of her was just that—an imagining, laden with its own misjudgments, presumptions, and projections. Death is the loss of a person, but it is also the loss of information.

The closest I could get perhaps was to triangulate her using what I understood about the time, the place, the women who had factored into her life, and the women who had influenced my own. My mother and Susan and Paula's sister Lynn had all come of age in the late 1960s and early '70s, the same era as Paula. They'd grown up in the same part of the country, Susan and Lynn in the very same town. Carol and my grandmother, my mother's mother, were born in the same decade; both stayed home raising children while their husbands worked, both came from poor families. The similarities bridged generations too. My grandmother and Paula both modeled briefly, both carried the badge and burden of beauty. Carol and my mother both left their husbands. We were different of course—my mother followed the rules as a teenager and I broke them; Carol left her bad marriage while my grandmother endured hers; Susan fled Cedar Rapids but Lynn stayed. Nonetheless, my hunch was that there were at least as many similarities as differences and that there was something to be gleaned from the choices all these women made, the opportunities they were afforded or weren't.

Maybe triangulate was the wrong word, though. For it wasn't the three points of a triangle I envisioned when I considered the ways in which we were connected but a spiral instead— Paula in the center, the rest of us moving outward around her, ad infinitum. Paula, then, was where I would begin.

• • •

I'd read the transcripts of the interviews Susan conducted with Paula's family, which she had posted in full on the Internet, but thus far I'd never listened to the audio. My brother-in-law had taken a handful of portraits during that trip in 2008. There was one of the three Oberbroecklings: Carol, Lynn, and Tim, the middle brother. They were in a tasteful light-filled living room with vaulted ceilings and wide picture windows. In the photo, Carol is facing away in an armchair. She appears to be wearing a green silk robe, something like a kimono. Her socked feet rest on an ottoman. Susan tells me she is seated this way because she'd just undergone knee surgery. Carol's thin white hair is translucent like dandelion fluff, her look faraway. Across from her, Lynn stares directly at the camera from a sectional sofa. She wears jeans and an Iowa T-shirt. Her arms are folded resolutely in her lap. Tim stands behind her, tall, handsome, and protective seeming.

With this photo before me, I played the recording. Carol died in 2011, and the sound of her voice in my ear was like a resurrection. I could hear bodies shifting, pauses in conversation, breaks for water, to go to the bathroom. I felt like I was in the room.

Paula Jean Oberbroeckling was born on February 25, 1952, six years into the baby boom. She arrived thirteen months after her sister Lynn Marie and was the second of five children. Her three brothers, Todd, Timothy, and Christopher, were born in 1954, 1958, and 1961, respectively. When relaying the story of Paula's birth, Carol began with the fact that Paula was born with "flesh warts" (or molluscum contagiosum, a common rash in newborns), which covered her face until she was a month old. She also said that Paula's jaw was pushed way over to one side, a result of the way she lay in utero, a temporary deformity that made her appear as if she only had the top half of a face. This also lasted for just a few weeks.

"She was the smallest and ugliest of my babies," Carol said. "When my mother first saw her, she said to me, 'Oh, honey, she's awfully sweet. Bless her little heart.'" The next beat of Carol's story was relief when Paula turned into a chubby, beautiful child. And so the myth of Paula's appearance began right there with her birth and with her mother.

Carol dressed her daughters in matching outfits like twins: Lynn in pink or blue, Paula in mint green or yellow, favoring stiff cotton dresses that puffed out from the waist and featured embroidery on the chest. She took pride in parading her girls through Cedar Rapids, where everyone oohed and aahed over them, such pretty little things with all those blonde curls.

Paula learned to walk early, at ten months, when most children don't walk until around a year. But then she threw out her leg. The family doctor had to build a brace to fit into the bottom of her shoe in order to right her joint. Later, her school flagged Paula as having a speech disorder. She had a muffled way of speaking. The Oberbroecklings took her to a speech therapist who diagnosed her with "lazy tongue," which meant her tongue wouldn't move fast enough to keep up with what she intended to say, resulting in slurring and stuttering. This was also something she would outgrow.

With such a small age difference, Paula and Lynn were inseparable, though they were opposite sides of the same coin. Paula was a shy girl; Lynn was the self-described "toughie." Lynn would take a blouse and smack at Paula to get her to go cower in the corner. Paula rarely defended herself. She was so passive and quiet that her father called her Spook.

On one occasion, Lynn and Paula had been bickering. Jim brought the two girls upstairs and told them that if they wanted to fight so badly, they could discipline each other. Though Jim would occasionally make noise about how he was going to spank one or the other of the girls, usually while waving a newspaper around, he never acted on it. The discipline in the Oberbroeckling house was left to Carol. On that day, though, he told Lynn that as punishment she could spank Paula and vice versa. Lynn was happy to swing at Paula with all her might. But when it came time for Paula to spank Lynn, she barely touched her. "Tap, tap, tap," Lynn said, recalling the incident. "Now, that's not fair," Jim had said before giving Paula another chance. But once again, it was just "tap, tap, tap."

If the myth of Paula's appearance began at birth, the myth of her destiny began not long afterward. The winter she was five, Paula was hit by a car while crossing the street on her way to kindergarten, which she attended in the afternoons. That day, Carol had bundled Paula in a heavy coat and snow boots before sending her out into the cold. The car's impact was such that she was launched into the air, a boot knocked right off her foot. Carol phoned Jim, and he rushed home to drive Paula to the hospital. There they took a set of skull X-rays (images that would be recalled during Paula's autopsy thirteen years later). Minus a few scrapes, the emergency room doctors declared her fine.

Another time, Carol, Jim, and Todd were in the front seat of the car, Paula and Lynn in the back. As they rounded a corner, Paula rolled out of the passenger side door. Her siblings cried out. When they turned around, they found Paula lying in the middle of the street. Miraculously, she was unharmed.

"She was doomed," Lynn said on the recording playing in my ear.

But to me these stories sounded less like the results of predetermination and more like the consequences of circumstance and the sort of benign neglect pervasive in the parenting techniques of the 1950s and '60s. When Paula rolled out of the back of the car, none of the kids had been buckled in— this being before state law required the use of seat belts and during a time when most cars didn't even have them. In addition to that, the family had just picked up Jim from a bar. In her version of the story, Carol said that she "was driving, and I moved over and I had Todd in the front seat with me, and Lynn and Paula in the back seat, and Jim got in the car." Does that mean Jim, presumably at least one drink in, was driving?

As for the car accident, the Oberbroecklings were living with Jim's mother, Vera, at the time. Vera's house, a two-story colonial with dormers, faced 1st Avenue, a major artery that connects the east side of Cedar Rapids with the west. During the week, Carol hosted a regular lunch date, so though Paula was only five, she made the journey to school alone.

That day, Paula stood with the crossing guard waiting, the traffic on the four lanes in front of them hurried and thick. When the light changed, Paula stepped into the street and the car hit her like a cue ball. Carol and her friend heard the screech of tires from inside the house and ran down the front lawn to find Paula lying in the middle of the road. It's difficult for me to imagine sending a five-year-old to school on her own. But this was typical of the Midwest in the 1950s. Susan tells me she walked to school alone. Lynn described herself and Paula spending most afternoons unsupervised.

They played outdoors—jacks, four-square, bike races. In the winter, they would drag their sleds up the hill at the end of their block, sail down, noses red and stinging. In the summer, they'd drown the ground squirrels out of their holes. For me, the story of Paula's being hit by the car spoke to more than just benign neglect. It also spoke to a certain level of trust the Oberbroecklings must have had in their environment. The block was safe. The neighborhood was safe. The town was safe. Or at least they thought it to be. Which means it wasn't that Paula was doomed. But that the world—the state, the city, the neighborhood—was simply not as secure as Paula's parents believed it to be.

Eventually the Oberbroecklings moved from Vera's house into a tiny two-bedroom Cape Cod with vinyl siding on Cedar Rapids' northeast end. As opposed to the southeast side, with its palatial homes and prominent families, the northeast was mostly working class.

Until the 1950s, the area had been rolling farmland, hosting row after row of Iowa corn. But in the wake of World War II, businesses like Downing Box Company, LeFebure Corporation, and Collins Radio Company, which designed and produced radio equipment and remains active today, opened plants or expanded. All of which brought jobs and a demand for cheap, easily constructed housing. Suburbs with cookie-cutter tract homes sprang up, drawing white-collar workers and their children, the baby boomers, the Oberbroeckling family among them.

The Oberbroecklings' house was one in a row of modest middle-class houses set deep in a development of the same. Theirs was a neighborhood where every house had a kid. The street they lived on, G Avenue, was wide and quiet. Regis, the Catholic junior high and high school where Lynn and Paula began secondary school, looked out like a sentinel over the whole neighborhood from a hill at the end of their block.

The area might have been associated with new wealth, but money was scarce in the Oberbroeckling household. Carol, like many mothers of the time, didn't work outside the home when her children were young. Jim sold insurance and worked as a shoe buyer for Killian's department store. Commissions were inconsistent, and any money Jim did make seemed to evaporate in his hands. To make ends meet, Jim sometimes sold the family's belongings. As Lynn put it, the Oberbroecklings had the first color television on G Avenue, and they also had the first television to be repossessed.

Exacerbating the problem, Jim liked to drink and possessed a charismatic generosity that had him buying rounds at the bars he frequented even when his bank account was dry. Jim would write a check to the bartender, and at home Carol's payment to the electric company would bounce.

Even when there were paychecks to cash, Jim found a way to squander the money. One fall when the insurance business was good, Carol diligently stashed away large percentages of every dollar that made its way through the front door. By the end of the year she'd saved nearly $1,500. Jim came home one night loose from liquor and good feeling and announced to Carol that he'd divvied up their savings among some of the guys at the bar. They'd been lamenting that they had no money of their own to spend on Christmas.

"No-good bums hanging around playing pool, and he bought Christmas for all of them, wiped me out in the process," said Carol. "He'd take bread from my mouth and put it in yours."

It's impossible to know whether the girls were cognizant of the tensions arcing through their household. Lynn, for one, was enamored with her father. As a child, she slept curled up with one of his shirts. If she was sick, she'd ask her father to go get her a cone from Dairy Queen. She even occasionally accompanied him when he sold insurance, the two of them flying along the black ribbons of asphalt that strung together the towns of eastern Iowa.

Paula wasn't as taken with her father as her sister was. Or at least she couldn't be described as a daddy's girl. And though she was more apt to stay home with her mother preparing Thanksgiving dinner, say, while Lynn would bundle up and go off with the boys to hunt or stalk the cornfields, Paula wasn't a mama's girl either. Carol said that she always felt closer to her boys than to either Lynn or Paula, but especially than to Paula. This was a truth that pained her when she looked back.

Carol and her own mother had been extremely close, partially because her father died when she was nine, but also because the two had had a special connection. Carol described arguing with other children in school over who loved their mother the most; she did. Carol confided everything to her mother and didn't understand why her own girls didn't do the same. Lynn admitted that she kept some things from Carol in order to shield her from pain, especially after Paula died when Carol was so fragile. Paula, though, Carol said, had naturally kept to herself.

Perhaps this was one reason why the portraits of Paula felt thin to me. Perhaps some people never really knew Paula. Teenage isolation is practically developmental, but maybe Paula's withdrawal went beyond that. Perhaps she put up her own walls, leaving those around her to extrapolate from the little that she did let on and from what they could see just by looking at her. Or maybe it was the opposite. Maybe no matter what she did, said, or felt, her appearance was centered, her self sidelined.

When she was fifteen, Paula entered a modeling contest sponsored by Seifert's, a women's clothing store. Thermo-Jac, a teen clothing company, had initiated a search for the next "Miss Thermo-Jac" whom they would feature in an upcoming issue of *Seventeen* magazine. They had set up a photographer in a makeshift studio. Out of all the girls photographed that day, Thermo-Jac chose Paula. They flew her to St. Louis to model in an advertisement that appeared in the February 1968 issue of *Seventeen*.

What I found interesting about this story was not that Paula won—she was beautiful!—but that it seems Paula hadn't wanted to participate in the contest in the first place. Lynn said the two had been at Seifert's that afternoon by coincidence, and Paula only agreed to enter the contest because the photographer cajoled her into doing so. He saw her—her blonde hair, her long legs, her bright eyes—and what he must have thought was: "model material." Read: something to look at, or, even more, something that people will *enjoy* looking at. Paula had no ambition to model, so said Lynn. What she wanted was new clothes. Paula loved clothes. One of the perks that came with winning the Thermo-Jac contest was a new wardrobe. Lynn said that they always had to pay for their own outfits but never had enough money to do so outright, so they'd put them on layaway. Meaning, Paula auditioned for Miss Thermo-Jac on a lark in the hopes of adding to her closet. But Paula's disinterest in modeling seemed not to matter. She was nice to look at, thus she should be in a position where people could look at her. Was this one more subtle communication that her beauty was the attribute people valued?

"[Paula] just wafted, she was so elegant. . . . She had this grace about her," said Kathy McHugh, a classmate. "When one of your classmates is in *Seventeen* magazine? That was the coolest thing ever."

• • •

I am an adult who knows that what is inside a person trumps whatever is on the outside, and still I want to be beautiful, mostly because I know that the whole inside/outside thing isn't completely true. Appearance is public. It is inescapable. Part of being a woman is being measured by your appearance—women spend their lives being looked at, appraised, criticized. Beauty as an aspiration is both insulting and, for me, an obsession.

I learned that physical beauty was something one wanted when I was twelve. My father was driving me to basketball practice. I was in the passenger seat of his hatchback, the seat belt cutting into my neck, the sky outside cloudless. He looked over and told me, as he often did, that I was beautiful. Then, after a beat, he asked whether I thought the father of one of my teammates ever told her that she was beautiful. This girl, though I'd never considered it before, was not pretty. I don't remember how I responded to my father—his question was asked quietly and out the window, as if to himself—but I do remember feeling bad for my teammate, as if she had failed somehow. The irony of this—that we were on our way to basketball practice where this girl was one of the best players on the team and where I mostly warmed the bench—strikes me upon reflection. Perhaps the question was my father's bungled attempt at bolstering my self-esteem. But of course, it was the wrong message: that appearance, a passive attribute, mattered, and perhaps more than skill.

The wrong message, and also, in many cases, true. Count-less studies have confirmed that attractive people are more fre-quently offered jobs, get promoted faster, and are paid more, as well as given other types of preferential treatment both inside the workplace and out of it. And this is today. In 1970, when for many women survival meant finding a husband for financial support, beauty was a special kind of currency, one that afforded security. Working women were also rewarded for their looks, more easily getting jobs in male-dominated fields, which happened to be all of them. Even fields like nursing and teaching had male gatekeepers in charge of hiring and manag-ing. In the '60s, a woman's appearance could legally serve as an employment qualification. Airlines could fire stewardesses once they turned thirty-two or got married. In *The Beauty Myth*, Naomi Wolf describes the "Professional Beauty Quali-fication" or PBQ, as "a commercial sexualized mystique of the airline stewardess, the model, and the executive secretary." So beauty did hold value; it was a boon.

• • •

Not long before she died, Paula chose to pluck her eyebrows into two thin arches, a child's drawing of two bird wings. Carol went berserk. She had always thought that Paula's eyebrows "looked like Brooke Shields," that they "made her face," because here Paula had this blonde hair and her star-tling eyes were topped with heavy dark brows. "I was heart-broken," Carol said. "Who knows who it was that talked her into that, but I hated it. I cried and cried, and I said, 'Paula! You've destroyed your face!'" Implicit here was the idea that "destroying one's face" was a risk, endangering opportunity—romantic, professional, social, or otherwise.

But beauty is double-edged, keeping people away as much

it draws them in. It is limiting precisely in the way it can become a woman's defining characteristic.

Steve Scheib, who dated Paula when she was a sophomore and brought her to prom, told Susan that Paula had for sure been beautiful. Scheib was a few years older, the type of dashing dark-haired nice guy girls clamored to go out with. His father owned a restaurant, his step-grandfather a bar. "I can remember the two or three different proms I went to, and you know how your buddies would pat you on the back and say, 'Boy, Scheib, she's good-looking.' It wasn't, 'Boy, Scheib, she's really smart.' Or, 'Boy, Scheib, she's gonna really make something of herself.' It was always, 'Boy, she's good-looking.'"

Beauty can lead to isolation. Beautiful women may be assumed unapproachable and thus left lonely. Beauty generates the presumption of a carefree life, an assumption that is occasionally met with resentment or deliberate withholding. Beauty can make men nervous. Worse, it can make them bold. It sets impossible expectations, standards. It breeds envy—in other women, in sisters, in mothers.

In one of Susan's interviews with Lynn, Lynn admitted that she and her mother often wondered what Paula might have looked like now, had she lived. Specifically, they wondered whether she would be fat. And I could hear in their words the complexity that attends relationships with pretty women.

Naomi Wolf identifies the "beating heart" of the beauty myth as its divisiveness. "At present, 'beauty' is an economy in which women find the 'value' of their faces and bodies impinging, in spite of themselves, on that of other women's. This constant comparison, in which one woman's worth fluctuates through the presence of another, divides and conquers. It forces women to be acutely critical of the 'choices' other women make about how they look."

But there is irony in this dynamic. Yes, many of us want to be the pretty girl. We assume that life is easier, better when beautiful. We imagine that beautiful people are safe from judgment. That they've won in ways the others of us haven't. What we don't consider is that beauty can be dangerous—danger born from attention, from never escaping notice.

The last photos I opened in Susan's file, taken by the first detectives on the scene at the culvert beside Otis Road, were wrenching: there was the grassy hill on which Paula's body was found; there were her gruesome remains.

At one point on the recording, as Carol was hypothesizing about what had happened to her daughter, she said, "I even thought at one time, that maybe it was Ted Bundy. I mean, I used to see pictures of him and I thought . . . 'Did you hurt my Paula?' Because, you know, he was a very charming character. And he would have picked Paula out."

Chapter 4

Her Birthright

CAROL HAD BEEN BEAUTIFUL TOO. IN 1945, WHEN SHE
was sixteen and still Carol Burks, she was crowned homecoming queen. The photos I found of her showed a woman
lithe and long all over: arms, legs, fingers, neck. She wore her
wavy dark hair in a pageboy with bangs and a soft curl that
rolled from her temple past her jawline to her collarbone.
Her upturned nose softened the sharp angles of her thin
face. In the Roosevelt High School yearbook she is seated on
the floor in the front of a class photo, unsmiling, demure, her
legs folded carefully to one side. In the *Gazette* around the
same time, she is crouching beside another young woman;
the caption says Carol is "autographing" the other woman's
skirt. In a later photo she is standing between her husband
and her brother-in-law wearing a dark dress with a scalloped
neckline. She has four-week-old Todd, donning the family
baptismal gown, in her arms, her two daughters in the fore-
ground so close in age and appearance they might be twins.
Lynn's gaze is off camera but Paula makes eye contact. Her
eyes are flashing, cheeky, the opposite of her mother's wide
earnest ones.

Our mothers are the first women we know intimately—from their aspirations and disappointments to their interactions, inflections, and gestures, the way they care for their bodies, their very smell. Our first inklings of what it means to *be* a woman come courtesy of our mothers. A mother is at once crystal ball, beacon of possibility, and cautionary tale. A mother sets the first bar. She represents the first hurdle. She is the original measuring stick. We want to be like our mothers. Or we do not. Either way we inevitably define ourselves by them.

When I considered all the events and decisions that led to Paula walking out the door that night in July of 1970— possibly pregnant, two men vying for her attention, living on her own—I wanted to know what she understood about what womanhood offered. What did she expect from her life? What had she internalized about gender roles, the choices offered women with regard to starting and ending relationships, the decision to have babies or to not?

• • •

Presumably, Carol's beauty was one of the qualities that attracted the attention of Jim Oberbroeckling. Carol had been raised on the west side of Cedar Rapids, and Jim on the east. While the southeast and northeast sides with their old and new money, respectively, made sport of looking down on one another, they were united in their disdain for the poor white west side of town, the wrong side, as it were. During those days, and some would argue still, people looked askance when the two ends of town fraternized. East siders didn't tend to date west siders, and vice versa. But somehow Carol and Jim found each other and together they flouted this unwritten rule.

Jim was a catch, tall and slim, rakish with brown hair he wore swept up and back like James Dean. Carol described him as the guy everybody liked, charismatic and game, a man who could "charm the birds out of the trees." Jim had quirky interests—playing poker, learning magic, and performing card tricks. His father was a watchmaker and jeweler who had owned his own shop until he relocated his family to Cedar Rapids. Once there, he gained employment at Siegel's Jewelry where he constructed and fixed watches until his death in 1954. Jim's mother also worked at Siegel's. Vera was an accountant. She was active in St. Matthew Catholic Church and all over town. Her obituary mentions the Altar and Rosary Society and the Women's Association of Creditors.

But it wasn't Jim's family that had attracted Carol; it was pure chemistry. She couldn't have helped falling in love with Jim; "he was such a handsome rogue." Carol and Jim married in July of 1950, when Carol was twenty years old. Eighteen years and five children later, they divorced.

Money mismanagement and alcohol weren't the only stresses on their relationship. The same attributes that had drawn Carol to Jim—his good looks, his charm, his easy way— had women happily receiving his advances. This was a fact that wound its way around to Carol many times over the years. When Susan asked Carol if Jim had been unfaithful, she'd laughed, "Oh, yes." So while Carol was at home watching, feeding, and cleaning up after their five children, the majority of the time having little money with which to do so, she was aware that Jim was carousing with his pals at the bar, spending the family's money, and chasing and catching women. At some point Carol must have realized that she could manage alone. That's more or less what she had been doing anyway. So in the summer of 1968, between Paula's sophomore and junior years in high school, Carol ended her marriage.

When I considered this fact, that the divorce had been Carol's choice as opposed to Jim's, it felt like evidence of incredible courage. Sure, the women's liberation movement was well underway by that time—there were more women entering the workforce, sex-based discrimination was being challenged, and empowered women were leaving their bad husbands in greater numbers (indeed, a third of the marriages of the 1950s eventually dissolved, African American marriages breaking up at twice the rate of white marriages), but divorce in practice was still extremely daunting.

Divorcees were labeled, gossiped about, abandoned by friends, shunned by their communities. Carol and Jim were members of the Catholic Church, which deemed marriage an unbreakable covenant. Divorced Catholics were forbidden from taking the sacrament of Holy Communion, forced to remain in their pews while the other congregants rose to take the body of Christ. By which I mean, everyone knew.

Beyond the shame, the process of separating was filled with legal hurdles and barriers. No-fault divorce didn't exist until 1970, so one party had to admit to and accept blame for the failure of the relationship in order for a divorce to be granted, and if the woman wanted any chance of receiving alimony, that party had to be the man. If there was evidence that both parties were at fault, the divorce might not be granted. Paula's classmate Kathy McHugh's mother had to get character witnesses to vouch for her in court so that she could keep her children.

But the biggest hindrance for most women was the enormous financial risk. "Head and Master" laws were still in effect, granting husbands the right to all earnings and all property acquired during a marriage. Until October 1974, it was legal for a bank to refuse a married woman a credit card or a loan without her husband's written permission. A man's financial outlook often improved after divorce, while women saw declines in family income up to 50 percent, African American women suffering the steepest drops of all.

Carol didn't have a job. She didn't have a college education. She wasn't independently wealthy. She had five children. For many women like her divorce meant destitution, a fate awful enough to keep them in their unhappy marriages.

This was, I had always assumed, the case for my grandmother. My mother's mother, who was born within years of Carol, was a teenage runaway. She had no college education and had dropped out of high school; indeed, having only graduated grammar school, she had barely any education at all. When she met my grandfather, she was living in an apartment in downtown Chicago. She had few friends and, as a waitress at a diner, fewer prospects. What she did possess was a striking beauty—long hair the color of molasses, high round cheekbones like plums pushed up under her skin, soft dark doe eyes.

My grandfather was a Peruvian immigrant. Family lore was that he'd fled his country in the middle of the night after he found himself on the subversives list kept by the military. He'd been flagged for his political engagement at the National University of San Marcos, and his father worried that for this he'd be imprisoned or worse. After arriving in the United States, he put himself through medical school (there's another family story about his stealing milk from a neighbor in order to survive; he would eventually repay her with free medical care). When he married my grandmother, he was a practicing physician, nearly forty years old, and she was nineteen, barely a woman. Nearly the same age Carol was when she wed Jim.

Once they married, my grandfather insisted that my grandmother quit her job and move with him to the south side of Chicago so he could be closer to his patients—this was the era of house calls. My grandmother had liked living downtown, being close to the art museums and to Lake Michigan. When she said so, my grandfather promised her they'd move back once he established his practice, but they never did. My mother told me the promise had been empty from the start. I don't know whether my grandmother knew then that she would never again live downtown, that my grandfather was prone to flying into rages peppered with Spanish, that he would castigate her and terrify her children into submission. That he would hit their daughter, my mother. But she would at some point. Unlike Carol, though, my grandmother would never leave.

Through our modern lens, it's easy to act righteous about relational dynamics that include violence or fear. From outside a relationship, the choice over whether to stay with an abuser or to leave appears unambiguous. There is no staying with someone who hits you, who hurts you. Except relationships are much more complex than that binary allows. There are many layers of attraction and need and entanglement. And women stay for many reasons.

That my grandmother had the strength to run away from her abusive home as a teenager (her own mother beat her with a hairbrush, pulled her hair until her scalp bled) but was unable to summon the courage to separate from her husband as an adult was complicated.

My mother tells a story of a winter night when she was about ten. My grandfather was in the basement cooling off after upending the house with stomping and screaming for whatever little thing. As my mother comforted my grandmother, my grandmother turned to her and asked whether they should leave. Yes, my mother said. Yes. My grandmother instructed my mother to check one of my grandfather's drawers in which he often kept money. It was empty.

"We don't have the money to leave," my grandmother said.

"Let's go anyway," my mother said.

But they didn't. Instead, they held each other and cried. My mother remembers their flannel pajamas, how the cold bit outside.

Money was clearly a factor in my grandmother's decision to stay, perhaps it was even the biggest factor, but it wasn't the only one. Like Carol and Jim, my grandparents were practicing Catholics: Good Friday, church on Sunday. (My mother received all the sacraments of Baptism, First Communion, Confirmation; she attended Catholic grade school, an all-girls Catholic high school, the whole shebang.) And the Catholic Church did not like divorce. Also there was this: when they met, my grandmother had been enamored with my grandfather—jet-black hair, glittering hazel eyes, a doctor with an accent at a time when there was a great Latin influence in America (see Desi Arnaz)—and it's possible part of her always was. This, even as she feared him. Love has its own laws. I think of Carol looking back on her marriage: "Jim could charm the birds out of the trees."

For my grandmother, my sense is that the risk was too great. She had no means and no family to support her. She had no education and two children at home. The difference between looking after oneself and looking after oneself with two kids is exponential. In the end she stayed for forty long years until my grandfather died.

When I place her story beside Carol's, I realize that perhaps there was another element at work. My grandmother's own parents had stayed together despite their awful fighting, both parties cheating. Maybe my grandmother thought that this was what a marriage was *supposed* to look like. And maybe it went even further. Perhaps she didn't know she *could* leave. Perhaps my grandmother literally couldn't fathom what her life might look like if she were on her own with two children.

Carol's mother, Alice, had herself been married three times. She was widowed by her first husband, Carol's father. Her second husband also preceded her in death, except when I looked up her third husband's obituary in the *Gazette*, I found that she and he had married four months *before* the death of her second husband. Had she ended that second marriage? I don't know for sure. What I did know was Carol's stated bond between her and her mother. Perhaps her mother's example, which proved that a woman could survive the loss (whether in death or in separation) of her husband, even if it was difficult, even if it was the hardest thing she'd ever done, was the wellspring of the courage that had allowed Carol to leave Jim. A gift, perhaps, from mother to daughter. *This is what is possible.*

It took four attempts over nearly a decade for Carol to make the separation stick. Carol told Susan that the day the Oberbroecklings' divorce was finalized, Jim, having already moved out of the family home, came over to the house on G Avenue. It was June and the weather was warm. He and Carol gathered the kids in the backyard and sat them down under the long arms of a weeping willow. Paula was a sophomore in high school then; Lynn was a junior. The couple spoke with the children, though Jim mostly cried. He could not believe that Carol had gone through with the divorce.

"Carrie, just promise me one thing," he said to her that day.

"If I can, Jimmer, I will."

"Promise me, if you ever marry again, it'll be to me."

Carol said, "Well, that's easy, honey. I promise." It was easy because she knew that she would never marry again. And, indeed, she never did.

Here Carol's story and my grandmother's intersected once again. My grandmother might never have mustered the courage to leave my grandfather, but she was twenty years younger than he was. She would live another thirty years after he died, during which time she could have remarried or at least embarked on another relationship. But, like Carol, my grandmother chose never to wed again. And she made this choice purposely, as Carol had, even fervently.

Once, while my grandmother and I were having dinner at a favorite Italian restaurant in Chicago, I couldn't help but notice the inordinate attention paid us by the little gray-haired maître d'. He hovered around our table, topping off our water glasses and attempting small talk.

"I think he likes you," I whispered to my grandmother.

She looked pointedly at me. *"That* is *his* problem."

Later, a single man who lived across the street rang her doorbell and asked my grandmother if she'd like to go to the movies with him. She responded with a terse, "No thank you." I asked her why, and she told me that she had "already *been*" married.

My grandfather forbade my grandmother from having a job or from driving a car; she finally convinced him to allow her a driver's license when she was fifty. *Fifty!* She was to keep house, care for the children, entertain, be beautiful. She volunteered at Christ the King church, took the bus to get groceries, cooked large Italian meals for their friends and for my grandfather's colleagues. From the front porch of her bungalow, she watched the comings and goings of the people who lived on her tree-lined street. My mother called her a caged bird. My guess is that my grandfather's death had set her free, and that she would not risk being caged again.

Elements of my grandmother's story would become formative for me. My mother's too. Of course. When I looked for them, I saw uncanny resemblances between the choices that the generations of women in my family made. I saw them in Paula's as well. But when I began to dissect them, I saw that these matrilineal influences were not linear, but circular, convoluted, and complex. Our mothers' choices shaped our lives but not in the ways I might have expected.

Like my grandmother, my mother also had an imperfect marriage. My parents, who'd been wedded by a priest in the Catholic Church, split up in the late '80s. I was twelve and in eighth grade then, four years younger than Paula was when her parents divorced. My father, not unlike Jim who was married and living across the country by the time Paula died, had moved from my mother's home in with his next partner, though my father's new partner was a man. My mother remarried when I was in college and remains married to the same man to this day.

When, at thirty-two, I told my grandmother that I was engaged, she said, "Oh Kate," shaking her head, "you have to be sure. You have to be absolutely sure." I didn't know how someone could be absolutely sure, but I was willing to take the risk. I hadn't always known that I wanted children, but I always knew I wanted to marry. I wanted a partner. This, in spite of what I had watched happen in my own family, in spite of what I knew about my grandmother's experience. One might think that I'd have sworn off marriage, but I hadn't.

Made to think about it, I attributed my willingness to chance being wrong about the match to the confidence with which my mother single-parented, with which she climbed the corporate ladder, with which she took care of the house and then eventually remarried. Even if my marriage didn't work out, I assumed I would survive, just as my mother had.

• • •

Paula was sixteen when her parents divorced, so maybe she wasn't yet considering the possibility of her own marriage, but certainly she would in the years to come. Women were still marrying young. The median age of marriage for a woman in 1968 was just over twenty. As Paula approached graduation she watched her friends couple up and then she attended their weddings. George Steinke and Kathy McVay, Paula's friends from high school, were married in June of 1970 when George was seventeen and Kathy was eighteen. Paula was Kathy's maid of honor. Marci Marie Sanchez, who graduated with Paula, married Bruce Allen Luedeman the summer before the girls' senior year. Paula's good friend Delilah Nollge married Steve Greene in August of 1968. Delilah was sixteen. But perhaps most potent of all, Paula's own sister, Lynn, married shortly after she graduated from high school the year before Paula. She was eighteen years old.

In a photo taken of Lynn's wedding party, Paula stood at her sister's side. She wore a pale peach cap-sleeved satin dress that fell, in the conservative wedding fashion of the time, from the hollow of her neck all the way down to her ankles where matching peach shoes peeped out. A short veil floated behind the crown of her head anchored with a large bow. A bouquet of orange flowers cascaded from the clutch of her hands. Lynn's dress was lace, white, and similarly staid, covering her from neck to ankles, shoulders to wrists. Her veil was longer than that of her maids'. She was shorter than Paula by a few inches. She looked small and young, swimming in so much lace and tulle.

Paula knew what it felt like to wear a long white dress. Younkers, where she was employed, held bridal shows in the Misses Department, and Paula had modeled wedding gowns in them. Among the racks, Younkers erected an elevated runway. They edged it in a garland of white flowers and placed a white runner down its length, then lined it with folding chairs and invited the community. Lynn and Carol went to support Paula.

As she walked down the runway in front of her family, her coworkers—the yards of fabric moving against her thighs, swishing around her ankles, the weight of the veil heavy on her head, the train dragging behind her—did Paula wonder what it would be like to walk toward a man wearing that dress? Toward a house and children and everything that came with them, the responsibility, the commitment? Toward a future as a wife? And, if so, how had watching the evolution and eventual dissolution of her parents' marriage colored her expectations?

The divorce agreement granted Carol sole custody of all five kids and ownership of the house and its furnishings. It stated that Jim must pay child support in the sum of $25 a week, five dollars for each of the five children, until they turned nineteen or became emancipated, married, or deceased. It also stipulated that he continue to carry medical insurance for the children. At that point the youngest child, Christopher, was not quite seven; Lynn, the oldest, was seventeen.

Without Jim's income, sporadic though it was, Carol was in danger of losing her home. She had been advised not to take a full-time job before the divorce. To do so would risk losing custody of her children. Though she didn't explain the connection between working and losing her kids, I took it to mean that if she had a job she might be painted as a neglectful mother: a woman at work couldn't simultaneously be at home caring for children. This was the type of coercion used to control women then and now. The best thing for the children, she was told, would be for her to stay at home. With that in mind, her attorney had insisted she apply for welfare before he would file her case. The idea of going on public assistance had been "horrible," but she was left with little choice if she wanted to both leave Jim and keep her house and kids. On the afternoon Carol went downtown to file the paperwork, she did not have to go alone. Her mother went with her.

The $385 allotted to Carol every month by welfare, in addition to the $100 that came from Jim after the divorce was finalized, allowed her to pay the utilities and to buy food stamps. But getting through the weeks was difficult. Carol worried constantly about where the next pair of shoes would come from, and there were nights the whole family went to bed hungry. At one point during that winter, Carol ran out of oil to fuel the furnace. She told the kids that they were going to play like they were pioneers, bringing all five children into her bed and piling it high with blankets and coats. They slept like that until morning when Carol's mother came over and, after witnessing their situation, called the fuel company and bought the family some oil.

Carol learned quickly that she would need to supplement her welfare income. The rules were strange. On welfare she was able to buy soft drinks but not toilet paper. She needed a stopgap. Without a college education, her opportunities were limited mostly to the service sector. During those tough years, when the children were still at home, Carol did myriad odd jobs. She offered services to her neighbors. She cut their hair and gave them permanents. She took in their laundry. She ironed their shirts and slacks. She cleaned a health salon at the shopping mall, arriving at the store by 6 a.m. so she could finish her duties before the mall opened. When she was done, she vacuumed her way to the door in an effort to erase any trace of herself. Returning home, she'd often see Tim on his way to school. Sometimes she cleaned a local tavern. She even tended bar occasionally at night for some friends. The owner's wife was afraid to be at the bar alone after dark. She offered Carol a dollar an hour to pour drinks. All of this, cobbled together, kept the family afloat.

Aside from the embarrassment they felt over the free lunches they were suddenly being given at school, Carol said that the kids were oblivious to the family's financial situation. Years later, though, Lynn told me, almost defensively, that the family had been very poor.

•　•　•

When my mother was young, she wanted to be a doctor. Her father had taken her on house calls, and she'd watched the tyrant from home morph into a caring, trusted presence in front of his patients. Magic. Miracle. And maybe this was the draw. But she also wanted to have a family, and if she had learned anything from watching her father, she knew that it wasn't possible to do both (today she tells me that she couldn't see that she could have done it differently from him—by which she means, she had no role model). Instead, she majored in medical technology and studied laboratory medicine. She began her career working as a phlebotomist, drawing blood. When I was born, she moved to third shift, working overnight in order to be home for me. She moved to the day shift when I was about thirteen, old enough to let myself into the house after school (which I did, every day), and worked her way up the ladder from there. At the peak of her career, she was one of only a few women vice presidents at the major US laboratory in which she worked. Today she consults on the openings of labs. She never became the doctor she wanted to be, but in her trajectory I saw the epitome of hard work and success as a woman.

When I was growing up, my mother told me over and over that I could be whatever I wanted. And I believed her. I am grateful for this, but here again I see how these lines are not straight but circling. When my mother told me that I could be whatever I wanted, she meant I could be a doctor or a lawyer or some other professional who would—critically—be able to support myself without a man. But I listened to only half of what she told me, the half I wanted to hear, the part about "whatever I wanted," and not the implication about supporting myself, which is how I find myself a writer.

This is something I struggle with. I am the writer I wanted to be, but if my husband dies in a car crash, if he leaves me, if I wanted to leave him, I would lose our house. No, I wouldn't have to clean a salon like Carol did, but there is no way, given my career choice, to make a salary that would support our current life. Certainly I would have to give up writing, which

I see now is a luxury. Were I a lawyer, a doctor, an executive at a bank—things that I could have accomplished with my privilege—I and my children would be fine. I heard my mother, but I was not able to apply her wisdom to my own life, despite how I saw it play out in her life and in my grandmother's. And it strikes me that in some ways I have put myself in a situation more like my grandmother's than like my mother's. Should I not have become a writer? Time will tell.

Paula witnessed her mother's inequitable marriage. She watched her parents' relationship deteriorate. She watched them separate and divorce. She saw her mother struggle to keep the family solvent; she watched her take menial jobs. Did she see these events as lessons in survival and resilience or as a warning against marriage and men? Or did her mother's life not factor? Did she see marriage as an inevitability, an imperative because of the time?

Carol said that Paula loved children and wanted "a dozen of them." To support this, she brought up Paula's spending her time volunteering with kids. But Lynn disagreed. She said that she never felt Paula's ultimate goal was to get married and have children. Had Paula lived, Lynn imagined that she would have been a world traveler, a businesswoman, perhaps. Or, as she put it, "the woman purposefully rolling a white suitcase through the airport."

Chapter 5

Her Coming of Age

IN THE SUMMER OF 1967, AS THEIR PARENTS' MARRIAGE
was deteriorating, Paula and Lynn discovered Bever Park.
Built up on a hill that rises 163 feet above downtown Cedar
Rapids, Bever is a wooded expanse east of the city adjacent
to the tony Vernon Heights and Ridgewood neighborhoods.
In the summer, Bever Park offered walking and biking trails,
tennis, and swimming. In the winter, kids came to skate on
an iced-over field or to sled Cannonball Run, which sloped
down from the reservoir, the park's pinnacle. There was a
candy pavilion where a bagful of sweets cost a quarter and
even a makeshift zoo, which was dismantled in the early 1970s
when more people began to consider the ethical treatment of
animals. In Paula's time, though, the tiny zoo's wrought-iron
cages were stocked with bears, monkeys, an ostrich, even a
lion, whose roar could be heard splitting the night in the surrounding neighborhoods.

For young kids—nine, ten, eleven—who were given the
freedom to walk from the neighborhoods abutting the park,
Bever was a magical place. But for the junior high schoolers
looking to while away late afternoons after last bell or yawning

weekend and summer days, what Bever offered was numerous secluded spots beyond the reach of adult eyes, where they could congregate at dusk, break off in twos, and head into the woods to make out.

For Paula and Lynn, Bever Park, just a couple miles from their house, was another world. The sisters attended Catholic school—an expense Jim had insisted on and which says a fair amount about the importance he placed on religion. Jim and Carol didn't have money to throw away. The girls started at St. Matthew elementary, where they'd been baptized and confirmed, and moved on to Regis. The student body there was made up of white kids from the east side almost exclusively. The school, located at the end of G Avenue, their very block, might as well have been in their backyard for the widening of the world it granted them.

But Bever Park was different. The boys who hung out there were from all over Cedar Rapids. They came from the public schools, from the moneyed neighborhoods in the southeast, from the working-class areas in the northeast, and from mostly African American Oak Hill. So different from the buttoned-up parochial-school boys at Regis, indeed the only boys Paula and Lynn had ever really known.

The sisters meshed easily with this group of kids, and before long they were begging their parents to let them transfer from Regis to Washington, the public high school most of their new friends attended. Jim was opposed to the move. He believed a Catholic education kept his daughters from distraction, their grades up, and their minds focused. But he agreed on the condition that both girls maintain their grades. And with that, Paula and Lynn changed their course, beginning their sophomore and junior years, respectively, at George Washington Senior High School.

For her part, Paula maintained her grades. Aside from the outlying A in English or American Study, or D in physical education, Paula earned mostly Bs and Cs. She graduated 192nd in a class of 506, in the top third with a GPA of 2.6. Her transcript, which tracked all three of her years at Washington as well as her time at Regis, indicated that she scored a 118 on the Henmon-Nelson IQ test given to her as a sophomore. While IQ tests are fraught for many reasons, her score indicates a "high average" intelligence. Which leads me to believe that Paula was smart and also that she could have done better in school.

On her transcript, a section on "personality and character ratings" says that her teachers found her alert and well groomed. She was mature, cooperative, and had leadership potential, but she scored lowest in industry and initiative. This assessment fits with what I heard from her classmates about how they respected and looked up to her, about how they found her kind. It fits with what I can glean from looking at her photograph—well groomed. And it fits with my hunch that she could have gotten better grades had she decided to. It also fits with what I intuit served as a distraction (from achievement in classes)—namely, boys. I'll add that this is a *normal* distraction, one I had in spades myself.

At Washington, there were no uniforms, no nuns, no chapel, no catechism. What's more, the boys were better looking than those at Regis, and they knew how to have more fun. That fascination went both ways. Lynn and Paula's arrival at Washington raised eyebrows. In the arcade, where the students collected in loose knots before school and in between classes, the Oberbroeckling sisters—tall and twiggy

with long, shining blonde hair—sparked whispers and elic-
ited sideways glances.

Kathy McHugh, Paula's classmate, told me that Washington was as cliquey as any high school. There were the "country club" kids, whose families had money, and then there was
everybody else. Paula was one of everybody else, by which
Kathy meant Paula wasn't popular. I had a hard time reconciling this idea. I equated beauty with popularity, but apparently having one did not guarantee the other. It was the girls,
though, who drew lines between groups. Whether or not one
belonged to the country club didn't seem to matter as much
to the boys.

At Washington the boys flocked to Paula. They stared at
her during class. They vied for her attention. At home, her
phone rang constantly. Boys from school calling to chat with
her, to ask her out, to hear her voice. So much so that she
couldn't field them all or didn't want to. Sometimes she tried
to pawn these boys off on Lynn. She once told her sister that
she'd heard a kid from school had plans to call and ask her
out.

"I don't want to go out with him," Paula had said to Lynn.
"So I'm going to tell him you're going to go."

To which Lynn responded, "Oh, no, I'm not!" But she did,
which was the first hint for me of their shifting dynamic. Paula
was gaining the upper hand.

• • •

All women receive male attention. Beautiful women, like
Paula, receive more. From catcalls and low whistles to bold
hands that snake around shoulders, that find the soft backs of
arms, that cup knees, conveying familiarity, entitlement, ownership. To outright groping and blatant staring. Being noticed

can be thrilling, or it can disarm. A male gaze can bolster ego or it can be awkward, threatening, sexualizing. It can come at too young an age. The awareness of appraisal affects behavior—how a woman walks, sits, touches her face. It can make a woman throw her shoulders back with confidence or curl into herself with discomfort. Attention and its lack play a role in a woman's very conception of herself.

It is difficult for me to guess what that type of unrelenting male attention might have felt like for a young Paula because my experience was so different. I was gawky—braces, glasses, bad perm. I turned no heads. I got no phone calls. I was certainly never so overwhelmed by interested parties that I had to pawn suitors off on my friends like Paula did. That said, in my seventh-grade class, there was a girl who'd captured the boys' attention. She was soft-voiced and round-shouldered. Like Paula, she had long blonde hair. She and I had math together, and when the teacher was facing the chalkboard, the boys in class would subtly turn their desks toward hers and proceed to stick out one leg, thrusting their flexed foot in her direction. It took me a while to figure out that this rigid leg was a metaphor for the boner they got when they looked at her. I can remember envying this attention both before and after I understood its meaning. At the time, when I'd watch the interaction between these boys and this girl, I wanted nothing more than to be her, or to be anyone who inspired so much lust and wanting. Now, when I think back with my adult eyes, all I can recall is this girl's reddened face, her lowered gaze, her obvious discomfort and disquiet, her complete lack of preparedness for so much provocation.

A boy from my middle school called another girl I knew a "butter face," which I learned meant she had everything (hot ass, great tits) "but a" pretty face. I overheard him say that she should wear a bag over her head. If he said this about her, I couldn't imagine what he'd say about me. I was so petrified by the thought of being noticed that I couldn't even will myself onto the equipment in the gym, unable to bear the idea of anyone seeing how my butt and thighs strained against my sweatpants. If I couldn't be beautiful, then I wanted to be invisible.

I have found that a central conflict of womanhood is the wish to be thought beautiful and simultaneously to go unnoticed. Being looked at makes me uncomfortable, that discomfort coming from the knowledge that I'm being appraised. I feel disgust for this person for daring to look at me at all and simultaneously a desperate desire for them to find me beautiful.

Historian and author Stephanie Coontz describes a study whereby modern middle-school girls "rejected the old behavioral norms for femininity. They did not feel there was anything they *must do* or *could not do* because they were female. But they held strong beliefs about how they *must* or *must not look* [italics Coontz's]. Appearing 'hot' was mandatory, although looking 'slutty' . . . threatened a girl's social standing."

These pressures aren't bestowed solely by men. They are enforced by women as well, who judge and, many times, do so more harshly than men. Remember Naomi Wolf's "beating heart of the beauty myth" where a woman's worth fluctuates through the presence of another? The difference is that male attention comes with greater risk. Homicides, globally, are carried out by men in stratospherically higher numbers than by women.

But that's not all. Coontz goes on to say that "an early emphasis on being sexy can not only push a girl into initiating sex before she is emotionally ready but can also stunt the full development of her other interests and competencies."

This recalls Paula's lack of "industry and initiative." It also makes me think of my own experience. I spent my teenage years certain that if only I were beautiful the world would open up for me. When, years later, after moving to New York, I felt beautiful for the first time, my life did change, but not in the way I had anticipated. Once my appearance was validated by male attention, I found myself suddenly able to contribute, say, to conversations in ways I hadn't been able to before. I could risk humiliation because even if someone thought me unintelligent, I knew they either wanted me, which was power, or approved of my appearance, which was respect. So, rather than being granted some universal acceptance, some implicit adoration that buoyed me past everyday discomfort and disappointment, what I found was that feeling beautiful allowed me to simply *be* me—the me who has opinions and thoughts and ideas. (Said another way, it allowed the full development of my interests and competencies. Ahem.)

So, attention can be a cross but it can also grant the potency of confidence, the bravery to engage in risk, the capacity to say what you think, to be who you are. Attention is validation. It is permission to do and be and act.

Admitting this embarrasses me. It makes me feel perverse and shallow and weak, but it is true. And it calls into question all the ways in which Paula changed after transferring to Washington and how much of her evolution was a result of her being the locus of relentless attention.

• • •

After the Oberbroeckling sisters started school at Washington, Lynn began dating a senior. The couple then introduced Paula to Steve Scheib so the four could double-date. Steve, a senior on the football team, described the Paula that he dated—the new girl who had just left Catholic school, just started public— as "a young stork that had not matured into adulthood. She was exuberant and really idealistic. She was trying to find her way because she had a sister who kind of called the shots."

Neither relationship lasted the year, and by June of 1968 Lynn met and fell in love with the boy she would eventually marry. Once together, Lynn began spending much of the time she might have spent with Paula developing her new relationship.

The sisters had always been close. Only thirteen months apart, they spent their childhoods traversing virtually the same developmental territory. This made them best friends as much as siblings. As little girls, they ran and played side by side. They shared clothes, purses, shoes, and a bedroom into their teenage years. As they got older, they moved together like swans. On Saturdays they headed downtown to visit their grandmother Vera at Siegel's. She'd give them a dollar to take to Woolworth's for a plate of fries and a Coke, which cost 35 cents.

But once Lynn met her future husband, she found that when the sisters were together, at home or on the way to school, they tended to bicker over borrowed clothes. It was from this strained distance that Lynn watched Paula change before her eyes.

No longer forced to dress like every other girl in class, Paula traded her Catholic school uniform for clothes like those worn by the hippies on the west coast. She chose polyester and platform shoes, jumpsuits in rainbow colors, clothes she likely saw in magazines and on television stars like *Laugh-In's* Goldie Hawn. She preferred heels to sandals, despite her height—she was five feet eleven inches tall—which to me underscored her confidence. Carol would sew clothes for her girls, perhaps to save money. For Lynn she crafted outfits that were "sedate and made of nice material." But for Paula she made clothes that were flashier. A favorite was a taupe velvet Beatles-inspired tunic. With it, Paula wore a billowy cream satin blouse, boots, and elephant-leg pants that were fitted to the knee. Carol sewed Paula headbands. Paula adopted a black fur coat Carol had deemed ugly and cast off as well as Carol's so-called squaw bag. On Paula they both appeared as if they were out of the pages of a fashion magazine.

Along with her newfound love of clothes came a heightened attention to her appearance. She bought makeup, mostly Avon and Maybelline. Numerous tubes of lipstick in light shades like peach frost, which she applied in such a way that left the tip pointed like a sno-cone. She wore mascara and patted Pond's Angel Face on her cheeks. She blew her hair dry and then rolled it up with curlers. She wore her fingernails long and manicured, and spritzed her pulse points with Lanvin's Arpège or My Sin. She hung big hoop earrings from her lobes, dangled bangles around her wrists. And she exercised. She maintained her 22-inch waist, something Lynn said was a point of pride, with "one of those wheelie things that you got down on your knees and rolled forward." She also had a "little bust exerciser."

These outward changes begat inward ones, or perhaps they simply laid them bare. Larry Martin was one of a group of boys with tricked-out cars and leather jackets who descended on Washington High in the early hours before first bell to peel out and "slide around doing burnouts." These boys with hot cars came to show off for each other and for the girls who stood on the sidelines and watched. Larry remembers that when he drove over in his yellow Pontiac 2+2 and leaned out his open window, Lynn hung back, primly, but Paula was playful. Once she approached him and asked, "Why do you beat your car like that?" Larry shrugged. It was a minor encounter. But the point was, Paula wasn't afraid to engage, to call Larry out, to voice her opinion. Outward and inward had fused.

The difference between the shy girl Paula had been and the confident young woman she was becoming was so stark that Lynn would see her across the room at parties and hardly recognize her. It was as if the two sisters had switched places, Lynn folding back into herself, becoming the quiet girl, the wallflower, while Paula metamorphosed into the brazen, beguiling one, the one people could hardly turn away from. Lynn said that Paula possessed this dual ability to charm and then turn around and act the little innocent, which provoked both fluster and fascination. She said that Paula's magnetism was unexplainable. But when I hear those words—magnetism, charm—I think immediately of Jim. Perhaps Paula was more her father's daughter than anyone knew.

One afternoon not long after Lynn met her future husband, the two were hanging out with Paula in the girls' grandmother's living room. Sitting beside Lynn's boyfriend on the couch, Paula draped her slender arm around his shoulders and turned to Lynn: "You know," she said, "if I wanted him, I could have him."

Lynn remained neutral. "Yeah, you think so?"

"Yeah, I could just do that," Paula said, then smiled. "But I'm not going to."

Everyone laughed. And Paula winked.

Lynn used this story as an example of the ways in which Paula could be funny. The humor lay in the fact that Paula would never steal anyone's boyfriend, much less her own sister's. The first time I heard this story, reading through Susan's interviews with next to no context, I found Paula's words appalling for their cruelty. I felt hurt on Lynn's behalf. They seemed evidence that Paula was a mean girl who, because she was beautiful, considered herself better than everyone else, including her own sister. But my judgment has evolved. I still don't see humor as Lynn did. But what I do see is a defining of roles. A drawing of lines.

Paula had spent her entire life up to that point living in relation to her older sister. She barely spoke as a child, allowing Lynn to do all the talking for her. She was shy, quiet, misunderstood. She looked up to and followed Lynn everywhere. But her experience at Washington had seeded and grown her confidence. It had allowed her to become herself, a woman with her own power, who didn't need to rely on her sister to usher her through the world. Paula no longer had to be satisfied with being second to Lynn. She could be whomever she pleased. She could be a woman who stole her own sister's boyfriend. She wasn't that woman, but she could be.

Alongside this new confidence, Paula began behaving in ways that shocked Lynn. She flitted from car to car at the free drive-in, talking to all kinds of people, making jokes, holding court. The sisters would invite their girlfriends to spend the night. Once Carol and Jim were safely asleep, Paula and their guests would sneak out the bedroom window. They would spend the dark hours running around the neighborhood, meeting up with other kids. Debbie talked about meeting Paula at Cedar Memorial Cemetery at night where they'd rendezvous with a group of boys they considered friends. They smoked cigarettes, zigzagged around the fountains, the shadowy statues. Lynn, though, never joined them. She stayed right where she was at home, pajamas on, waiting for the girls to return. It seems Lynn worried about getting caught, about repercussions. Paula, though, acted fearless. Perhaps she no longer cared, if she ever had, what her parents thought.

Part of this disregard was likely the result of the slow burn for life and love that starts at thirteen, fourteen, fifteen, with puberty and a gradual awareness of the possibility of sex. This potential heightened by the dawning realization that one doesn't necessarily *have* to do everything one's parents say and of course also by Paula's newfound self-confidence. Though perhaps there was another factor at play, something that was exacerbating her brazen behavior. Perhaps Paula's actions were also punishment.

After the divorce, Jim wasted no time in marrying one of his old girlfriends. By the time Paula graduated high school, her father and his new wife had moved across the country to Grand Junction, Colorado. Thus magnifying the loss: her father had not only left the house, he'd left the city and the state. Steve Scheib, that sophomore-year boyfriend, said that Paula didn't often talk about her parents' divorce but that when she did, she seemed hurt. The way he put it was that she didn't understand why her dad didn't love her mother anymore.

In the 1950s and '60s nearly half of American households were comprised of nuclear families. On television and in magazines, women stayed home baking cookies and cleaning house while their husbands rushed off to work. This was the era of *Good Housekeeping* and *Ladies' Home Journal*, of *The Adventures of Ozzie and Harriet* and *Father Knows Best*, *Leave It to Beaver* and *The Donna Reed Show*. All of which unsubtly set up expectations for children of living with both parents. There were no popular television shows that portrayed single motherhood despite the fact that the war had left many women widowed.

The point being, there was stigma then to having divorced

parents. Children of divorce were often looked down on by their teachers, by their peers, by the adults in the community. Kathy McHugh, Paula's classmate, described being mocked by other students. "My best friend in sixth grade told me, 'My family is better than yours because I have a daddy,'" McHugh said. It wasn't uncommon for parents to forbid their children to hang out with the children of divorce.

Certainly the stigma wasn't as great when my parents separated in the late '80s, divorce being that much more prevalent. I don't recall being castigated by our community. But looking back I can think of only one other kid from school whose parents were divorced. She and I were close friends, and so were our mothers. Probably this was no coincidence. But judgment aside, I was gutted when my father left. I had believed that my family would remain intact forever. My parents had let me down on the ideal I had come to expect. They had broken my trust. And for that I was furious.

My father moved into a small apartment across town after my parents separated. Once the divorce was finalized, I saw him on Wednesday nights and every other weekend. Rather than turn my anger at the dissolution of our family on the person who had left, the one who had sought the divorce, my father, I turned it on the person who was there, the parent who was present, my mother. I punished her with a relentless sour disposition, sharp tongue, and rampant disobedience. We fought constantly.

In the wake of my parents' separation, I hung out with boys my mother disliked, engaging in behavior I knew she disapproved of. I began running with a group of kids who rode skateboards and listened to hair bands. They hung crosses from their necks, emblazoned skulls on their skin and clothing, cut holes in their black jeans. They wore their short hair long in front so that it covered one eye and flew back like wings when they skateboarded. They were harmless, but their appearance was intimidating and that's what drew me to them. I also wanted to intimidate, to make the anger I felt for my parents' divorce manifest.

I'd invite these kids over after school when my mother was still at work, my father living across town. This despite my mom's explicit instructions forbidding me from having anyone in the house when she was away. These boys and I experimented with smoking and drinking. I let them kiss me, sneak their clammy hands up my shirt, under my bra. Like Paula, I slipped out at night, boldly coming in through the garage door in the morning as if I'd only been out for an early walk. I got arrested for vandalism. I came home drunk in the middle of the afternoon and, when my mother threatened to call the police, I did so myself. I did all of this as much to show my mother that I couldn't be controlled as to differentiate myself from her.

My mother-in-law rebelled against her parents during her teen years too. And, like Paula, Susan's rebellion also included Bever Park. In high school she'd lie about where she was going and then meet up with friends at Bever, especially boys. Or she'd sneak off to her boyfriend's house to have sex while his mother was at work, throwing it in her father's face when she returned just to make him angry. She says she did this in order to get back at her parents for their arguing and hard partying. Susan's behavior eventually got her shipped off to boarding school, an event she says set her on her life's course. Her behavior was worse there—she began smoking, both marijuana and cigarettes, and drinking too—but what she gained was a widening of scope. Her lens was no longer Cedar Rapids and all the people she had always known. Now it was kids from all over the world, most of them with a lot of money and ambition. So much so that Susan grew her own ideas—growth and potential by proximity. Privilege by proximity in addition to privilege because of privilege; her parents could afford to outsource her when they felt they couldn't manage her. Carol never could have afforded to do that with Paula.

• • •

Teenagers are meant to cleave from their parents. It's biological and imperative. But this necessity makes the process no less turbulent. Mothers and their children begin literally as one. Even after birth, after the initial separation, mother and child often act as halves of the same whole, moving, eating, sleeping in tandem. Which means separating from the mother represents the loss of a portion of one's original self, a piece that has sadly outlasted its function. Acting out by making choices counter to the ones their parents might make for them is one way teenagers initiate this split. It's the way I did it. It's the way Susan did it. It sounds like it was the way Paula did it too.

Carol was the parent who initiated the Oberbroecklings' divorce, but she did so in response to Jim's actions. I don't know whether Paula was aware of that fact. I do know that as Paula entered her junior year in high school, her parents recently divorced, a rift opened up between her and her mother. Or perhaps, it already being there, it widened, eventually becoming insurmountable.

In the end, Paula would pack her belongings and move out of her mother's home. She would separate herself from what should have been a support. The distance between Paula and her mother became so vast that on the night Paula disappeared she was living, more or less, on her own.

During her conversation with Susan, Carol considered her relationship with Paula: "When she died, Paula and I weren't close. I just felt like I had lost her," Carol said. "Paula sometimes didn't like to follow the rules, and of course I wasn't happy about the Robert thing."

Chapter 6
The Black Boyfriend

"THE ROBERT THING" REFERRED TO ROBERT WILLIAMS. Those three words were code for Paula's choice to date an African American. They were code for Carol's choice to disavow Paula's decision. And they were code for everything that resulted from the showdown between mother and daughter that ensued. But I would learn that that phrase, "the Robert thing," went beyond Carol and Paula. Tied up in Carol's choice of words were so many particulars about the pressures that existed in the middle of the country in the 1960s. In them I heard defiance and dismissiveness but also embarrassment, regret, even shame.

Robert met Paula for the first time in the Washington High School cafeteria. He'd found her in tears. When he asked what was wrong, she told him that someone had taken all of her lunch money. Robert consoled Paula by buying her a Coke.

Weeks passed before he was able to squirrel up the nerve to ask Paula out on a date. When he finally did, she accepted, and the couple made a plan to meet downtown at the Iowa

Theatre. *Bullitt* with Steve McQueen, *Funny Girl* about the life of comedienne Fanny Brice, *Night of the Living Dead*, and *Romeo and Juliet* with its star-crossed lovers were some of the highest-grossing films in the fall of 1968. Perhaps they saw one of those. After the movie, Robert called Paula again and then he called her again. And easy as rolling down a hill, the two became a couple.

Robert wore thick black glasses, which made him appear studious if a touch goofy. His friends described him as affable, said that he liked to party, to dance, that he was a sharp dresser and someone who was always up for a good time. He told Susan during one of several conversations they had in 2008 that his relationship with Paula wasn't "racial"—him dating a white girl, her dating a Black boy. "Paula was just someone that I got to know. And I got to know her well. And I got to understand her. And she got to understand me too. She was someone that I cared about very deeply, and we grew closer and closer and closer as time went on. And we fell in love."

Initially, Robert had been drawn to Paula's appearance. He described Paula as having a terrific smile and eyes that woke him up whenever he looked into them. But it was her personality that he fell in love with. She was unfailingly positive, he said, so much so that it was impossible to cling to a negative mood in her presence. She possessed an emotional radiance that was contagious.

Early on, Paula confessed to Robert that she didn't think her mother would approve of their relationship. He asked what she thought they should do about it. She answered by admitting that she really liked him. She said she didn't want to lose him as a friend. He smiled. He liked her too.

That Carol might disapprove wasn't a surprise. Robert was well aware of how interracial relationships were regarded in Cedar Rapids. At Washington, where the student body was more progressive than the city's population as a whole, it was becoming more common to encounter mixed-race couples. But generally in Cedar Rapids the consensus was that the mixing of races was unnatural. Even George Steinke—a white classmate of Paula's who grew up living among Black families in Oak Hill and who claimed to have been part of a racially mixed group of friends—knew the rules: "You did not date a Black." But I sensed that it was more complicated than this, because the fact was that there *were* interracial couples in Cedar Rapids. So, if the assessment depended on the person speaking, then how had each come to his or her conclusion?

• • •

At this time the whole country was crackling with protest and civil disobedience. In 1954, the U.S. Supreme Court had struck down the "separate but equal" doctrine that had allowed for state-sanctioned discrimination. The following decades saw sit-ins organized to desegregate lunch counters in the South; clashes between nonviolent protesters and police in Birmingham, Alabama; and the 1963 March on Washington, 250,000 people strong. In 1964, the Civil Rights Act, prohibiting discrimination on the basis of race, sex, color, religion, or national origin, was made into law. There was Martin Luther King Jr.'s "I Have a Dream" speech and, barely six months before Paula and Robert's relationship began to blossom, King's assassination in the spring of 1968. In its wake, rebellions, termed "riots" by the police, shook entire cities—Washington, Chicago, Detroit. But not, it would seem, Cedar Rapids.

An article in the *Des Moines Register* from 1968 reported that Harold Hughes, the governor of Iowa, had claimed that rumors of impending racial violence were prompting citizens to arm themselves. He said that women and children were afraid to go out after dark. But from everything I could tell, Cedar Rapids remained mostly quiet.

"Cedar Rapids was in a bubble. We weren't protesting. No one was burning down shit. No one was doing nothing. Everything was business as usual," Lovie Bassett, a Black student who was in the class ahead of Paula's, told me.

The population of the city at the time was just over 110,000, of which African Americans made up less than 2 percent. That's fewer than 2,000 people, which is to say the community was very small. Most Black families lived in Oak Hill. The houses there were modest, sometimes rundown, usually brilliantly painted, a rainbow of wood-framed homes sitting on dirt yards. The community was strong. Kids played in the streets or at the Jane Boyd Community House, located just up the hill. More than once, I heard Oak Hill described as a great place to live and to be a kid. But the reality was that most of these families hadn't had a choice. They'd been forced to live in Oak Hill systemically because their blue-collar jobs, often the only ones they could get, wouldn't afford them more, or they were forced overtly by real estate agents who refused to show them houses in so-called white neighborhoods.

Percy Harris, who would become a well-respected doctor and the town medical examiner and who also happened to be Black, attempted to buy a parcel of land from St. Paul's United Methodist Church in one such neighborhood after completing his internship at St. Luke's Hospital. His plan was to build a house for his family of fourteen. There was an uproar. Many white people fought the sale, claiming they feared their property would devalue if Harris moved into the neighborhood. After taking a vote counted 460 to 291 in Harris's favor, the church approved the sale in 1961. Progress! But this didn't stop someone from throwing a rock through his window once he'd moved his family in.

One of the women who helped to put the first African American on the police force in Cedar Rapids described a similar event: a rock through a window, death threat attached. There were a handful of men and women who were actively engaged in fighting this type of hostility and in improving the situation of the Black community in Cedar Rapids. In 1942, they formed a chapter of the NAACP in order to desegregate the Ellis Park pool, which had refused entry to a Black student from nearby Coe College. Their action included marches and appeals to the state government. They also lobbied to diversify the staff in the public school system, and succeeded in placing the first Black teacher in a classroom in 1964. There were other successful progressive grassroots projects aimed at community building and improving race relations, but unlike in the bigger American cities, there were no protests or sit-ins. No fire, as it were, in the air. There was just the status quo: a mostly segregated city, and a marginalized community's careful attempts to eke out small civic improvements for itself.

"To many of us in Cedar Rapids and in Iowa, many of us African Americans, we were really not affected by [the civil rights movement] so much," said Rick Williams, who was a teammate of Robert's (and no relation). "I think the thing that had the most impact on me at that time was the Vietnam War. That was probably the greatest motivation I had to study a little bit more and to get into college. But the civil rights movement? I mean it was there, and I was aware of it and paid attention to it, but . . . and we had problems here in Cedar

Rapids, but they were minor. We didn't have any riots and things like that here. I was aware of it, but it was a time and it never did affect my life."

The Washington High School district was comprised of both the northeast and southeast quadrants of Cedar Rapids. This included Oak Hill, thus making a small portion of the student body Black. For the most part, the races there self-segregated but there was a core group of students who intermixed. In 1968, the students came together to elect Lovie Bassett homecoming queen. According to Kathy McHugh, "*Everyone loved Lovie.*" Sports brought the boys together and a mutual curiosity drew the Black guys and white girls. Rick Williams hypothesized that this was a result of the sheer size of the Black community. It was so small and tight-knit that, just as the public-school boys were a revelation for Lynn and Paula after years of Catholic school, the white girls proved novel for the Black boys who'd grown up like siblings with the girls in Oak Hill. Lovie, who dated a couple white guys in college, echoed this: "For a Black girl growing up in Cedar Rapids, the little handful of Black guys, you know, they're like brothers. You know them all your life. . . . I didn't date anyone in Cedar Rapids because there was nobody to date."

Robert and Paula took it slow at first, keeping a low profile while the people around them got used to the idea of their hanging out together as friends. Paula didn't tell many people that she and Robert were romantically involved. She kept the secret even from Lynn. As I read the interviews and began to conduct my own research, I found evidence that the couple had done a good job keeping their relationship under wraps, and a few people, fifty years on, even claimed to be surprised that Paula and Robert had dated at all, which in turn surprised me. Steinke, who was in Paula's class and who regularly spent time at the Oberbroeckling house, said he didn't find out that the two had been dating until the end of his senior year. Larry Martin, who hung out with Paula frequently in the months before she died, told me he didn't know about Paula and Robert either. But then Kathy McHugh told me that everybody knew about their relationship because "they made such a striking couple."

For their part, Robert said, Paula and he met in quiet out-of-the-way places, mindful that the mere fact of their company—a white girl, a Black boy—might earn them sideways glances. They spent a lot of time in dark movies where their hands brushed over popcorn and candy, where they had their first kiss. They grabbed hamburgers and malts at Henry's after school. They went out under the cover of night. Paula occasionally went to Robert's basketball games to cheer him on. They went to parties where the races were mixed and where no one cared about the color of their skin. When they danced, they were so good that everyone cleared the floor in order to watch.

What must it have felt like to have to hide their feelings for each other, to not be able to share their happiness (their dancing!) with the people who were closest to them? I wondered if there was shame, undeserved but generated from acting outside the social code. Maybe there was some excitement. A thrill born from keeping a secret, in meeting in clandestine places. A buzz that heightened the chemistry already arcing through their teenaged bodies. There had to have been fear. Fear of being found out by the wrong person. Fear of whatever repercussions might accompany the exposure of their relationship—ostracism, conflict, punishment. Because secrets almost always find their way out. And this one was no exception.

As time passed, more people began to catch on. Robert said that Lynn, for one, saw him and Paula talking, perhaps a little too closely, in the hallway at school and put it together. Lynn was lovesick herself and maybe she noticed in her sister the same symptoms that had been roiling within her. The two shared a bedroom, after all.

When she found out, Lynn was shocked by the relationship. She was opposed to interracial dating on principle, something she had likely been taught at home and something she seems embarrassed about in retrospect. "I know that she didn't tell me right away because . . . I didn't . . . I know this sounds horrible, but I just didn't agree with that," she said to Susan.

One time Paula convinced Lynn to accompany her to a party in Oak Hill. There was dancing and mingling in someone's dark basement. One of their Black classmates tried to coax Lynn away from the wall and onto the dance floor. She bristled at the notion, telling him, "I can't do that."

Robert and Lynn were both seniors; Paula was a year younger. Robert said that after Lynn learned about him and Paula, she would glare witheringly at him from across the classroom. One day, Lynn approached him, asking what exactly he thought he was doing with her sister. Knowing better than to engage, Robert raised his hand, he said, and asked for a hall pass.

Though Lynn didn't agree with Paula's decision to date Robert, she did help her sister in one crucial way. She kept Paula's secret from their mother, whom both girls knew would be furious.

Carol was aware that Paula had a new boyfriend, but she didn't know who he was. The only information she had was that Paula talked to this boy on the phone, that Paula liked him, and that he played basketball. She also knew his nick-name: "Mr. Basketball."

It wasn't until the spring of 1969, during the televising of the state basketball tournament, in which the Washington High School team had earned the right to play, that Carol learned Robert was Black. The whole family was crowded into the living room of the Oberbroecklings' house on G Avenue. As they watched the game on television, Robert came into view and someone said, "Oh, there's Mr. Basketball!"

Carol's eyes went wide. "That's him? That's him? Oh my God, is that him?"

Interracial dating might have been accepted among a certain progressive set of young people. But Carol, like many in the older generation, remained resolutely closed-minded, ingrained in her racism, and she did not want her daughter dating an African American.

"I was born in Oklahoma. And in Oklahoma, when they approached you, they got in the street so that you could walk on the sidewalk. It was a whole different world for me when I came up to Cedar Rapids to live," Carol told Susan. "I don't believe in the interracial marriage. I just don't believe in that."

I can't help but point out here that Carol and Jim's relationship had also been frowned upon—she from the west side, he from the east. A match that, at the time, raised eyebrows. But Carol seemed not to put this together or, if she did, she didn't mention it.

The disapproval of romantic partners on the basis of lineage was a storyline in my family as well. My father's parents, committed Dutch Reformed Protestants, had always hoped that marriage might lead their nonpracticing son back to the church. When my father announced his plans to marry my mother, who was not only not a Protestant but a Catholic of all things, they made no secret of their disapproval. My grandmother badgered my mother for years over ensuring the "right religious course" for my brother and me. My parents raised us without religion, which drove my grandmother mad. But then in the '80s, when my mother became very ill, my grandmother took a Greyhound bus to Kansas City to care for her. She stayed for weeks, made multiple trips. My mother says she is forever indebted to her.

Regardless, there it was. Paula was trapped. Either she disobeyed her mother or she disobeyed her own heart. The decision was complicated. On the surface there was the blinding fact of love and attraction that can bring two people together despite nearly everything else. An attraction one could argue that is even more overwhelming in youth. There was, perhaps, a righteousness surrounding the certainty that she and Robert were doing nothing wrong. But there was also the fact that Paula and her mother had been on shaky ground for months. The tensions raised during the divorce and from the fact of Paula's maturing had long been simmering beneath the surface of their relationship. Dating someone her mother so vehemently disapproved of could have been one more way Paula was asserting her independence, or perhaps more simply it was a rebuke. Either way, when faced with this decision, Paula chose to flout her mother and follow her own heart.

The reveal of Robert's race magnified the stress on Paula and Carol's already tenuous relationship. Carol found out that Paula had let Robert drive her car, which "broke her heart." The tit for tat reached ugly levels. According to Debbie Kellogg, Carol communicated her disapproval by forbidding Paula the use of the dish towels lest she "contaminate" them.

As the rift between Paula and her mother widened, it would appear that Paula found solace with Robert and his.

Robert's mother was part Native American and was light-skinned with red hair; his father was from the West Indies; his relatives were African. As a teenager, Robert, raised among "all sorts of people," seemed to have a solid sense of self. Robert's mother embraced Paula. She would take Robert, his sister, and Paula shopping at Killian's downtown where there was a coffee shop in the basement, or across the street to Armstrong's department store, where there was an animated Christmas display. They'd stroll, pop in and out of shops, stop for a soda, for lunch. Robert said Paula confided in his mother, felt close to his sister.

Meanwhile, the more Carol tried to control Paula's behavior, the more Paula writhed within her grasp. According to Detective James Steinbeck, who worked on Paula's case, Paula began sneaking out at night to see Robert. In the back of Robert's house there was what Steinbeck called a "lean-to shack," but which I envision as a covered porch, where Robert and Paula would often hang out. Rick Williams said most of the Black guys didn't have cars, so it was up to the white girls to come to them. Plus, he said, interracial dating was more accepted in the Black community. Steinbeck said that a couple of times, when Carol suspected that Paula was at Robert's, she called the police. "I went and dug her out of that place," Steinbeck said. Did Carol's calls contribute to the CRPD's initial indifference to Paula's disappearance? Maybe the police were accustomed to them.

Lynn didn't punish her sister in the same way that her mother did. "I stuck up for her. I stuck up for her to my mom," said Lynn. She recalled one evening after Paula moved out. Paula had stopped by the house after clocking out of work, and Paula and Carol got into an argument. Paula didn't own a car. Rather than wait at her mother's house for the person with whom she had arranged to drive her home that night, Paula decided to leave on foot; the more than three-mile walk would have taken over an hour. When the door closed behind her, Lynn said to her mother, "I'm not letting her walk." She got in her car, picked Paula up, and drove her home. "I wasn't like my mom," said Lynn. "I didn't agree with it, but it wouldn't make me change my feelings for her in the slightest. . . . I would defend her to my last and I would talk to her and I would never stop loving her."

Carol's type—white, not well educated, sheltered, likely brainwashed by the biases of her own parents, her own teachers, and her own community—was prevalent in the middle of the country in the 1960s. Fifty years seems not so long ago, and yet the United States had only *just* legalized interracial marriage in 1967. The same year had both Sidney Poitier in *Guess Who's Coming to Dinner,* about an interracial couple engaged to be married, *and* Secretary of State Dean Rusk offering to *resign* if his daughter's marriage to a Black man caused embarrassment to President Lyndon B. Johnson. In some ways Carol was just following suit. Unable to break new ground. To think for herself. I began to think of her as merely a cog in the giant wheel of racism, Carol blindly pushing it forward. This isn't meant to excuse her behavior. It is only an attempt at understanding her for who she was. A person who was the product of the people who had raised her and of the culture she witnessed around her, a person who was uninterested in or afraid of questioning the status quo, a status quo that she undeniably benefited from.

Carol never met Robert. "I never wanted to. Never wanted to even look at him. Nope. I just have an absolute closed mind.

I mean, things are different now than they were then," she said. She quickly added that she had changed. She listed a handful of African Americans she said she "adored," including a man who helped build her house. She also mentioned the nurse who cared for her in her old age, a woman who was white but was married to a Black man. "I just love Sarah, you know, and what she does is fine. It's just that I didn't want it for my family.

"But bless [Paula's] little heart, you cannot pick and choose who you fall in love with," said Carol a little later. "I think her heart belonged to Robert."

And so Paula—Paula, whose mother was a racist, whose sister and best friend didn't approve of her relationship—Paula chose to follow her heart, to date a Black boy, to not be a cog, to think for herself. It wasn't even a simple case of not being able to "choose who you fall in love with." Her heart, her judgment, were open from the beginning. She accepted Robert's Coke, his invitation, his kindness, all before loving him. She was the strong one. She was the change-maker, the person willing to face down where she came from, to call foul and form her own opinions and to show empathy and kindness to another human being. In this, Paula was ahead of her time. Or, at the very least, on the right side of history.

To me this was evidence of conviction and courage regardless of whether its catalyst was born of teenage hormones, because for Paula and Robert to date each other *was* to risk. There was the potential of damaging familial relationships that Paula faced. There was the threat to her reputation. "[Interracial dating] was the biggest 'no' there was," said Debbie Kellogg, who also had Black boyfriends in high school. "That made you a bad, slutty girl." And there was the risk to one's physical well-being, for despite the openness of some and the general fact of the civil rights movement happening elsewhere, racially motivated conflict still sparked, like flash paper, out of nothing at all.

One night after a basketball game hosted at Washington, Warren McCray, a white student, jumped Albert Carr, a Black student, outside the gymnasium. McCray used the N-word and knocked Carr to the concrete, leaving him unconscious. Onto Carr's closed eyes McCray dropped a handful of snow with the words "cool off." Albert Carr, only fifteen years old, was hospitalized and given ten stitches above his right eye; he had lacerations inside his mouth. Though the *Gazette*'s coverage doesn't specify a motive beyond teenage ribbing, it was widely understood that Carr's crime had been that he'd dated a white girl.° This occurred in 1963, a few years before Paula entered Washington, but the lesson had not been forgotten.

"In the back of our minds, with me and some of the other guys that had dated white girls, we had the scenario of what happened to Albert Carr. We were always concerned about getting around some white guys who maybe didn't approve of any interracial dating and having them say something and then having that whole scenario all over again," said Rick Williams.

It wasn't just Robert who risked violence from sanctimonious onlookers. Paula risked being hurt as well. Lynn, Rick Williams, and Kathy McHugh all described friction between

---

° McCray, who was seventeen and married, initially pleaded innocent to charges of assault and battery. But in the end, the charges were dropped at the behest of Albert Carr's parents. Carr's mother is quoted in the *Gazette* as saying, "My husband and I both agree that we do not wish to cause Warren McCray to feel that we are interfering with his education." This makes me wonder how much contact the McCrays and the Carrs had during this experience. And how much contact did the Carrs have with the school? Were they encouraged to back off? Threatened? Or were they just extremely forgiving and kind?

the white girls and the Black girls, each considering the other competition, for boys, for friends, for attention.

"Those Black girls did not like us white girls," said Lynn. "I got kicked. I got the books knocked out of my arms. They were the same with Paula." Kathy McHugh remembered this as well. And here's Rick Williams: "One thing that we had to be a little concerned with was that there were African American girls that didn't like the fact that we were going out with white girls too. I'm sure there were African American girls taking on a white girl too."

Lovie, whose best girlfriend was white, doesn't recall this tension, saying, "That's not my style; that's not something I'd have done. . . . I wasn't raised that way, I just think whoever people fall in love with, that's who they fall in love with." But in the police file, one boy told police: "There were some colored girls who were not appreciative of some of the white girls occupying the Black boys' time." The report said that this boy "believed that Paula Oberbroeckling and Robert Williams were part of this group who were not too well thought of in this black/white relationship."

In spite of all this, Rick witnessed many interracial relationships at Washington. The trick, he said, was in keeping them quiet—from the other kids at school and also from objecting parents. After Paula moved out of her home, Rick circumvented a girlfriend's disapproving parents by mailing her letters care of Paula's new address. Paula would host the couple at her home when they couldn't find anywhere else to go. The police report said that Paula's house was "the place where the white girls met their Black boyfriends." These couples knew that there was a potential price to be paid for their affection.

Robert and Paula did pay for their relationship. Nearly everyone remembered Paula as being universally liked, as a kind soul with a generous heart who was adored by everyone who knew her. But when the police came to interview Carol after Paula's disappearance, one of the things she told them was that Paula didn't have many friends. This disconnect confused me at first, but as I moved my way into her story, I came across multiple statements in the police report that gave me a sinking feeling. Ben Carroll told the police that after Paula started dating Robert, he made a point to "lose contact" with her because he knew that the relationship upset her mother. Debbie Kellogg also told the police that Paula had kept few friends since she started dating Robert because they didn't approve of his race. Paula was eighteen, barely an adult, on the outs with her family, and it turns out she didn't have many friends at a time when she really needed them.

After reading Robert's interview for the first time, I said to Susan that I felt bad for him. Their love had seemed real. He had seemed so broken.

"Yes," Susan agreed, "unless he killed her."

Robert admitted to the police that he and Paula had had arguments during the year and a half that they were together, and that he "did probably strike her on one occasion." A friend of Paula's said that she saw Robert "beat Paula up once in the yard at the 15th Street address, however, [he] did not beat her too badly." Lynn said, "I always thought way back then, thirty years ago, that Robert had something to do with it. That he was mad because she was dating Lonnie Bell and smacked her a little too hard. . . . But then people said how he just cared too much for her, to do something like that. That he just . . . there was no way that he could hurt her." Carol, for the record, said she never thought that Robert was involved.

Not long before Paula graduated from Washington, in the months after her eighteenth birthday and before her disappearance, Paula came into the kitchen while Carol was fixing supper. She asked if they could talk. "Mama," Carol claimed Paula said, "I'm going to get my own place."

Maybe Paula had realized that as long as she lived under her mother's roof she wouldn't be able to grow into whomever it was she was meant to be. Or maybe she just couldn't bear any more conflict.

Carol said her heart sank when she heard her daughter's words, but she tried to remain neutral. "Why are you doing that?" Paula was noncommittal, saying only that she felt she needed to be on her own.

"Does it have something to do with Robert?" Carol asked.

Paula told her it did not. Carol said she knew that this was a lie. Indeed, within weeks Paula moved into a house in Oak Hill just around the corner from where Robert and his family lived. But even this wouldn't be for long.

Chapter 7

The Detective

WHEN MY SON WAS A YEAR AND A HALF OLD, AND I WAS four months into the piecing together of Paula's story, one of the detectives who had worked on Paula's case stumbled onto Susan's website. He was incensed. "I cannot believe that there is all this conversation about this crime was not solved," he posted online. "The case was solved."

James Steinbeck proceeded to roughly sketch a story I'd read in the last entry of Paula's police file. The report had been composed by Assistant Police Chief Kenneth Vanous. The information therein, Vanous wrote, had come from a "reliable informant." Steinbeck's version went like this: Paula had been pregnant. The pregnancy was "going to ruin her big modeling career." Her "boyfriend" knew a pimp who expedited abortions for his girls. The pimp arranged for Paula to visit this man, a local chiropractor. During the procedure something went wrong, and Paula began to bleed. The chiropractor was unable to stop the hemorrhage, and Paula bled to death right there on the table. The chiropractor then called the pimp to dispose of Paula's body. The pimp and one of his henchmen bound her wrists and ankles so that it would look like a murder. The men threw her in a drainage ditch where the winter snow obfuscated her body until the spring thaw, at which point she was discovered by a couple of kids. "Case closed," Steinbeck might as well have written. "Move on."

Putting aside the fact that his timeline was wrong (Paula disappeared during the summer, and her body was discovered in November just as it was getting cold, not the other way around), and that the details that had failed to make sense the first time I heard this scenario continued to sound improbable (Why had she set out in the middle of the night? Why was she dressed as she was? Hers was the era of giant maxi pads suspended from women's waists by belts. Not the kind of thing a woman who was miscarrying could conceal under a flimsy dress), Steinbeck's proclamation was exciting. What if there was an answer to Paula's death? What if Paula had died during an illegal abortion?

The most common method of inducing an illegal abortion in the years leading up to *Roe v. Wade* was to introduce a foreign object like a catheter into the cervix. The invasion acted as an irritant that, in the way a speck of dust in the eye elicits tears, induced bleeding and ultimately miscarriage. The bleeding could last anywhere from an hour to a few days. When it worked, the catheter came out with the pregnancy and the bleeding eventually stopped. When it didn't, the practitioner had to start over with a larger catheter.

That was *if* there was an opportunity to try again. Because just as easily the catheter could puncture the wall of the uterus, blood-rich in pregnancy, and the woman could hemorrhage. Or it could puncture the uterus *and* the bowel, allowing fecal matter to leak into the abdomen. Or the woman could suffer an embolism, the obstruction of an artery by a blood clot or air bubble. Or the implement could become infected. The infection could remain local in the fallopian tubes, ovaries, uterus, or vagina, or it could spread throughout the body, invading the bloodstream and causing septicemia, whose chills, sweating, fever, and weakness could end in septic shock in the form of circulatory collapse. In 1968, the University of Southern California Los Angeles County Medical Center admitted 701 women with septic abortions, one for every fourteen deliveries.

According to the official reports (meaning those in which the cause of death was listed as abortion), in 1965, before the passage of *Roe v. Wade*, 200 women died yearly from illegal abortion. However, that number is likely much higher. Septic shock causes the blood pressure to plummet, the skin to go pale and clammy, the pulse to be fast but weak, and respiration to slow. Oftentimes it results in kidney or liver failure. This massive collapse of the body's systems has been used by doctors and families to disguise abortion death. Renal failure, for example, was often listed as the cause of death rather than the illegal abortion that led to it.

Susan reached out to Steinbeck immediately, but, in spite of his need to air his exasperation over our pursuit, he quickly grew reluctant to speak. Reading back issues of the *Gazette*, I thought I understood why. I learned that when Steinbeck left the Cedar Rapids Police Department in August 1973, the force was in chaos. The year leading up to his departure had seen the apprehension of a detective, Kenneth Millsap (who'd also investigated Paula's case), on charges of intoxication and resisting arrest. After being unceremoniously benched (read: embarrassed), Millsap turned around and sued the city for half a million dollars. Though he lost and then was eventually reinstated, the drama served to expose the culture at the CRPD.*

According to a front-page story in the *Gazette*, a "veteran member of the force" believed that morale in the department was "the lowest in more than a decade" and "service to the public [had] suffered." The piece asserted "intentional lack of cooperation among officers," "poor" communication, and personality conflicts. The list went on. A probe of police wrongdoing initiated by the county attorney led to the police chief's voluntary disability retirement and the unexplained resignation of the assistant chief, who was also head of the detective bureau.

Less than a year later, six members of the department—both current and former, and including Steinbeck himself—were indicted for some combination of conspiracy to injure the reputations of fellow officers, perjury, and obstruction of justice. These officers were also suspended and then reinstated and eventually vindicated. But there had been a lot of backstabbing and blame-throwing, reputations had been damaged, careers undermined. Steinbeck's for one. After leaving the CRPD, he ran for and won the office of public safety commissioner, overseeing both the police force and the fire department. But this too would be fraught with political drama, and he would last only two years in the position before

---

* Susan spoke with Kenneth Millsap, who is now deceased. Nowhere in his interview does he mention the drama that surrounded his tenure on the police force or the fact that he sued the department for $500,000. When Susan asked him whether there was corruption in the department, he said, "There was a departmental strife once in a while . . . there's always . . . in any quasi-military organization, you have the ins and the outs, you know, and one election you might be on the ins and the next one you might be on the outs. So, you always have two competing factions."

packing his family up and moving to Texas to retire from law enforcement altogether.

Perhaps Steinbeck's commenting on Susan's site had been reactive (his post appeared at 11:23 p.m.) and, on second thought, he had found himself reticent to reopen those wounds forty-five years on. But for me, this new window into the shambolic CRPD pointed toward one of the potential reasons no one was ever arrested for Paula's killing. How could these men deliver justice if, like squirrels, they spent all their time squabbling among themselves?

Indeed, Susan finally convinced Steinbeck to talk, and he told her, and then he told me, a story focused not on Paula but on the hubris of and mistakes made by the Cedar Rapids Police Department in the years surrounding Paula's death.

To hear Steinbeck tell it, the whole place had been corrupt. He, the only straight arrow, an idealist and a true believer in the righteousness of police work, was struggling to be effective in a department of betrayers and Machiavellian law enforcers. He called himself the Serpico of the CRPD, by which he meant the whistleblower, rule follower, persona non grata. He told me the reason he'd been subpoenaed by the district attorney was that "Millsap knew I wouldn't lie," but that his honesty had gotten him thrown out of favor with those in power—the once "fair-haired son" now the bad apple. Be patient, he said a few minutes into his spiel. "This [has] something to do with why the Paula case . . . ended, because there were some terrible things."

He started with Jean Halverson, a seventeen-year-old girl who had been in Paula's class and who had disappeared the fall before Paula did. (Yes, Washington High School had *two* missing girls in *one* graduating class.) Halverson had been shot to death in a clearing in a Cedar Rapids park. Thanks to some crackerjack detective work, much of it accomplished by Steinbeck (he ingratiated himself with key sources, and matched power pistons found at the scene of the crime with those of a gun stock for sale at a gun show, leading him directly to the suspect), the police narrowed in on one Richard Zacek. The police chief asked Steinbeck to interrogate Zacek himself, which led to a confession, the best-case scenario. Zacek admitted to Steinbeck that he'd spotted Halverson exploring a wooded area. He then ran home for his gun so that he could come back and rape her. But when he found himself face-to-face with Halverson, Zacek chickened out, and he shot her instead.

In April of 1970, Zacek took a plea deal in order to avoid life in prison and received 75 years for the murder of Jean Halverson. But not long into his sentence the ruling was overturned. Apparently, around the same time Steinbeck was getting Zacek to confess to killing Jean Halverson, two other members of the CRPD were illegally breaking into and entering Zacek's apartment in order to search for evidence. (Steinbeck said this happened without his knowledge.) The illegal search came up during the trial into police misconduct I mentioned earlier. Zacek's lawyers heard about it and pounced.

Zacek would be tried a second time, and he would enter a second plea deal. But this time he had leverage. With it he bought himself 35 years on the outside, reducing his sentence from 75 to 40 years. With a different judge he might have evaded his sentence altogether and the fault would have rested squarely on the shoulders of the CRPD.

Halverson wasn't the only victim to risk justice served because of police misconduct. There was also Maureen Brubaker Farley, a seventeen-year-old newlywed who lived in Cedar Rapids and whose body was found splayed across a junked car on the southwest side in 1971. Steinbeck claimed that the CRPD had a good suspect, but the police once again executed an illegal break-in that prevented the district attorney from using found evidence. It's been forty-nine years and, like the Oberbroecklings, Maureen Farley's family still has no clue what happened to their daughter.

"Naughty things," Steinbeck said over the phone about what the police department was up to. "There were so many things that went on . . . back then that whenever they would wrap up a case, they'd wrap it up because they couldn't tell all of the things, policies, and procedures that were illegal and unethical. And they had a very difficult time sweeping these matters under the rug."

What he meant was not that the police were trying to bury information but that they were trying to cover up their own mistakes with regard to how they procured said information. Steinbeck said that a lot of this was the result of the changing times. Many of the cops resented new laws governing police behavior. The Miranda warnings, for example, passed in 1966, guaranteed an arrestee's right not to self-incriminate. And *Escobedo v. Illinois*, passed in 1964, guaranteed a right to counsel. Often, officers would "forget" to employ these warnings or fail to administer them properly. These mistakes and oversights resulted in mistrials and justice going unserved. Just one more crack for a victim to fall through.

Although Steinbeck was clear with me—he knew of no such mistake made in Paula Oberbroeckling's case—he still seemed to be implying that it was possible. He, after all, hadn't been privy to everything. Had I been keyed into it, this might have led me down a different path: an investigation into police corruption, the ways in which their misdeeds were concealed, and the effects these cover-ups had on society, say. But at the time I was so blinded by the potential that Paula's homicide could be solved, indeed, that it *had* been solved, that I was incapable of seeing beyond this revelation. All I could think about was the chiropractor and the henchmen and the nurse. Where were these people? What if I could prove Steinbeck's theory?

Steinbeck told me a version of the abortion story, which he said he believed to be true. In it, he ID'd the chiropractor as Thomas Chester Sturgeon, "Doc" to his friends. Sturgeon died in 1999, so there would be no confronting him. The pimp was also dead. And Susan had already interviewed one of the men Steinbeck mentioned as dumping Paula's body. (He denied his involvement and spoke mostly in circles, pointing out intricacies that appeared to absolve him of culpability.) The nurse, however—the one from whom the chiropractor sought help, according to the informant in the police file—she was alive.

• • •

An Internet search revealed the woman's full name, address, and home number. I called the nurse half a dozen times—pacing the living room of my Brooklyn apartment, seated at the oak writing desk I'd wedged into my bedroom—at all hours of the day and evening—while my son was napping, after he'd gone to sleep, while he was out strolling with his sitter. Each time I left a message, spelled my name, slowly recited the digits of my phone number. Each time I hung up less hopeful that she would ever call me back.

Then one night, seconds after I'd tapped "end call," my phone startled me by ringing in my hand. I answered immediately and found on the other end of the line, not the nurse herself as I'd expected, but her daughter. The daughter told me that her mother hadn't returned my calls because she didn't have long-distance phone service. But if I could call her mother back in about ten minutes, then she would be there waiting to answer.

Heart hammering in my chest, I endured ten long minutes and, on the nose, dialed the nurse once again. This time the ringing yielded a hello, twangy as a banjo but with the timbre of a gravel road. I launched into who I was—a reporter—and what I was after—information about the death of Paula Oberbroeckling.

"Who?" the nurse asked, cutting me off mid-sentence.

This surprised me. I hadn't anticipated having to explain who Paula was. I took a deep breath and started over, beginning by telling her that Paula was a Washington High School graduate who went missing in July of 1970. But before I could finish my sentence, the woman interrupted me again. "Oh! That dead girl!"

Yes, I said, that dead girl.

Once we were on the same page, I asked the nurse if I could record our phone call, and she said yes without hesitation.

For someone who suffered an initial failure of memory at hearing the name Paula Oberbroeckling, the nurse knew a lot about Paula.* She knew that Paula had had a Black boyfriend and that it was likely that she had been pregnant when she disappeared. She had heard the rumor about the abortion, and she knew of the chiropractor, except she repeatedly got his name wrong even after I corrected her.

She told me that the chiropractor's office had been located just down the hill and on the same block as the apartment

---

* When I mentioned this to Susan as suspicious, she pointed out that there was a chance the nurse never even knew Paula's name. That around her community Paula had always been referred to as "that dead girl."

she'd occupied in 1970. This was something I had known and which added to the plausibility of the chiropractor bringing a bleeding Paula to her door. In addition to the chiropractor, whom she did not like (among other aggressions, she said he used to broadcast an audio tape of barking dogs in order to irritate his neighbors and dissuade visitors), she also knew all the other players involved.

Then she told me something I didn't know, which was that her own husband—ex- now and deceased—had been one of the men rumored to have helped dump Paula's body beside Otis Road. When I asked if she knew for a fact whether he had been involved, she told me she'd pressed him on it over the years, and he'd always denied it. When I asked Steinbeck about this, he told me he'd never heard anything about her husband being involved, though he knew him as a "naughty guy who always carried a gun." This was likely an apt characterization, but that of course wasn't the whole story. According to the nurse, her husband was a man who had spent most of his life unable to read or write. A man who was desperately afraid of small animals as a result of the rats that climbed into his infant crib, by which she meant that her husband was someone for whom life had been very difficult. He would eventually serve time for a different murder, which occurred during a gunfight at a local bar, and for which the nurse said he was wrongfully accused. The way she said this seemed to imply that whether or not he had had a hand in Paula's death, he had served his time.

The woman told me that after Paula's body had been found, the police had knocked on her door. They asked her whether she worked at the VA hospital, whether she would have known what to do were someone hemorrhaging. This was another surprise—there was no mention of this visit anywhere in the police file. As far as I knew, no one had ever spoken to her, and I wondered briefly if she were lying. But in this anecdote I also saw my opportunity. Her admission provided an opening for my punch.

"I know why the police came to your door," I said carefully. "The reason I've called you is because your name appears in the police file. There is a source who said that Paula was brought to *your* house the night she died and that whoever brought her thought that you'd be able to help save her because you were a nurse. The source said that she died in your home."

Over the phone, the nurse yelped and called out to someone in the next room, "They think that girl died here! Oh my God!" She repeated this, oh my God, oh my God, breathing heavily into the receiver and sounding as if she might lose consciousness.

I waited for her to calm down and then asked, "Did Paula Oberbroeckling die in your home?"

"No! Oh my God," she said. "No!"

My heart sank. Her shock sounded real. She'd agreed to my taping our phone call. She'd seemed forthcoming during our conversation. She told me that the police had it wrong; she had never been a nurse, only a nurse's aide, which she described as a "glorified candy striper"—"bed pans and baths"—and not even in Cedar Rapids but in Iowa City where she'd lived when she was younger. She'd told me about her husband and his conviction. About everything she'd heard about Paula. And now this response. My gut was telling me that this wasn't the reaction of a woman who had been hiding her involvement in a homicide for forty-plus years.

I allowed her to settle down and then I gave her the line I'd been planning about the possible irony that whoever had killed Paula had been trying to help her by giving her the abortion that she potentially needed. But the nurse was not sympathetic to that idea. "I'm all for choice," she said, referring to a woman's right to choose, "but it doesn't mean you have to run out and do it."

In the days and weeks after my conversation with the nurse, I began to feel gullible for believing her so readily. The nurse told me that after the police had banged on her door, she went to Percy Harris, the town medical examiner and her doctor (the same man who'd purchased property in the so-called white side of town and had a brick thrown through his window for doing so), and he called the police off. Why would she approach her doctor about a problem with the police? Why would Harris hold sway over the actions of the CRPD? Steinbeck said that, as the medical examiner, Harris worked closely with the police department, which was likely why the nurse went to him. But still, would the police put aside a credible lead because Harris told them to move on? And why would he vouch for one of his patients over a "dead girl" in the first place? Steinbeck also pointed out that maybe the nurse had sounded so convincing because it was true: Paula *hadn't* died in her home, because maybe Paula had died in Sturgeon's office *with* the nurse present.

The nurse may well be innocent, but I worried that I was suffering a kind of journalistic Stockholm syndrome. She'd agreed to talk to me and was seemingly forthcoming, which conveyed a level of trust. Did I unconsciously repay that trust with a trust of my own? Because who *wouldn't* deny their involvement in a crime? There was no statute of limitations on murder. Paula's case might be cold, but it was still an open investigation. Perhaps the passage of time had overwritten the truth with whatever story she'd had to repeat in order to absolve herself. Or maybe the nurse was simply an excellent actor.

This lack of resolve left me adrift. In the time it took me to reach the nurse, I'd built up the potential of our conversation. My hope had always been that somewhere out there was someone who had been waiting to come clean about what had happened in Cedar Rapids in the early hours of July 11, 1970. That an admission of guilt or of knowing would serve as a relief from a truth that had been festering inside of them in the same way its absence had left a hole of need in me. They were ready to talk, if only anyone cared to listen. Here I was, I thought. So where were they? And then came the nurse, who could easily have slotted in for this character. Except she hadn't.

The thing that struck me now was that nearly everything this woman told me fit with the scenario that Steinbeck had laid out, which in turn matched the story that ended the police file. But the nurse had not read the police file. And she had never spoken with Detective Steinbeck. So where did her story come from? And what did it mean that she knew it?

The journalist David Aaronovitch writes that humans depend on the construction of stories; they need narrative explanations of experience. He explains that this phenomenon is biological, a cognitive imperative, both innate and beyond our control. Humans must establish causality in order to process the things that happen to us and around us. We need this so acutely that when there is no story, when something goes unexplained, we build the story ourselves, oftentimes out of nothing at all.

A novelist and a professor in the department where I got my master's degree liked to say to our class, "Coincidence is a word we created in order to explain holes in reality." I'd always liked this idea, but whenever I repeated it I inevitably found myself on the other end of a blank stare. But having read Aaronovitch, this assertion took on added meaning. Humans needed to understand experience so badly that we made up a word in order to explain the unexplainable.

Whether the abortion story had its roots in police work or on the streets of Cedar Rapids (the first mention of abortion in the police file came four days after Paula's disappearance when a friend of Paula's told the police that "she had received word that Paula had wanted an abortion"; I will never know when it first appeared in the community—chicken or egg?), and whether it was true or not, it now had a life of its own. The nurse knew the story because she lived it or she knew it because it was the conclusion that the people around her felt comfortable coming to, the narrative that made sense, the story that, for whatever reason, the community was willing to accept. I can't help but take this one step further and point out that implicit in the acceptance of this story, the mythologizing of it, is a warning about what happens to women who have abortions: They are punished with death.

Like the nurse, I also was guilty of participating in this willful acceptance of things I didn't know to be true. There were holes to Paula's story that I'd put aside, things that I'd taken on faith, problems that I hadn't yet interrogated. Take Robert's alibi. That he was at an all-night party at Butch Hudson's house (Butch was a foster son of Democratic Iowa state senator John Ely°). As far as I could tell, this story wasn't relayed to the police until December 2, 1970, three days after Paula's

---

° Coincidentally (ironically? presciently?), Senator Ely introduced a bill in 1967 that would reform abortion law in Iowa, legalizing the procedure when it was administered early in pregnancy by competent physicians for reasons deemed physically or mentally appropriate. The bill died in committee but not before a public hearing, which allowed Ely to state his case for the general population and for the media.

body was discovered. And this, when *Ben Carroll* mentioned that on the way to get Paula for work on the morning of the 11th he'd picked Robert up and dropped him off downtown. Ben said Robert had been hitchhiking home from Butch's party with a couple other kids. It wasn't until five days after Ben told the police this story that they corroborated it with Robert. And then when they tried to check it against the stories of other kids who'd attended the party, no one could quite say that Robert had been there the whole night."* But Robert's being the culprit was an idea that didn't sit well with me—I liked him as the loving boyfriend willing to risk so much just to be with Paula. I liked thinking of him as the one support at a lonely time in her life—what with being the new kid in high school, her dawning coming of age, her parents on the outs, the tension between her and her mother—so it was easy for me to accept the shaky ground on which his alibi was built and move on.

The thing was, the abortion story made sense to me too. I could understand what might drive a teenage girl with few options to the office of a seedy chiropractor. When I considered all the ways Paula could have died—strangled in anger, or raped, or beaten, out of jealousy or desire or because she was pregnant, by a boyfriend or an acquaintance or a stranger—it was the abortion story that I wanted to be true. This seemed to me the least scary, and by least scary I mean for her, as if I could ever imagine her experience, which I could not. But somehow, from the shadowy place where I lived with limited knowledge and only my own insight, I was able to twist my understanding of the story so that if Paula were with people

---

* John Thomas, who also lived at the Ely's with Butch Hudson, told police that he "believed" Robert had been there.

she believed were trying to help her, even in the smallest parts of their hearts, even doing something that had to have been *very very* scary, rather than with people who clearly wanted to harm her, then maybe this brought the littlest comfort. I needed to believe that her death hadn't been as horrifying as it most surely was. And it appeared I wasn't the only one.

"Bleeding to death is a very peaceful, quiet way to die. Very peaceful. I mean, she would not realize she was dying; she just went to sleep and died. As opposed to some horrible reason why she was all tied up. So, I mean, it would be peaceful for me to know that my child just laid on a table and died. Bled to death and didn't know she was dying. As opposed to being . . ." Carol does not finish her sentence, the other possibilities too awful to give voice.

With no cause of death listed on the autopsy (remember, her body was too badly decomposed), and with the case yawning wide open and unsolved fifty years on, the abortion story, even unconfirmed, was easier to believe than the *real* story, the *official* story, the story told by the police department and the judicial system and the media, which was that there was *no* story. After all, the messaging from the detectives, who had suspended their investigation; from the judicial system, which had failed to force anyone to stand trial; and from the media, who had ceased covering Paula's case after three short stories, boiled down to one idea: Let's just forget "that dead girl" and move on with our lives.

This story asks us to accept that there is no answer. It requires that we put Paula in the past. Which implies that how she died doesn't matter. Which implies that Paula doesn't matter. Which implies that women don't matter. *Why is there so much talk about this case?* Steinbeck had asked. *This case has been solved.*

But, for whom, exactly, had it been solved? For the detectives? For the police department? Did they believe they had their answer and thus felt they had done their jobs? (For the record, Steinbeck wasn't the only officer who felt confident that he knew what had happened on the night Paula disappeared—i.e., the abortion scenario. Kenneth Millsap said, "We had a pretty good scenario, which we had really kind of, off the record, confirmed of what really happened." And Charles Jelinek, Millsap's partner, said, regarding the department's failure to arrest anyone, "You know who were involved with it. But nothing you could do about it.") I'm fairly certain that the police don't do police work for themselves. The job of the police and the judicial system is to ferret out whatever happened and then to ensure that the public, and the family, are informed by way of an arrest and ultimately a trial. And that certainly had not happened. In fact, the Oberbroecklings were left completely in the dark.

"I can remember a lot of times we would have to call to find out where they were, the detectives . . . 'Do you have any new information?' They weren't forthcoming. And I just remember that they said it was 'unsolved,'" Lynn said to Susan. "And my mom got some information somehow. And I don't know if it was the detectives, but Mom heard the same rumors I did. And Mom said, 'I don't know why they didn't tell us this.'"

I asked Detective Steinbeck how the Oberbroecklings would have been informed of police progress. Was there some sort of family liaison? Someone assigned to keep the people who cared about Paula apprised of any new developments? No, he told me, at least not in those days. What happens then when a case is considered internally solved but unprosecutable? The short answer: Nothing. Steinbeck pointed out that if there wasn't enough evidence to prosecute, the police would be out of line sharing their theory with the family because the family would then "take it to the media" and tell the newspapers that the police had failed. Instead, the police just stopped making contact.

"I heard that she was in a basement. They left her in a basement dead for eight days. And then somebody else said they heard she was in a basement dead for three days. . . . When I say that, it's all things I've been told. And I don't know if they said dead because they thought I might rather hear dead than laying there and no one doing anything. Like I said, nobody's given me a straight answer. Like, this is what really happened to her; we can tell you this for a fact. I don't know any of that," said Lynn.

The systems that had been put in place to protect the Oberbroecklings, to protect us all, had failed and then they had ghosted.

I considered the injustices of Jean Halverson and then of Maureen Farley and of Paula: a killer nearly going free on a technicality and then serving a reduced sentence because of police misconduct, or living a lifetime and never knowing whom or what was responsible for a loved one's death.

The man who raped, sodomized, and killed Stephanie Schmidt, my old babysitter, fled Kansas immediately after the crime. Two weeks later he gave up and turned himself in to the police after a national television station broadcast a story about the case. He pleaded guilty, forgoing a trial. What happened to Stephanie was appalling, but it was not cloaked. The Schmidts knew every awful detail surrounding the fate of their daughter. With this knowledge they were able to create a narrative for her that they could use as a lens through which to interact with the world.

Jeni, Stephanie's younger sister, faced her sister's murderer at his sentencing hearing. She looked him in the eye and told him what the loss of her sister had done to her. The opportunity to unburden this to him had been so therapeutic that, when I asked her to tell me the story of her sister's murder in the way she might tell someone she'd just met, I was shocked to hear empathy in her words. I heard it in the inclusion of the details of Donald Ray Gideon's life—his mental health, the help he asked for but never received after his release from prison, his traumatic upbringing, his time in a juvenile detention center. "He didn't have anyone, and I realized that was his story too," said Jeni. "So while [Donald Ray Gideon] is the one person who killed Stephanie, there are a series of actions that we as humans took in order to create him."

When I asked what it might have been like to *not* know, to never know, she took a sharp breath. She wasn't sure but she sensed she would not be who she is today, a wife and a mother of two daughters who manages her husband's music career and works part-time in a library. Jeni presents as empowered, positive, hopeful. She has come through trauma. It exists and it has formed her but it does not define her. If she had never known what happened to her sister, she doesn't think she would have been able to find compassion for the killer, as she has for Gideon.

"If you can be grateful for anything in a tragedy, it's to have closure," she said. "There is already a void when someone is out of your life, a void in such a big way. . . . I just think it would be a constant hole of fear and self-destruction. I think I would always be looking over my shoulder."

The Oberbroecklings, the Farleys, the families of the estimated 200,000 homicides that have gone unsolved since the 1960s have no idea what happened to their loved ones. These people have been left to stare into a gaping abyss where nothing is true and everything is possible. And so, by considering a homicide internally solved but never informing the family or arresting the culprit or even closing the case, the powers that be have denied the Oberbroecklings and anyone else who cared about Paula closure. This, I rationalized, was why there was "all this conversation."

Chapter 8

The City

AFTER MONTHS SPENT FEVERISHLY READING THROUGH Susan's interviews, the witness statements, and the police file, and after the disappointing interview with the nurse, I arranged four days of childcare for my son, who was then nearly two, and booked a flight from New York to Cedar Rapids. Susan agreed to join me. It was February, and I knew that the biting cold and blanket of snow would evoke a mood opposite that steaming summer of 1970 when the whole city was slick with sweat and girls ran around without shoes, but I couldn't wait any longer. I had to go.

While I still didn't really know what I was doing—whether I could solve the case or resolve it with some sort of meaning or understanding—I also couldn't walk away. I thought maybe what I needed was proximity. That if I got closer, spoke with the people who cared about Paula, met with the key players, saw the ground on which she'd walked, walked it myself, then maybe the story would crystallize. This was a risk. It was money out of my pocket, time away from my child and from embarking on paying work—all things that might have stopped a more rational me, that definitely would have stopped the old pre-mother me. But I could not shake the sense that there was something important out there for me to find. So I told myself, just this. Just this trip. And if nothing materialized, I'd go back to New York, care for my family, find new work. I would move on. I couldn't lose myself down this rabbit hole forever.

From 35,000 feet above, I watched the patchwork plains pass slowly under our aircraft. Last season's spent crops stood petrified white with winter. The grid, all right angles and studded with farmhouses and their requisite barns and silos, recalled circuitry—the great American motherboard, I thought, though not for the first time. The landscape was familiar to me, having grown up in Kansas and having flown to this fly-over country my entire childhood. But I no longer had family in the Midwest and had barely been back since graduating from the University of Missouri in 1999. Seeing this part of America again as an adult—as a mother and a wife with a career—made me feel as if I were traveling back in time. I suppose in a way I was.

I knew the Midwest. I knew its determination—the back-breaking, stiff-upper-lip, awake-before-dawn work ethic handed down over generations of people who'd coaxed wheat and corn from the earth, who'd stretched and scrimped and saved to feed families. This mindset transcended the farmers who'd embraced it out of necessity and now appeared in grandkids and great-grandkids and great-great-grandkids who worked desk jobs and raised their own kids in the suburbs. My father's penny-pinching—his willingness to pick overripe produce out of the sale bin, to use a binder clip to secure his cash—is a direct result of his parents' poverty and their having survived the Great Depression.

I knew its pride, in the value of hard work, in the importance of kindness toward others, in its open doors, its hospitality. And I knew the irony that too often this kindness was only extended to a certain, white, homogeneous variety of stranger. When I was growing up, Kansas City and its surroundings had constituted one of the most racially segregated cities in the country. My public schools were almost completely white.*

I knew the Midwest's reserve. Its commitment to keeping up appearances, its straight line, steady pace. Living farthest away from the tastemakers on the coasts produced an underlying feeling of being forever behind the curve. It was a remove that was even greater in the pre-Internet days of my childhood and certainly greater still in the pre–cable television days of Paula's. A feeling that necessitated holding one's head high. That reserve produced a sense of security, at least in the suburbs, which felt shielded from the problems of the rest of the country. It was a false security—engendered by the secret keeping, the never complaining, the putting on of a happy face—but it made a person feel safe nonetheless. Growing up, I had always felt safe.

These forces shaped my childhood in suburban Kansas, but I also had a connection to Iowa, and I saw them there too. My father had been born and raised in the tiniest of rural Iowa towns. Hull had one stoplight, a pizza joint as its only restaurant, and a library so small my father had read every single one of its books by the time he left for good at eighteen. The town's population was white, Dutch, ardently religious, and unapologetically xenophobic. It smelled like manure.

---

* A 2019 article in the *Kansas City Star* states that, according to the Brookings Institution, the KC metro area has gone from being the 11th most-segregated city in the country in 2000 to 27th among 51 cities with populations of one million or more.

When we were children, my dad would strap my younger brother and me into the car, and we'd travel the seven hours from Kansas to the northwest portion of Iowa to visit my grandmother, a gentle woman with sparkling blue eyes. She was built like a body pillow, huggable and soft, and wore her eyeglasses on a glittering chain. She had worked as a dental hygienist when she was younger but had since retired and spent her days baking with lard and sewing giant needlepoints. Lung cancer had killed my grandfather, whose job keeping the books at a gas station had him passively inhaling gasoline fumes for much of his adult life.

Once I was old enough to drive, my father let me take the wheel, then put his head back and snoozed. The first time I was given this privilege, my father slept assuming I knew to watch for the county road signs; the route jogged. I didn't know, and by the time he awoke I'd driven us more than an hour off course. But who could tell? It was only one farm after another after another, the rows of corn flying past like a shuffled deck of cards, the quiet country road offering up only the occasional tractor whose flat of hay bales I could practically swing the car around without looking as there was never any oncoming traffic.

Out of the window of the plane, I watched as a handful of tiny towns and their playing-card fields gave way to a small proud city and the fat gray ribbon of river that runs through it. Cedar Rapids is a stark contrast to the country around it, different and yet defined by it. The city is held in by farmland, populated by people who had been raised on farms or by their ancestors, populated by their ideas. I'd been equating Cedar Rapids with Kansas City by the simple fact of their midwestern geography, but when I looked up the city's demographics, Cedar Rapids was so much smaller. Kansas City proper has close to half a million people. With a population of about 132,000, Cedar Rapids doesn't even make it onto the list of the two hundred most populous cities in the country. The town I grew up in, thirty minutes outside of Kansas City, is bigger. So are Paterson, New Jersey, and Syracuse, New York.

One has to work to get to Cedar Rapids. The city is served only by a regional airport, so there are few direct flights from anywhere outside the immediate vicinity. (From New York, I flew through Chicago.) The converse is also true: one has to work to get out. Chicago, around a four-hour drive and a 75-minute flight east, is the escape hatch. Cedar Rapids has no major sports teams, so its citizens root for the Cubs and the Bears, and teens grow up dreaming of that big city. They identify as Chicagoans. We did the same thing in Kansas. Or I did because of my mother's mother and our trips to Illinois. Long before the dream was New York, it was Chicago.

The first thing I did after coming off the jet bridge was to call Lynn Oberbroeckling. More than anything during that trip I wanted to meet her. I wanted to tell her face-to-face that I was sorry about what had happened to her sister and that I hoped my research might uncover something that the police had missed, something that would break open the case, something that would confirm the going theory or disprove it.

Lynn knew that I'd taken the story over from Susan because Susan had told her. But when I left a message on Lynn's voicemail a couple weeks before I left New York informing her that I'd be in town and asking if she'd let me buy her coffee, lunch, whatever she wanted, I didn't hear back. Instead, a few days later, Susan did. In an email, Lynn apologized for failing to return my call. She told Susan that she had some things going on, which had prevented her from reaching out. She said she planned to be in town during our visit but wasn't certain of her availability; I could try her again once I'd arrived. But she didn't answer her phone when I did there in the terminal, so I left another message.

Susan had flown in from Colorado the day before and was waiting for me when I landed. I spotted her immediately. She's tiny—just five feet tall with the body of a ten-year-old boy— and so she stands out in a crowd. Her light eyes bright with excitement, she walked toward me with arms outstretched: "Yay," she said. "You're here!"

She'd rented a pea-green Kia Soul, which stood out from every other car in the lot, looking ridiculous and like a bread-box on wheels. We laughed at it for a minute to cover our nervousness, or I did. On top of my awareness of how far out on a limb I was, throwing myself at something so uncertain, I also feared that I was leading Susan on. That if I failed to make something of Paula's story, I'd disappoint her. She and I had had a rocky start—cliché mother- and daughter-in-law stuff mostly; no one was good enough for her firstborn, me included, and she let me know by disapproving of my every move and voiced opinion. Our relationship had improved immensely in the years since the wedding, but our history had me wary of the repercussions of damaging whatever bond we'd managed to create.

We drove from the airport toward downtown Cedar Rapids to eat lunch and come up with a plan. The air was frigid as I'd expected, the ground covered with snow. As we exited the highway a short fifteen minutes later, I picked up an odor. It was alternately sweet and yeasty—which Susan said was cour-

tesy of the cereal manufacturing, molasses, and corn syrup—
and gamy and metallic from the meatpacking. It was a smell
that made me the slightest bit nauseated. Susan told me that
Cedar Rapids had always smelled that way, had smelled that
way when Paula was alive.

In Paula's day Cedar Rapids was booming. The decades
that followed World War II saw the expansion of longtime
local companies like Quaker Oats, which milled cereal, Cargill and Penick & Ford, which both processed corn into starch
and syrup among other industries, and Wilson & Co., which
packed meat. Those companies, eager to feed the progeny
of the baby boomers, saw in Cedar Rapids land on which to
grow, proximity to farms, waterpower for milling, and rural
manpower at the ready. Jobs were everywhere. The city's rapid
sprawl northward was evidence of its prosperity. People were
marrying, having children, buying houses, TVs for their family
rooms. Cedar Rapids was a microcosm of what was occurring
all over the country in those years.

As we entered it, the city felt deserted compared with New
York. Downtown, tallish buildings flanked wide, open streets.
There was a trickle of traffic and hardly any sidewalk activity. It was freezing of course, and the car culture had everyone inside, but even in the Cuban restaurant we found, we
were practically the only customers despite the fact that it was
lunchtime and the food was delicious.

I'd scheduled interviews with some of Paula's friends and
with a couple of people who had had experience with missing
girls in the 1960s—other families, other sisters, other armchair detectives. But before all of that what I wanted to do was
to see.

Feeling conspicuous in our boxy grasshopper car, Susan and I took the Soul up and down what felt like every street in Cedar Rapids. We drove to Lindale Mall, which had been enclosed in the years since Paula had been employed there. From the parking lot, Susan pointed out where Lonnie and Ben would have waited to pick Paula up on the night she disappeared. Younkers, which would close in 2018, had been an anchor store. I saw where Paula would have exited and where the Misses Department she worked in had been. We drove to Washington High School, which had been expanded since Paula was a senior. Susan pointed out where the boys would show off their cars before school, where the girls would congregate and watch. We circled the building on foot, passing a coed group of cheerleaders presumably heading to practice. They looked so young. We peered in the windows and saw a soda machine standing in the same place it had when Robert bought Paula that first Coke.

We drove to the border of Oak Hill, to the spot where Debbie's car had been abandoned. Past Mercy Hospital across the street from where the chiropractor had had his office. We went past Robert's house, to the house in which Paula lived briefly right after she left her mother's home, and then to the one she disappeared from on the west side. Both of Paula's former homes were ramshackle and lonesome-seeming. When we stopped in front of the house she'd grown up in on G Avenue, it was clear it had been cared for—painted mustard yellow sometime in the interim, its shutters black. A carport hung off the left side; beyond it was a detached garage. A cluster of bushes stood under the front windows, a burst of green in the snowy landscape. Above them hung a holiday wreath; a sweet red heart was placed on the front door. It exuded warmth.

As we drove, Susan barely stopped talking. She spouted

names and dates and histories. She connected people by marriage or friendship, by work relationship. She relayed anecdotes about buildings we passed, neighborhoods, specific homes. Events that made it into the *Gazette* and rumors that had flown around town. Webs of information that I could hardly keep up with. Everything related, however tangentially, to Paula. I kept asking, "Who was that again?" And, "How were they connected?" Susan's knowledge of Cedar Rapids—its inner workings and its dynamics, its history and its people—ran so deep I feared I would never have a true handle on its complexity, much less begin to understand where Paula fit within it.

Susan ended the tour at Mt. Calvary Cemetery. We circled the grounds, squinting across the icy dunes in search of the stand of trees she remembered as being within walking distance of Paula's grave. We found it, skeletal against the cloudless sky, and parked, instinctively growing quiet. There was no point in getting out of the car; everything was buried under six inches of snow. The dry heat wafted out of the Soul's vents and onto our faces. After a few minutes passed, we looked at each other as if to say, "What now?"

I felt overwhelmed but didn't want to let on how much. I don't know what I expected—to feel Paula? to be moved? to gain some new understanding? Here I was, closer to Paula than I had ever been and she had never felt more enigmatic.

Chapter 9

The White Boyfriend

IN THE SPRING OF 1970, AS THE CROCUSES PUSHED UP
through the thawing ground, Paula boxed her things and
moved out of her mother's home. She'd rented a room in a
house around the corner from Robert in Oak Hill. At Washington, she was enrolled in a school-to-work program called
DECA (Distributive Education Clubs of America). The program, geared toward filling management and hospitality jobs,
allowed her to leave class after lunch to go to work at Younkers.
She deposited her salary in her own personal bank account
from which she wrote checks. I have a copy of one made out
to McDonald's for two dollars. The paltry sum is dignified by
her gorgeous signature, a giant spacious swooping P and an
O that curls outside of itself like a wrought-iron trellis. It was
a signature that spoke confidence, never losing steam despite
the length of her last name.

Paula had no plans for college—Debbie Kellogg told me
she couldn't afford it—but she was considering buying a car,
which would have added to her independence. And so, having just turned eighteen and with her graduation imminent,
Paula had effectively liberated herself from all authority (her

mother, her teachers) and was perched on the cusp of the rest of her life. It was around this time that she began hanging out with Lonnie Bell.

Robert and Paula's relationship had frayed in the year since he graduated. After finishing school, Robert had envisioned a future where he played college basketball and then moved on to a professional team. At some point, he and Paula would marry. He gave her a promise ring and said the two fantasized about moving west. They'd head to Grand Junction, Colorado, where Paula's father lived. Paula could work, maybe model. Robert was content to be patient and wait for Paula to graduate.

Over the course of that year, Robert made several trips to Fort Dodge, Iowa, to try out for the local junior college basketball team. Though he and Paula wrote letters and made plenty of phone calls to bridge the distance, he sensed something was changing while he was gone. Whether it was the result of a waning affection or a reevaluation of the relationship in light of the pressure her family had put on her is unclear, but Robert heard that while he was away, Paula had been dating other guys. Lonnie Bell confirmed this, telling police later that he and Paula had gone out about half a dozen times while Robert was out of town.

One night, late, after Robert had returned to Cedar Rapids and while Paula was living in Oak Hill, she ran out to Lonnie's Porsche to grab something and found Robert standing outside. Lonnie told police that Paula had refused to let Robert in at first, but after some thought she asked Lonnie to wait in the back room so that she and Robert could talk. Robert said that night Paula asked if she could date both him and Lonnie.

Robert told her she could not; it was either him *or* Lonnie. A couple days later, Lonnie said Paula told him that she had decided to end her relationship with Robert. She solidified her resolve by moving yet again.

I found the timeline during this last year of Paula's life difficult to nail down. Robert told Susan that over the holidays in 1969 he visited Paula's dad at the shoe store where he worked in Lindale Plaza. If that was correct, it meant that Jim didn't move to Grand Junction until sometime after. Which also meant that Paula and Robert couldn't have discussed relocating to Colorado to be near him until then. But that was the time that Robert said he and Paula were on the outs, which made it all sound suspect, nothing more than Robert's wishful revisionist thinking.

What is clear is that in a very short period of time, Paula lived in three houses: her mother's house, then the apartment in the house near Robert on 11th Avenue and 15th Street, and then the house on the west side into which she moved with Debbie Kellogg in early June and from which she disappeared just over one month later.

Despite the grand gesture of moving, it appeared that Paula and Robert never completely stopped seeing each other—theirs was the type of relationship that couldn't quite resolve itself with an ending. Robert told police that the last time he hung out with Paula was on July 4, a week before she disappeared. She and Debbie had come over to his house and ended up staying for dinner. He saw her again the next day driving what he thought was Lynn's car; he thought he saw Debbie in the passenger seat. The last time they'd had sex was in June. One of Paula's coworkers at Younkers told police that even after Paula started dating

Lonnie, she continued to receive phone calls from Robert at work. Debbie confirmed this, telling police that even though Paula had committed herself to Lonnie, she continued "slipping out" and meeting up with Robert.

Shortly after I became interested in Paula's story, my husband told me that when he was working on the documentary film, he'd found himself uncertain whether he liked Paula. He thought Paula was duplicitous, callous for going back and forth between two men who loved her. He admitted that this had become a conflict for him, changing how he felt about her story. I defended Paula instinctively. I told him that she wasn't beholden to anyone. She could date whomever she wanted whenever she wanted in whatever way she wanted. But privately I worried about what he'd said. I wanted to like Paula. I wanted her to be a symbol of feminine power, a woman who'd exercised choice and freedom, someone ahead of her time who'd become a casualty of being born too soon.

I knew that by 1970 the sexual revolution was well underway. The advent of the pill at the beginning of the decade had given women control of their own fertility, allowing sex without pregnancy and, by extension, sex without the threat of marriage. Women were starting to speak freely about sex, about wanting it, about having it outside of the confines of matrimony, outside of commitment. Helen Gurley Brown published *Sex and the Single Girl* in 1962. One year later, Lesley Gore sang "You Don't Own Me." And three years after that Nancy Sinatra released "These Boots Are Made for Walkin'." In 1962, Gloria Steinem wrote "The Moral Disarmament of Betty Coed," her debut piece for *Esquire* magazine. The story claimed that college women across the country were collectively rejecting the status quo in which the decision to have premarital sex came with the inevitability of being judged and branded (loose, slut, amoral). Instead, these women believed sex was personal and no one's business other than those having it. All of which constituted important advancements toward the emancipation of women.

Except, the more I read, the more I intuited that the sexual revolution's effect in the moment and on everyday lives had been overstated. The pill could be difficult to obtain unless you were married. There were laws in several states that prohibited doctors from prescribing it to single women and, in states where it was legal, there were doctors who refused to prescribe it, citing "moral grounds." Some women would circumvent this by pretending to be engaged and some doctors would turn a blind eye in order to help them, but this presupposed access to doctors. The chances of teenage girls with little financial means, family support, or connections—i.e., girls like Paula—having actual access to contraception were slim. (Robert told police that he occasionally used condoms but not always, and when he asked Paula whether she used a "preventative" she told him it was "none of his business.") In addition to these logistical barriers to contraception, there were emotional ones, namely shame. In 1968, for example, the Catholic Church's position on birth control was that it was "intrinsically wrong." So, empowered women might have been having more sex but they were also getting unintentionally pregnant more often.

While on college campuses an open dialogue about sex might have paved the way for women's sexual autonomy, only 15.2 percent of women aged twenty to twenty-four were enrolled in college in 1970.* For teenage girls living in small

---

* The National Center for Education Statistics didn't start breaking out female college enrollment by race until 1972. When they did, white women were enrolled at a rate of five percent higher than Black women.

cities like Cedar Rapids, frank conversations about sex were next to nonexistent. There was no "sex talk" with mom or dad, as most parents disapproved of or were squeamish around the topic; and if there was sex education in school it revolved not around how one's body worked and how to control fertility but around basic anatomy and expectations of gender roles within a family unit. Indeed, it was during the sexual revolution that whole (conservative) movements erupted to protest sex education in schools. The fear was that educating women about sex would lead to them actually having sex, so young girls were intentionally kept in the dark. This didn't keep women celibate; it just kept them ignorant.

"I didn't know anything about birth control. I didn't know what a rubber was. And there were scares," Susan told me about deciding to have sex with her high school boyfriend. "There were times I was afraid I was pregnant. I didn't take precautions because I didn't know how."

This doesn't factor in the social ramifications. While white girls might have been able to get away with having sex with the person to whom they were engaged, having sex with more than one person still got a girl labeled "bad"—neither marriage nor mother material—and that even by other young people. Black communities tended not to pillory their girls in the same way white communities did. Rather than alienate, they usually brought these young girls into the fold. Black women who engaged in premarital sex suffered another type of shaming that came from outside their community, one that painted unmarried Black women as draws on the welfare system, as sexual deviants, and as responsible for the population boom.

Both major political parties, PTAs, church groups, and coffee klatches all still condemned premarital sex. Having sex was to risk ruining one's reputation, something that was often irreparable. The way I saw it, if Paula could look this in the face and shrug—either because she was aware of the changing cultural norms or because she knew inherently that part of personal freedom was the ability to act out one's sexuality or because she simply didn't care—then she was brave, a forerunner.

I liked this version of her, but I knew it wasn't complete. I wondered whether I was giving Paula too much credit, whether I was projecting onto her the things I thought would help condemn society for her death. Was dating both Robert and Lonnie an act of empowerment? Or just deceitful? And what if Paula wasn't sympathetic? How did that change the narrative?

• • •

It wasn't immediately apparent what Paula saw in Lonnie Bell. When they began dating, Lonnie was twenty-one years old and still lived at home with his mother and his stepfather. He had no job and no immediate prospects. He wasn't well liked, including, according to Debbie, by Paula herself.

In the police report, a friend of Paula's said that she, the friend, "didn't care for" Lonnie, even going so far as to call him "crazy." Robert detested Lonnie for obvious reasons, but he also had this to say: Even if she didn't love me, "I didn't want him to even be around her . . . I knew he wasn't good for her." Debbie Kellogg told police that Lonnie was "excitable and violent" when he was drinking or on "reds," meaning amphetamines. She said that he "dislikes women," that once, at a party she and Paula had thrown at their house, he'd gotten angry and chased Debbie outside. She said Lonnie pushed Paula to the floor that night. She said he threw a chair across the kitchen. She said that she, Debbie, was afraid of him.

It's possible that Paula was using Lonnie for access—to

people (he was older and ran with a different crowd) or to drugs. The police file noted that Lonnie had been arrested for a violation of the state narcotics act on July 14, 1968; the charges were ultimately dismissed.

While I don't sense that Paula had a drug problem, the interviews lead me to believe that she was open to experimenting with whatever was around. As Susan put it, "It was the seventies!" Robert said he'd heard she was "on grass," though he'd never seen her smoke it. Lynn told a story about Paula and Debbie trying speed (Lynn had passed) and then going to ride the roller coaster at CeMar Acres, an amusement park. She made a joke about how Paula cleaned their room afterward and if that were going to be the case then Paula was welcome to do all the speed she wanted (Paula wasn't big on tidying up). Carol told police that, though Paula had tried drugs, they weren't her "bag."

A friend of Paula's told the police that Paula was using Lonnie for money. That he could afford to take her out, whereas Robert never could. Or maybe Paula, like Debbie, feared Lonnie. Debbie told police that Paula was the only girlfriend Lonnie had ever had, and that one time Paula confided in Debbie that Lonnie had threatened to kill himself if Paula ever left him. Debbie said Paula wasn't sure whether to believe him on this or not.

But then there was this: Debbie also said that Paula was using Lonnie to resolve the rift that had formed between her and her mother. Because there was one person who liked Lonnie Bell, and that person was Carol Oberbroeckling. "Oh, remember him with that hair?" Carol once said to Lynn. "He was the cutest boy, and he had the prettiest white teeth."

Lonnie was cute. He was shorter than Paula and slight as a whippet with strong arms and tan skin. He dressed like a hippie, snugged tank tops into bell-bottoms, tamed his scraggly blond hair with a leather headband that he wore like a crown. And, of course, he was white. When, years later, Carol and Lynn spoke about Paula's relationship with Lonnie, they framed it as Paula's attempt at "doing the right thing."

"I think that she wanted . . . to please you [Carol], to please all of us. And that's when she moved in with [Debbie] Kellogg and started dating Lonnie," said Lynn. "And in her heart it was always going to be Robert, but she was going to do the right thing."

The "right thing," it would seem, constituted not dating an African American. Or maybe it was the opposite, maybe doing the right thing was dating a white guy whom one could marry and thus be "respectable" in the opinion of others. Or perhaps the right thing was following her mother's directive despite what Paula knew to be true, that she and Robert had a connection that had nothing to do with race, a human connection. In any case, it appeared that the right thing had Paula spending time with someone few people liked, someone *she* didn't even like, someone who was angry, someone who might have been capable of violence.

When Paula was alive, domestic violence wasn't treated like a crime. A man beating his wife was considered a private matter, a family affair. In 1964 *Time* magazine published an article titled "Psychiatry: The Wife Beater & His Wife," which likened domestic abuse to a "mental quirk" and made this statement about the results of the study that inspired the story: " 'The periods of violent behavior by the husband,' the doctors observed, 'served to release him momentarily from his anxiety about his ineffectiveness as a man, while giving his wife apparent masochistic gratification and helping probably to deal with the guilt arising from the intense hostility expressed in her controlling, castrating behavior.'" Reading this made my blood boil. Not only could women expect to be beaten by their husbands should their husbands feel "ineffective as men," and not only did these women lack recourse as this abuse was regularly ignored by authorities, and not only should they blame themselves for being "controlling, castrating," but they receive gratification from being beaten.

Over the course of my research into Paula's death, I'd encountered evidence of dozens of cases of violence against women in the area surrounding Cedar Rapids in the years just before and after Paula's death, but it was all violence against *white* women. Violence against women of color was virtually invisible. Even when I went searching for examples, I had a hard time coming up with them, but I highly doubt this was because they don't exist. A series published in collaboration by a group of Iowa news organizations, including the *Globe Gazette* and the *Des Moines Register*, highlighted 75 cold murder cases in Iowa. But only two—two!—of the victims, Linda Mayfield and Angela Marie Altman, were African American women; for comparison, there were 40 white women, 29 white men, and one African American man. The article wasn't comprehensive (Paula hadn't been included), so there were more, but someone had chosen which people to include and which people to leave out, ultimately deciding that other dead African American women weren't worth mentioning.

The number of references to violence against women made in Paula's case file, in the police report, and in the interviews—references that didn't even involve Paula herself—is shocking. Their prevalence and offhandedness are evidence of the ways society tolerated, even accepted, said violence. There were stories of rape and detailed anecdotes of boyfriends beating girlfriends and of husbands hurting wives, right alongside throwaway comments of inferred abuse that somehow, because of their flippancy, read as doubly damning.

When she was a child, Debbie Kellogg watched her own father regularly beat up her mother. "I thought that meant they loved you," she told me. Her conception of romantic relationships was so dependent on that early impression that even though her mother kicked her father out of the house when Debbie was in the sixth grade Debbie still found herself in a relationship with a man who hit her.

Debbie described calling the police on this man, something she did many times. The responding officers would listen to her story and then tell her that she needed to go take a walk, to cool off. "Can't you just leave for a while? . . . Can't you just stay overnight somewhere?" she told me they asked her. "I told them, no! This is my house!"

Debbie's intimate experience with domestic abuse was no anomaly. Paula had a high school girlfriend who was in an abusive relationship as well. According to the police file, this girl's boyfriend went so far as to break her jaw. The girl was admitted to Mercy Hospital where she stayed for weeks while she healed.˚

That this level of abuse occurred between high school

˚ Less than three years later, that boyfriend was convicted of the shooting death of a deputy US marshal in Oak Hill. The murder occurred outside Big Ruthie's, a notorious house of prostitution, which also happened to be next door to the house that Debbie Kellogg grew up in. The narrative that was initially put forth was that the marshal had been killed in the line of duty while looking for a "federal fugitive." But at the trial it became clear that the marshal had frequented Ruthie's. She testified that he had paid her $15 to masturbate and had asked her for "a girl who is not experienced and had not had kids." According to Steinbeck, the marshal was an "old horny white guy" who had been rolled for his wallet by one of the girls who worked at Ruthie's. He then opened fire on the house, and the boyfriend returned it.

sweethearts was appalling. But what made it corrosive, infective, was the way it was discussed. Here was what Debbie Kellogg told police regarding the girl's broken jaw: "[the girl] had an argument with her boyfriend . . . and got her jaw broken." And here was the way the police recorded the event during their own investigation: "[the girl] had received a broken jaw by her boyfriend. . . . This required her to be hospitalized." Later in the report, ". . . [the girl] said before she met with her accident and moved back home. . . ." Neither Debbie Kellogg nor the police made the boyfriend the subject of their sentences, the active participant. Neither said: This girl's boyfriend broke her jaw. They said she "got" her jaw broken; she "met with her accident"; she "received" a broken jaw (like a gift!). As if the girl, not her boyfriend, had been the person responsible for her injury. This framing recalled the *Time* magazine article, and it was an example of the pervasive subtext that had women believing that any abuse they incurred could be blamed only on themselves. In this climate, it was possible that Lonnie's behavior—shoving, chasing, throwing furniture—didn't even register as something Paula should complain about. This was what relationships were. This was what a woman could expect.

In his statement, given after Paula's body was discovered, Lonnie told police that the subject of Paula's potential pregnancy had come up twice between them. The first time, Paula asked Lonnie what he would do if she were pregnant with Robert's baby, specifically would he continue to date her. Lonnie told police that he had joked that she should have the baby and sell it or have an abortion. In the second instance, she informed Lonnie that she had just missed her second period. Lonnie told police that he suggested she go get a test "before she got too upset."

In 2005, in a national study that was the first of its kind, the CDC found homicide to be a leading cause of traumatic death among new and expectant mothers. The numbers only go up when factoring in a woman's age and race: If the woman in question is African American, her risk is seven times greater than that of a white woman. But women age twenty or younger of both races experienced the highest ratio of pregnancy-associated homicide. Even without a pregnancy, nearly half of female homicide victims are killed by a current or former intimate partner. Victimizations are at their highest when women are about to leave a relationship.

Of course, Lonnie wasn't the only one of Paula's boyfriends who might have been capable of violence. There was also Robert. Which was, I was beginning to realize, the axis on which Paula's story spun. Paula had danger lurking around every corner. Because of the era and because of her familial situation, there was no one to advise Paula on how to respond to domestic peril, nor did she likely have the voice or the vocabulary with which to combat it herself. Place this climate of normalized violence adjacent to the movement toward sexual liberation and you have a dangerous dichotomy. On one hand, violence was implicit and accepted; on the other hand, the push toward sexual freedom necessitated trusting the opposite sex. These forces were in direct opposition. Women were encouraged to embrace the very people who could hurt them without repercussion.

This dissonance recalled Stephanie's murder and my own refusal to truly contemplate what it might mean. How could I?

How could I do both, live and be afraid? The two states contradicted each other.

When I was fourteen, I lied to my mother in order to attend a high school party thrown by a girl I barely knew. Somehow I wound up willingly following a boy upstairs into a bedroom. He was in high school. He was cute. He seemed to like me. No one ever liked me. I wanted to kiss him and to have him kiss me back. I wanted his hand under my shirt. I did not want to have sex with him. I had never had sex before. As our interaction grew heated, and I said no for the second time, maybe the third, he became angry. He stood up and from above pointed his finger down at me and said, "You are lucky I'm not another sort of guy." Then he stalked out of the room.

I've never forgotten his words—the idea that there were two sorts of men, men who would walk away when I said no, albeit angrily, and men who would not. And everything those words implied—that women who escape sexual assault were lucky and those who didn't were not; that the man claimed no responsibility; that some men "had" it—by which I mean the capability of violence—and some men didn't, and that women would never know until we brought out this nascent quality or, "lucky us," did not. Because there was no way of knowing which type of man we were dealing with, we were left with two options: put aside this knowledge and trust, or don't.

An adult might say that this necessitates finding a balance, living with that knowledge, which I suppose I actively do today, but at sixteen, seventeen, eighteen, when everything—the potential for romance, the freedom to move about on my own, the complexities of social hierarchies and gender dynamics—was new? Impossible. I could only be myself—a reasonably intelligent, boy-crazy girl, with her first job and, by extension, her own money for the first time, who simmered with anger at her parents and was as curious about alcohol and drugs as anyone else—by setting aside the knowledge that there were men out there who would, given the opportunity, hurt me.

Perhaps this was what Paula was doing too. Perhaps she was a girl who was in love with one boy and using another to regain her mother's favor. A girl who was reveling in her youth and the fact that she had just graduated, determined to have fun during this last summer of freedom before the responsibility of adulthood set in.

• • •

And so it went. Paula told Lonnie things were over with Robert and in early June 1970 she moved out of Oak Hill and into the rooming house with Debbie Kellogg at 116 10th Street, on the forbidden west side of town. Paula's new home wasn't much—one room in a run-down, white-sided, four-bedroom house with a shared living room, kitchen, and bathroom—but the price was right, $12 a week, and it afforded her the ability to move about as she pleased.

Paula brought along with her a piece of her past: the mint-green, flowered bedspread that Carol had sewed for her when she and Lynn were girls. The spread matched a set of curtains that had hung in their childhood bedroom. She covered her new walls with posters; her clothes lay wherever she shed them. While she was home she often left all the doors open, all the lights burning.

Jimi Hendrix and Janis Joplin both played Woodstock the summer before. Jefferson Airplane and the Band were on the radio. And violence was in the ether. The Vietnam War was in its fifteenth year. Richard Nixon had just invaded Cambodia, setting off protests across the United States, including those that ended in the massacre at Kent State on May 4. As of December, for young men, the potential for violence—inflicting it or having it inflicted on them—was a lottery number away.

To combat their fear, the seniors at Washington, Paula among them, frittered their free time in the ways of those aware that the end of youth is near. During the day they cooled off at Lake McBride just outside of nearby Solon. They congregated at Henry's Hamburgers, driving through, parking and eating, then dawdling until the owner kicked them out. At night, too young to gain entry into bars, they cruised 1st Avenue, the main drag that bisected the city north and south. Lined with all-night diners, pizza joints, and other hot spots, 1st Avenue was rife with opportunities to meet up. Sometimes the kids cruised all night long, hopping out of one car and into another, agreeing to rendezvous later in the evening. So-and-so had pot; they could chill at such-and-such a house. When they grew tired of driving, they stretched their legs on the 1st Avenue Bridge, milling in the parking spots that flanked the street, the Cedar River roiling beneath them.

On a weekend night two weeks before Paula disappeared, Larry Martin, Paula's friend from school, drag raced 1st Avenue. He stayed easily ahead of the cops who had neither radios nor fast cars and thus no recourse against his flagrant speeding. Around two in the morning, he was standing on the 1st Avenue Bridge, bragging to some of the guys about smoking this car or that, when Paula tapped him on the shoulder.

"Want to take me for a ride?" he said that she asked him when he turned around. He said sure; she got in his car. Larry couldn't help noticing her outfit, he told me, she was wearing "that blue nightie." The same dress she had on two weeks later on the night she vanished. When he commented on the dress, flimsy and high-waisted, Paula pointed out that it covered a lot more than her swimsuit did, which Larry figured was a fair point. Her choice of clothing didn't surprise him. He had always considered Paula to be more comfortable in her own body than any of the other girls he knew.

That night, Larry and Paula drove up and down 1st Avenue for an hour, an hour and a half. Under the blink and flash of intermittent streetlight, they alternately talked and didn't. Then Larry took her home. Paula never said a word about being pregnant, nor about Lonnie or Robert. That night, Larry said, he and Paula just "bullshitted." Larry considered her to be the most regular of girls hanging out on the most regular of nights.

Chapter 10

The Timeline

SEATED AT THE DINING ROOM TABLE AT HER FATHER'S house in the farm country outside of Cedar Rapids, Susan and I allowed ourselves to become consumed by the case file. Laptops open, legal pads scattered, we sat adjacent to floor-to-ceiling windows that overlooked the great expanse of her father's emerald yard, his wife's small stand of apple trees, her swimming pool–sized vegetable garden, her swimming pool. We were building timelines.

Everyone had a story for the night Paula disappeared— Lonnie, Debbie Kellogg, Ben Carroll, Lynn Oberbroeckling, the merchant policeman, and the girls who saw Paula stalled in front of the post office. As did each person who crossed paths with each of these people. The web was incomprehensibly wide and complex. Each story was constructed around time, the hour that person last saw Paula, last spoke with her, where that person was when and with whom. *Rashomon*-like, the only person who had no story, who could not speak, was the person at the center of the web, Paula herself. And she was the only one who knew the truth, except of course for the person who killed her.

Susan and I did our best to construct Paula's story for her based on everything we knew for sure—the time she clocked out of work (9 p.m.), when she came and left the Austin & Garf show (9:15 and 11:45 p.m.), the time we estimate she drove off in Debbie's car (around 1 a.m.), and when the merchant policeman stopped to help her reset the gears on the Nova (1:15 a.m.). We placed her timeline beside Lonnie's, which changed between his initial statement, given the day after Paula's body was found, and the statement he gave four days later when he was asked to return to the police station to discuss the inconsistencies present in his first statement. We then used the timelines given by Ben and Debbie and the people Lonnie encountered that night to cross-reference his telling.

Lonnie's story went like this: He and Ben picked Paula up from Younkers sometime after 9 p.m. when she clocked out of work. They caravanned to the Nowhere, hanging out until just before midnight when Paula asked to be driven home. Lonnie left his Porsche at the Nowhere and rode with Paula and Ben in Ben's Mustang. The boys dropped Paula off at her house and proceeded to cruise around town. They went to the East Side Maid-Rite, a classic-style checkered diner, and to Pizza Pete's in Marion, about ten minutes away. And then they headed to Angie Nejdl's house. Angie, an acquaintance, told police that she ran into Lonnie and Ben at the Maid-Rite and suggested they come back to her place to hang out.

But on their way to Angie's, Ben and Lonnie got lost. As they searched for her address, they ran into a friend of Lonnie's who had recently returned from a tour in Vietnam. Lonnie's friend agreed to escort Lonnie and Ben to Angie's house, after which he drove off. Ben and Lonnie hung out with Angie, her roommate, and her roommate's boyfriend for a few hours. As the night wore on, Ben passed out in his chair. Angie fell asleep on the floor. Eventually, Ben woke up, and Lonnie and he left at 1:30 a.m.

On their way back to Paula's, they ran into Pat Conway, a boy from school. Pat followed them. Lonnie got out of Ben's Mustang at Paula's house, and got into Pat's car. Ben went home. Lonnie said he and Pat went to a "Bob's Place," an establishment Susan and I could find no record of.

For reasons he does not explain, Lonnie returned to Paula's house and began banging on the front door until Debbie and Barb Besler, Paula's other roommate, woke up and answered. Lonnie demanded to know where Paula was. Debbie told him she wasn't home. He forced his way past the roommates, went upstairs to Paula's room, and returned with his stereo and "stereo tapes."

This had always seemed so damning to me. When I was a kid, my mom would deem a squabble childish by saying, "I'm taking my dollies and going home!" It was the emotional equivalent of a middle finger. This seemed like what Lonnie was doing when he retrieved his stuff in the middle of the night. He was pissed (because Paula wasn't home? because he thought she was with Robert? because she was pregnant?), and he wasn't hiding it. After he had his tapes, he got into his car and headed east for home.

Here was the big inconsistency. Something I noted, and something it seemed the CRPD noted too. After leaving Paula's, Lonnie ran back into the friend who'd just returned from Vietnam. Lonnie parked his car in front of Rapids Chevrolet, got in with the friend, and the two boys "drove around" until 8 a.m., at which time Lonnie said his friend took him back to Rapids Chevy. He got into his Porsche and drove home. But this was impossible.

"Look," I said to Susan, pointing out one of the first bullets on our timeline, my eyebrows raised. Lonnie couldn't have taken his car from Paula's house east toward Rapids Chevrolet because according to his own story his car would *still* have been at the Nowhere Lounge. At no time during his first statement did Lonnie mention retrieving the Porsche.

When the police called Lonnie back into the station less than a week later and presumably pointed this error out to him, Lonnie changed his story. Instead of going from Pizza Pete's directly to Angie Nejdl's house, Lonnie now said Ben first took him back to the Nowhere to get his car. He said he then drove his Porsche to Paula's, parked, and got in with Ben to head to Angie's. In this scenario, his Porsche would have been at Paula's for him to zoom off in after barging in on Debbie and Barb. (This works with the timeline save the fact that Debbie, Barb, and Ben all said that Lonnie burst in around 3:30 a.m., not 1:30 a.m. as he initially claimed.)

But then there was another problem, which came from his friend, the Vietnam vet's, statement. He said that when he crossed paths with Lonnie in front of Rapids Chevrolet, Lonnie was driving west. If Lonnie were coming from Paula's on the northwest side heading toward his house on the northeast side, he would have been driving east. Driving west meant that he could have been coming from the Nowhere, where perhaps he had picked up his car, but then the question remains: who drove him there and why didn't he tell the police? This raises the second problem with Lonnie's revised statement. Ben Carroll went home after he dropped Lonnie at Paula's. And Pat Conway, present in Lonnie's first story, disappeared during his second story. But Pat Conway *does* appear in Debbie's statement; she said that when Lonnie woke her up, beating on the door and charging through the house, she saw who "she believed was" Pat Conway and a couple of girls standing across the street. Was Pat Conway the one who drove Lonnie to go pick up his car at the Nowhere? Who were the girls? I had no idea. The police never interviewed any of these people.

This was part of the frustration of this case. The loose ends were everywhere. The police tried and failed to reach out to Pat Conway two times, and then as far as I could tell, never again. The police also never circled back to Ben to clarify whether he had in fact driven Lonnie back to the Nowhere to get his car after they went to the Maid-Rite as Lonnie claimed in his second statement. Speaking to either of these boys would have gone a long way toward nailing down Lonnie's timeline. Ben Carroll died in 2011. According to Debbie Kellogg, Pat Conway is also dead,* so the window of opportunity to ask this question, to talk to them at all, is closed forever. The dead take everything with them.

The investigation file is rife with infuriating oversights like these. There was Robert's missing timeline. He was cleared as a suspect by a Lt. Byrne, who believed that he didn't show any "guilt reactions" during his lie detector test. And the police never documented officially clearing Lonnie as a suspect. When I pointed this out to Susan, she said, "They didn't think Paula would fit in Lonnie's trunk."

There was a report from a Detective Staves regarding a visit he took to a car dealership that sold Porsches. While there, Staves measured the size of the trunks in those cars built between 1960 and 1966. In the earlier models the trunks were 6 inches deep and housed under the front hood, the engine in the back; the later models had trunks both in the front with

---

* I haven't been able to verify this since I haven't been able to locate any record of him.

the engine as well as in the traditional place at the rear of the vehicle but still were only 9 inches deep. Staves closed his report by writing: "In my opinion an adult body would not fit in this trunk and certainly not Paula Oberbroeckling."

Staves was probably right. Paula was 5 feet 11 inches tall. She had a size nine shoe. She likely couldn't have fit in Lonnie's trunk. But could she have fit in his friend's trunk, the vet? Or what about the trunk of the Nova? Or what about the back seat of either car? (Don't forget that the right rear window* was down when the Nova was found outside the Eagle parking lot. Automatic windows were years off. Someone— more than one person?—had been in that back seat and had rolled that window down.) Or what about the passenger seat of Lonnie's car? Or the passenger seat of his friend's car or Debbie's car, for that matter? Who says you have to transport a body in the trunk?

As far as I could tell, these possibilities were never raised, much less answered. I knew my body language—eyebrows up, palms to the ceiling—spoke disbelief, incredulity. I could feel Susan humoring me. She had been down all these roads before. She had tested these hypotheses, flushed out all the inconsistencies; she had been incredulous, too, and now she was vindicated.

"See?"

---

* In Debbie's statement given to the police on November 30th, after Paula's body was found, she said that the back window was down. She reported being annoyed by this as she'd asked that Paula not have anyone in the car. The police report that detailed the officers' response to Carol Oberbroeckling's call outside Eagle on July 11th states that all four windows in the Nova were down. But remember, this report was written five months after the fact, which goes a long way to show how seriously the CRPD took Paula's disappearance. Read: not at all. Further, December 9th was more than a week after Paula's body was found. So, in this case, I'm inclined to believe Debbie's account.

I did. So many holes.

No matter how I looked at it, it was clear that there was a problem with Lonnie's timeline. There were whole chunks of that night that lacked detail. There was a chance that he truly couldn't remember the sequence of events. He had been drinking, plus his statements were given more than four months after the fact. I would have had a hard time providing a timeline for a night four months ago when I was all over town and under the influence. My instinct says that his girlfriend going missing forever would be potent enough to sear an evening into one's memory, but trauma studies show how frequently victims misremember even the most obvious details of a life-changing event. So maybe he had truly forgotten.

There was also the potential that he'd lied. But even that didn't mean he was culpable. Maybe he was skittish of the police for other reasons. A couple summers before, he and seven other teenagers had been arrested during a narcotics raid at what police dubbed a "marijuana party." He was charged with violating the state narcotics act and contributing to the delinquency of a minor and then arraigned in municipal court. The charges were eventually dropped. The judge said there was "no showing [Lonnie and his cohort] actually had narcotic drugs in their possession." But the ordeal was weeks long, and likely stressful. Perhaps Lonnie had taken pot to Angie Nejdl's house the night of Paula's death. Maybe that was the reason Angie invited him over in the first place; as far as I could tell, the two weren't friends. Maybe Lonnie was frightened that if the police began digging, he would find himself in violation of the state narcotics act once again.

Lonnie Bell was the only person who refused to submit to a lie-detector test during the investigation into Paula's death. The file said he lawyered up. However, when I reached out to

Fred Dumbaugh, the attorney mentioned in the investigation file, Dumbaugh said he had no recollection of advising Lonnie. On December 12th, a couple weeks after Paula's body was found, the police file said that Lonnie had become unavailable for questioning because he was in the hospital. Lonnie was in St. Luke's Hospital for at least four weeks.

All of this together—that Lonnie was unaccounted for in the very hours during which Paula disappeared; that he had been demonstrably angry with her; that he was unavailable during the investigation; that he refused to take a lie-detector test; that he thought she might be pregnant; that he knew she'd been sneaking out on him with Robert—reeked of guilt. He was the boyfriend. It's always the boyfriend!

Lonnie had been reluctant to talk to Susan in the past. He'd hung up the phone when she called him the day before I arrived in Cedar Rapids. We had few options other than to go visit him.

I didn't know much about what had happened to Lonnie Bell in the intervening years. He made an appearance in the crime blotter of the *Gazette* in 1979 when he was thirty. According to the item, he'd been charged with public intoxication and criminal trespass. He'd entered a Pizza Hut at lunchtime on a Tuesday with his roommate and threatened an assistant manager with bodily harm. Lonnie and his buddy yelled obscenities at the restaurant's employees and customers, turned over a couple of tables, and threw a jar of cheese into the parking lot. For this, Lonnie spent the night in jail and was released on cash bond the next day. In 1981, he filed for a marriage license with a once-divorced woman who had been crowned Miss Cedar

Rapids in 1965. Other than that, all I knew was that he was sixty-six years old and lived in government-subsidized housing.

Lonnie's apartment complex lay off a solitary, moderately forested road with few turnoffs and even less traffic on the southwest side of Cedar Rapids. The community had no gate and no security guard. Beyond the entrance, Susan and I found a smattering of two-story buildings, brown-shingled, brick and drab, in a sea of asphalt. I was afraid, though I couldn't pinpoint exactly why. There was the potential that Lonnie had played a role in Paula's death and had kept quiet all these years and would go into a fury at our prying. Or possibly he wasn't involved in her death at all but then there I was holding up to the light an event that was likely a great source of pain for him. But also, and perhaps most certainly, there was the simple fact that he was a man whom I did not know, and I was willingly stepping onto his turf. A move I had been warned against over and over again in varying scenarios throughout my entire life.

Susan had met Lonnie before. On an earlier reporting trip she and my father-in-law showed up at Lonnie's door with a tape recorder. The audio was scratchy and difficult to decipher, but Lonnie, after initially saying he didn't want to talk, allowed Susan a few words. In order to ingratiate herself, she told him that she felt he'd been unfairly persecuted. This did seem to open him up. He made a few suggestions as to culprits and motives and then said he had to go.

I parked the car beside Lonnie's building. When I looked at Susan, I was met with resigned confidence. Despite her size and age—she was in her sixties herself, by which I mean she would not be fighting anyone off—she seemed unfazed by our mission. "Ready?" she asked. I nodded, knowing I needed to give Lonnie a chance to tell his side of the story.

We entered through an air lock in the side of the building and found in front of us a set of carpeted stairs that led both a half flight up and a half flight down. Lonnie lived up. The hallway outside his apartment reeked of stale smoke. A TV's blare echoed from inside. Sirens and gunshots told me he was watching a cop show. It was early afternoon on a weekday. I widened my eyes at Susan. She was holding an already-running tape recorder and I, in an attempt to generate goodwill, a leaking bag of hot dogs and fries we'd picked up from the Flying Wienie. We rang the doorbell three times before we heard someone shuffle to the door.

"Hi Lonnie," said Susan, stepping forward as the door began to open. "I called you yesterday. This is my daughter-in-law. . . ." She motioned to me, but before she could finish her sentence, Lonnie cut her off.

"I don't want to talk about it," he said as he shut the door, not hard, but resolutely—though not before I saw him.

I had a couple of photos of Lonnie and Paula together, which had been taken not long before she disappeared. The two were attending a friend's wedding. They were standing outside on a lawn with another couple, effectively braided together. Paula had one arm around Lonnie's waist and the other around the waist of the other boy, who had his arm around Paula's shoulders and the shoulders of another girl. The sun was bright. Paula was wearing a canary-yellow jumpsuit with a halter top and wide legs. Her feet were obscured by the green grass, her shoulders bare. Her hair was teased a little higher than normal, special for the occasion. It was luminous, reflecting the sun right back at the camera, like light off water. She was radiant but she didn't smile. One hip cocked forward, steady gaze, straight face, she appeared to me the most confident woman who had ever lived. Self-possessed and comfortable. The other people in the photo didn't even read, eclipsed as they were by Paula.

Beside Paula, Lonnie stood shorter by a hair and thinner too. He wore a navy-blue tank top pulled tightly into blue jeans, which were held up by a thick brown leather belt. His hair was long, dishwater and dull next to Paula's gleaming blonde. But his face was what glowed. His head tipped affectionately toward Paula's, he was positively beaming. He looked so happy.

This ecstatic, tan picture of youth was not who opened the door. Lonnie as an adult was average-sized, no longer thin, with a shock of frizzy hair that appeared dyed, the brown of a tea stain rather than the blonde I'd expected. His pupils were huge, impenetrable, and dull, not sparkling like the kid in the photo. And in place of that wide grin, Lonnie the adult was moving a set of false teeth into place.

Four years after that day, Susan and I tried again with Lonnie, and this time he let us in. He'd moved; his new apartment was also in government-subsidized housing but this community was for older residents. The building was institutional, high-rise, not well maintained. There was a sign on Lonnie's door forbidding smoking. Inside, compressed oxygen was in use. But when we entered, we found the apartment—one dimly lit room with a Pullman kitchen and a bathroom attached— fogged with cigarette smoke. Lonnie sat on a recliner and didn't move to get up. An air-conditioning unit blew cool air from the apartment's only window, which was obscured by a drawn shade. Outside it was midday, close to 90 degrees. The TV set was on at high volume. In spite of the smoking and the compressed oxygen, Lonnie seemed better cared for than I could tell in the ten seconds I had seen him while holding the leaking bag from the Flying Wienie.

When I asked him what happened in the early hours of July 11, he said that he'd always believed the abortion story. That during the four months he had dated Paula there had been "no periods." That she had asked him what he would do if she were pregnant with Robert's child. And also, he pointed out, why would she have been crying in the living room with Debbie Kellogg if she weren't going to "take a baby's life?"

But that was still to come. Here, with the door firmly closed in my face, I finally dared glance at Susan. I held up the hot dogs in question, and she shrugged. I placed them on the mat in front of Lonnie's closed door, hoping maybe he'd eat them. On our way back to the car, Susan turned to me and said, "Oh my God, I'm shaking." I was both relieved to not be alone in my fear and doubly afraid to realize that this had been a stretch for her too. What if something had happened? I had a child. Where were my priorities? But I wasn't given time to dwell. We were through it and Susan was pointing to the trees opposite Lonnie's building. Through them, I could just catch the glint of moving water. If I could see through buildings, down the sheer bluff that ran to the Cedar River, I'd be looking directly at the culvert where Paula's body had been found. How Lonnie avoided thinking of Paula every single day was beyond me.

Chapter 11

The Flood

I INSTINCTIVELY PUT OFF DRIVING PAULA'S FINAL
route until the end of my trip. As if it were within my power to
stay her death. As if by not tracing her last steps, I could keep
her alive, everything before her, if only in my head. But as the
days passed, pressure mounted, and I knew I needed to go.

Susan and I pulled up in front of the ramshackle house
on the west side. Its dull white exterior was exacerbated by
the gray skies above and by the heaps of browning slush lap-
ping the curb. We debated where Paula might have exited the
house—the front door? the side?—and where the Nova would
have been parked. There was an alley that ran along the left
side of the house. A small driveway. I pulled into it and said,
"Ready?" before backing out just as Paula must have.

We headed toward 1st Avenue. There was a gas station on
the corner. Susan thought there had been a gas station there
when Paula was alive too. There were no cell phones in 1970,
and no landline in Paula's house. If she were going to alert
someone that she was en route (the chiropractor? Robert?
someone else?), she might have used a pay phone. Did she
stop at the gas station to make a call?

We made a left onto 1st Avenue's four lanes, which were lined with storefronts in various states of survival—convenience stores, diners including the West Side Maid-Rite, other ephemera. We passed over the 1st Avenue Bridge with its gracious lanes and concrete arches, which reminded me of the trajectory of the bouncing ball on a follow-along song. We turned right on 1st Street SE on the other bank, which took us past the spot where the old post office had been and where the Nova had fallen out of gear, where Paula had pulled over and received help from the merchant policeman, where the girls who had been cruising saw her with the car's hood up. We drove a few blocks and there we could go no farther. Facing south, parallel to the river, looking toward the high-rises downtown, where there should have been open road, instead there was a giant glass-and-stone edifice built right over the center of the street. As we got closer, the writing on a retaining wall outside came into focus: "United States Courthouse, Northern District of Iowa."

Seven years before that morning, in June of 2008, the swollen Cedar River crested its banks, sinking ten square miles of the city in muddy water. The flood washed away a railroad bridge that connected the east side of the city with the west. It devastated the municipal buildings on the island in the middle of the river. It drowned homes and yards and neighborhood streets. The flooding was some of the worst since Hurricane Katrina. The city received $848 million in assistance from FEMA. Ten thousand people were displaced.

I happened to be in Cedar Rapids just after that flood when the city was still reeling. That was when I joined my husband's family on their initial Paula research trip, long before I'd gotten involved myself. It had only been three weeks since the storm, and the flood was inescapable. On our flight's descent we witnessed the scope. Mirrored floodwaters reflected the blue sky, clouds, our very aircraft right back up at us. The element one would normally take for granted was reversed—the sky in the earth—but so subtly that it wasn't immediately apparent, beautiful and unsettling, like a Dalí.

When we landed, we found that all of Cedar Rapids was focused on the present. People were getting through life minute by minute, day by day. Every hour was spent cleaning out or taking stock or donating time or money or supplies. The flood was the topic of every conversation, the locus of every action. Amid all this, my husband and his family were trying to dredge up a then-thirty-eight-year-old killing. Even the director of photography on the film seemed more taken with the flood than with the subject he'd come for. His plan was to juxtapose footage of the floodwaters with the voices of Susan's interview subjects. The crew walked away with hours of flood footage and only a handful of still images of the people who had anything to do with Paula Oberbroeckling.

But who could blame them? The practice of triage states that you address the most acute problem first. The flooding was a fresh wound necessitating immediate attention; Paula's death was an old one. A wound that, even without a flood, the community and the police department seemed content to leave in the past, to forget and move on from.

Now, seven years after that flood, Susan and I continued to contend with it. Water damage had led to a sort of municipal-building musical chairs. City Hall, which had been underwater on May's Island, was relocated into the former U.S. Federal Building on 1st Street. Then the federal courthouse moved into this brand-new building constructed right across Paula's path. On the other side was Oak Hill, a bend in the river, the neighborhood where some notorious gangsters had lived, the store in front of which Debbie Kellogg's car had been parked, and the hill on which Paula's body had been found, but we couldn't get there, at least not in the way that Paula had.

"Just imagine," Susan said, waving her hand in front of the courthouse, "that the road goes through."

I tried. But all I could think was here the flood was again passively working against us, serving to further obfuscate Paula's death. And this time, ironically, it had help from the judicial system.

I am aware that we can't live mired in every single hurt from the past. That would be paralyzing. But to move on from a wrong before there is resolution connotes tacit approval. In *Trauma and Recovery*, psychiatrist and researcher Judith Herman writes, "When the traumatic events are of human design, those who bear witness are caught in the conflict between victim and perpetrator. . . . It is very tempting to take the side of the perpetrator. All the perpetrator asks is that the bystander do nothing."

When I spoke with Jeni Schmidt, Stephanie Schmidt's sister, about how she'd weathered the trauma of her sister's murder, she differentiated between moving on and moving forward. Moving on in her parlance signified forgetting; the perpetrator here has won. But moving forward meant progressing with the conscious awareness and consideration of the infraction incurred. Taking deliberate steps to do things differently. To rectify. To improve.

In the years since the flood, Cedar Rapids had moved forward. The city reconstructed or rehabilitated those flood-damaged municipal buildings, placing City Hall out of the river's reach. It repaved roads, reinforced bridges, shored up banks. There was even a trendy new neighborhood with breweries and bookstores that had sprung up in the abandoned warehouses and factories a couple blocks in from the water. Many Cedar Rapidians had also found their way forward. They had cleaned up, a few had rebuilt, more often they had moved. In any case, they had survived.

The city's leaders and their constituents had come together to rezone, to commission and plan, to gather and communicate and collaborate. And while the methods weren't always agreed on, it was a way forward nonetheless. This banding together across class, race, and religion was common after natural disasters. I had witnessed the phenomenon in New York City after 9/11. Shared trauma engendered feelings of solidarity, of we're-all-in-the-same-boat, which led to an increase in social capital—basically goodwill between neighbors. It was this strength in numbers that allowed a city to move forward, a people to carry on.

The Oberbroecklings had also endured trauma, but they did so with no such support. The city did not rally around their cause. Those whose job it was to help them—the media, the police—neglected to do so. They couldn't even find refuge in the people who had arguably suffered the trauma with them—Paula's friends and her boyfriends. Because Paula's killing went unsolved, no one knew whom to trust. Rumors flew. Everyone was a possible suspect or accomplice. Some of the theories that made the rounds sounded insane to me. Debbie Kellogg and Lonnie Bell had conspired together to kill Paula because they had been in a secret relationship. The Black girls who didn't like Paula because she was dating Robert jumped her when she entered Oak Hill. All this speculation only sowed distrust and division.

I couldn't imagine the isolation attendant in such circumstances. The one narrative the Oberbroecklings *had*
been given—that of failing social services, ineffective police
departments, judicial systems, media—could lead to a feeling
of hopelessness, of futility. Who will support us? From this
vantage point, being failed by the systems set in place to protect and level justice might erode one's faith in others. I wondered if this was why, as the hours and now days ticked past, I
still had not heard from Lynn.

Lynn wasn't the only person I contacted before my trip. I also
reached out to Robert. Over the phone, his voice had been low
and kind. He told me he would be in town and encouraged
me to call when I arrived. But, like Lynn, once I got to Cedar
Rapids, he became too busy to meet with me.

Susan interviewed Robert in 2008. He showed up to their
meeting carrying a black trash bag filled with tools. He said
he'd come from a job laying bricks, but he wore white pants
and white shoes, both of which were spotless. He refused to
sign the film release form Susan offered him. They spoke for
a while sitting on the grass and then agreed to meet later that
night for dinner. Susan bought him a steak and, after, Robert
followed her to her rental car and allowed her to interview
him with a tape recorder. Outside it poured. On the recording
I could hear the rain pelting the roof of the car.

Robert told Susan that he thought about Paula constantly. "I
could be just like sleeping and, pow, she's right there," he said.
"For a long time I thought about her every day. We got robbed.
Of a relationship and a deep love for each other, of wanting to
grow together and be together. And I suppose that will always
be in the back of my mind. And always in my heart."

I found irony in the fact that as much as Lynn and Robert disliked each other, their experiences had commonalities. Lynn also spoke about being an adult, more than forty years past her sister's death, and not being able to get through a day without thinking of her.

This recalled something I'd learned recently that had shocked me about the way the body works and the long-term presence of injury. Our bodies employ vitamin C to produce collagen, which binds our wounds. This knitting together is not a one-time event but a continuous biological process that repeats throughout our lifetimes, binding and rebinding, replacing old collagen as soon as it wears out. So that, in advanced cases of scurvy—vitamin C deficiency—old wounds will literally reopen, flesh coming apart. This for me meant that, metaphoric or otherwise, healing was impossible. Once wounded, we were always wounded. Destined to carry around every past hurt for the rest of our lives. Our body's literal maps of our pain.

It seemed I wasn't far off. The psychiatrist Bessel van der Kolk describes "the imprints of trauma on body, mind, and soul" manifesting as "the crushing sensations in your chest that you may label as anxiety or depression; the fear of losing control; always being on alert for danger or rejection; the self-loathing; the nightmares and flashbacks; the fog that keeps you from staying on task and from engaging fully in what you are doing; being unable to fully open your heart to another human being." How then were the walking wounded to move forward?

During college I interned as a reporter in the features section of the *Kansas City Star.* That summer, Stephanie Schmidt's family was in the news. They had successfully lobbied for a state law that allowed authorities to keep some sex offenders in mental health facilities after they served their sentences. The law, which was highly controversial (the Kansas Supreme Court overturned it, but the U.S. Supreme Court upheld it twice), had been named for Stephanie and was being amended slightly. I offered to cover this latest development for the *Star*.

When I arrived at the Schmidts' house, just blocks from where I grew up, Stephanie's parents greeted me at the front door. Inside, I found nowhere to sit, barely anywhere to stand, every surface was covered with paperwork. There were multiple telephones, binders on top of binders, press clippings. Jeni, who was a year older than I, stood solemnly at her parents' side. Together, they explained the importance of the law and enumerated all the work they'd done in order to get it passed. And it was an accomplishment. It had probably saved women's lives, would save women's lives. But at the time, when I was twenty, all I could see was how the Schmidts had been calcified in time, how they continued to experience Stephanie's death as if it had happened yesterday rather than six years before. I listened to Jeni, who should have been on the cusp of her own life just as I was, and I ached for how her existence seemed to revolve around her dead sister.

More recently I read an update on the Schmidts' work, and I began to see things differently. Stephanie's family spent eighteen years working to pass legislation to protect women. The piece said they had decided to "retire" in 2011. They did this because they saw change. They cited advancements like AMBER Alerts, the invention of cell phones, and the creation of sex-offender registries, which made them feel that, had Stephanie been faced with the same horrifying circumstances today, she might have survived. This work, their advocacy, hadn't hardened them in time, in fact it was the very thing that had allowed them to move through it. Their action had carried them forward.

This theory fit with what I was beginning to understand about trauma. Herman wrote that of women who'd been raped, those who "made the best recoveries were those who had become active in the antirape movement. . . . In refusing to hide or be silenced, in insisting that rape is a public matter, and in demanding social change survivors create their own living monument."

But when I asked Jeni about that time in her life, telling her what I'd observed of her solidarity with her parents and how I'd evolved in my assumptions of it, she both validated what I saw and negated it. My conclusion was correct and also it was too easy. She told me that she believed she and her parents *had* done good work, *had* maybe saved lives—"for all you know a person is alive today because of you"—and that work *had* helped her and her parents organize their own day-to-day, but also it *had* served to harden her in time. She told me that for years after Stephanie's death she lived for her parents, for her sister, for everyone but herself. That she felt misunderstood and without a support network. Everyone was focused intently on her parents, and that *included* her parents, who were so locked inside their own trauma that they once said to Jeni, "We don't think you understand what we've been through." Which on the one hand was probably true, but on the other was a complete negation of Jeni's experience.

For years, Jeni worried about her own death, assumed that she wouldn't live past twenty because her sister hadn't. She found it difficult to form relationships. She described starting college and all the getting-to-know-you, including questions about whether she had siblings. "The answer isn't no. But if I said yes, then there were follow-up questions. 'Well, where is she?'" Dropping something as heavy as Stephanie's murder on someone she barely knew was usually a showstopper. Rather than endure those conversations, she cloistered herself.

The ten-year anniversary of Stephanie's death proved a turning point for Jeni. She had recently met her husband. She stopped focusing on her own vulnerability. She stepped back from the work she had been doing with her parents, gradually embracing the idea that her sister would want her to live for herself. That the best way to honor Stephanie was to be Jeni. This was her way forward.

When I finally heard back from Lynn, she sent me an email that said that her schedule would preclude her from meeting with me. She also told me that she didn't understand what I needed from her anyway, she had already told Susan everything. My heart sank. For me, it wasn't about learning more. I mean, there would always be more, and I had lists of questions, but what I wanted most from her was solidarity. I wanted to cooperate with her; I wanted her to cooperate with me. I wanted to have a shared goal. In many ways I thought I was embarking on this project for her.

There was a heartbreaking moment in Lynn's interview where she fantasized about reaching out to someone in the police file who might know what happened to Paula. "Would you just tell me?" she said she would ask. "I promise I won't tell anyone." *I promise I won't tell anyone!*

Both of Paula's parents died without knowing what happened to their daughter. So did Paula's brother Christopher. Layer upon layer of pain. What if the police and the community weren't the only ones who were willing to forget Paula's death? What if moving on was what Lynn wanted as well? Then what was I doing? And who was I doing it for?

During that initial reporting trip in 2008, my husband and I took our rental car down to the river's edge to see the flooding for ourselves. The east side of the river with its factories and warehouses had been devastated, but the worst of the flooding in terms of people's houses, their everyday lives, occurred on the west side in Czech Village and in Time Check, both close-knit, blue-collar communities made up of modest homes.

It was nearly impossible to navigate the neighborhoods. Some streets were barricaded. Lakes of muddy water stretched for blocks making others impassable. As we circled closer, we saw homes that displayed their scars on the outside. Dirt and grime stretched to high-water marks two-thirds of the way up the siding of some houses. Yellow police tape obstructed entryways. Rusted appliances sat junked on the curbs. The area was mostly vacant, but at one point we saw a group of people removing debris. I instinctively lowered my eyes. I felt like a disaster tourist, like I should get out of the car and help.

But here's the thing. When I returned to New York and tried to talk about what I had seen in Cedar Rapids, most people were unaware there had been a flood. And if they did know, they had no idea of the extent of the damage, the effect on people's lives. The problem was, without having been there, there was no way *to* know. Most national news outlets had covered the flood as it occurred and then never again.

"We really feel that we are the forgotten disaster," Greg Eyerly, the city's flood recovery director, was quoted as saying. "We don't make sexy products. We make starch that goes into paper, we make foodstuffs, ingredients in crackers and cereal.

We make ethanol. The sexiest thing we make is Cap'n Crunch. We're not a beachfront property. We make an anonymous contribution to our country, and people forget about us."

It is easy to brush aside trauma when it is happening somewhere else, to someone else. The manner in which Paula's death was framed, by foregrounding her supposed transgressions—the way she was dressed, the fact of her relationships, whatever ridiculousness—ensured that it would be filed under personal trauma, something that had affected the Oberbroecklings only. Her death isn't ours because she is not us. But set Paula's death among the hundreds of thousands of other deaths of women, women who had been thrown away (in recent memory I can recall the stories of women whose bodies had been tossed into fields, into bodies of water, buried under leaves in the forest, run over by cars, chopped up, put in trash cans, stuffed into suitcases and left at the side of the road; in 2017 alone, 3,222 women were murdered in the United States), and here is one giant gaping wound that, never triaged, is festering just beneath the surface of American society. Covering it up, or better, sinking it under the notion that it is not our trauma, not our concern but someone else's— in this case, the Oberbroecklings—is a silencing. One that affects all of us because it is, in fact, all of ours.

Judith Herman puts it this way: "Remembering and telling the truth about terrible events are prerequisites both for the restoration of the social order and for the healing of individual victims."

• • •

Having no other choice, Susan and I drove around the U.S. Courthouse. On the other side the buildings were lower-rise; the streets felt wider. Back on course, we made a left onto 8th

Avenue SE, which turns into Mt. Vernon Road. Within ten blocks I found myself once again in front of the parking lot adjacent to which Debbie Kellogg's Nova had been found.

We sat for a second, taking it in, and Susan said, "Now watch this. Turn around."

I did, driving south through Oak Hill, taking a couple natural jogs and suddenly I popped out onto Otis Road. Within minutes I was trudging toward the culvert.

Concrete, cream-colored, hard, and enigmatic, the pipe ended in a small stand of trees. Everything was blanketed in snow. I recalled the images from the case file—a decaying pair of arm bones held together with rope, the polished nails, the skeletal feet. I·pictured Paula lying there among the rocks. Alone. In the dark. I hoped that by that point she was already dead. Or at least delirious from blood loss. I felt empty and sad. A woman had been thrown away here. Maybe there were people who could forget this, but I was not one of them. I was a woman, and I was too angry to walk away.

Coming to Cedar Rapids, I had told myself that solving Paula's homicide would allow me to give Lynn and all the people who cared about Paula closure. But I was beginning to realize that in truth my aspiration was more compulsive, more subconscious than that, it was outside of me or maybe deep inside.

What I couldn't reconcile was that something *had* happened that night. Paula went somewhere, and she met someone who killed her, intentionally or not. And then that someone, or maybe a different someone, tied her arms and legs together, if they weren't tied together already, and then dumped her body like so much garbage beside the Cedar River. The elusiveness of those somewheres and someones left me on existentially shaky ground. Accepting that we may never know who or what was responsible for Paula's death meant also accepting something fundamental about the world order. Namely, that life was not fair, that power rested in the hands of a few, and that those few could inflict violence on others without recrimination while those others were left with no recourse.

Perhaps because I was a new mother and because motherhood is, if nothing else, a hopeful pursuit, I needed to believe that young women were not disposable and that when a rupture like what happened to Paula occurred, the world would bend and stretch to repair it, to stop it from ever happening again.

Looking down on the very ground on which Paula had lain alone for four long months, I knew deep down that I wouldn't solve Paula's death. Simultaneously I had the strong sense that airing her story was important, that it was a step toward that "restoration of the social order" Judith Herman was talking about, toward setting things right, toward creating a world into which I was comfortable launching my own child. And that was worth giving myself to this story for as long as it took.

There, in the silence and stillness of winter, a goldfinch as blonde as Paula alit onto a branch just above the culvert. Soft suede feathers and glinting black eyes, it looked as unbound and beautiful as I imagined Paula to have been. Paula who had lived. Paula whose death was unjust and untimely and unfair, but also Paula whose suffering ended the night she died. The dead need nothing. Her pain was ours now to grapple with until we too died.

I'd told a friend that I was considering giving up on the Paula project if my Cedar Rapids trip proved unfruitful, if I didn't think I could solve the crime. She'd laughed. "Are you kidding?" she said. "You're looking at it all wrong." It didn't have to be solved or not solved, she said. That was reductive.

She and her husband were both people who made their livings coming up with new ideas—he in the art world and she in architecture. She had told me that over years of brainstorming together, they'd begun to call the gray space in between givens—meaning things we all take for granted, things we all agree to accept—the Flim. It was in this space where concepts weren't fixed, but fluid, where it was possible to experiment, to question, to think. This was where change could be made, where attitudes could shift, where there was room to evolve.

Maybe the Flim of Paula's case rested somewhere between the things we knew: that Paula had been discovered with her limbs bound and that her death had been largely forgotten, the silencing of her story an added injustice, a second death. Because maybe even if we knew how Paula died it wouldn't solve the fundamental question I'd been circling. Maybe this wasn't a mystery of *one* woman's life and why *one* woman died but the mystery of why women die.

Chapter 12

The Double Bind

AFTER I RETURNED TO NEW YORK, TO MY HUSBAND AND
son and to our tiny Brooklyn apartment, I found myself discussing Paula's case with anyone who would listen, with
friends, with my husband late into the night, with people I'd
never met before but who asked what I did for a living and
then what I was working on. I laid out what I knew, outlined
a couple of scenarios, and then elucidated the community's
response—the disinterest of the media, the chaos within the
CRPD—with little consideration for how engaged my listener
was, though most people asked questions, posited answers,
and entered my rabbit hole willingly.

This was before "grab 'em by the pussy," before Hillary
Clinton's loss, before #MeToo and the Brett Kavanaugh hearings, but not much. Barack Obama was president and all the
hope and great expectation generated by his first election had
dissipated into a feeling of generalized disappointment. We
were still at war. Guantanamo was still open. The Affordable
Care Act had passed but only as a paltry version of its original self. Obama's hands had been tied by a Republican con-
gressional majority. It wasn't all bad—especially in hindsight

and with what was to come—but it was all double-edged. Hillary Clinton had announced her candidacy (!) and was greeted with misogyny and sexism. A triad of women started the #ShoutYourAbortion meme in an effort to normalize the decision (!), and then one had to go into hiding because her address had been leaked and wingnuts were sending her death threats. Same-sex marriage was legalized on the federal level (!); meanwhile, Republicans were able to enact more than fifty restrictions on abortion nationwide. *New York* magazine put thirty-five of the women who'd accused Bill Cosby of sexual assault on its cover (they were being believed!), just as more women materialized with accusations every day. Push. Pull. In. Out. Forward. Backward.

When I talked to people about Paula, I felt a generalized rage in the air, ready to spark if given a striker. And Paula's story worked virtually every time, enraging women and men alike with its injustice. How could the police have turned away from a young woman? From her family? Why? Was it because they thought she'd transgressed? Potentially had premarital sex? Dated a Black man? Possibly gone for an abortion? Was it because she was seen as somehow unimportant? Because her family had no money? No standing in the community? This response confirmed my choice to turn from the obvious question of who had killed Paula toward the bigger mystery of how society could have allowed her to die. Something it seemed I was far from alone in caring about.

The first entry in Paula's investigation file was conducted on July 15th, four days after Carol reported Paula missing. Carol told the responding officer that Paula had been "upset" because she "thinks she is about one and a half months pregnant." Where Carol got this information is unclear. It's unlikely that Paula would have shared a potential pregnancy with her mother; the two were on shaky ground. Debbie told police a couple weeks later that Paula had been "quite desperate" about being pregnant. Meaning, it's possible that Debbie told Carol after Paula went missing. Or Debbie could have told Lynn who told Carol. Debbie and Lynn were in the same grade at school and were actually friends first. The other person who claimed to have knowledge of a potential pregnancy, of course, was Lonnie. So Lonnie also could have told the Oberbroecklings. Robert seems not to have known.

A counselor at nearby Franklin Junior High School who had once boarded at Vera Oberbroeckling's house told police that "the family all knew that Paula was a few months pregnant." But because Paula's body was nearly completely decomposed when it was discovered, the coroner was unable to prove during the autopsy that Paula was pregnant, which means that there was a chance that she wasn't. What seemed likely was that Paula believed she was pregnant. Though perhaps the more accurate verb was worried or feared.

The social ramifications of bearing a child outside of marriage in 1970, only fifty years ago, were harsh. Single mothers were stigmatized and shamed, deemed loose, and shunned. Under the law, pregnant girls could be expelled from school. They could be fired from their jobs. Their children had "illegitimate" stamped on their birth certificates. They experienced abandonment—by their friends, who feared guilt by association; by the men who impregnated them, who wanted not to be fathers; by their families, who were afraid of being judged by their neighbors. The same type of treatment that was bestowed on women who divorced. Both choices, I'd add, condemned by the Catholic Church.

After Paula's body was found, Carol told Captain Vanous that she didn't know the paternity of the pregnancy nor, she said, did Paula. There was Lonnie, and then there was Robert, whom she had called "a colored boy," though she'd been quick to tell the officer that Paula had stopped seeing Robert some time ago. Debbie told Susan that the reason she had been vague with the cops was that she was trying to protect Paula's reputation. She said it was bad to be with two guys in the first place and a Black guy to boot.

If Robert were the father of the baby, if Paula's child were Black, Paula would likely have been banished from her community, relegated to living in Oak Hill. She would have had a hard time finding a job or gaining assistance of any kind. Historian Rickie Solinger explains that in postwar America, single white girls who became pregnant were shamed and then hidden. They were given the benefit of social services to get them through their pregnancies, then they were asked to give up their babies and reform (read: marry and get pregnant the "right" way). Black women, on the other hand, were punished for their transgression by being made to keep their children, then being disallowed the social services with which to support them. The population boom was then blamed on them. The prospect of such repercussions had to have been terrifying to a teenage girl.

More than once during her interviews with Susan, Lynn said aloud, seemingly to no one in particular, that the thing she didn't understand was why, if Paula were pregnant, she hadn't confided in her sister. For Lynn, this failure seemed both a tick in the "not pregnant" column as well as a potentially fatal mistake—maybe there was a world in which Lynn could have helped Paula. Lynn's questions also, heartbreakingly, contained a hint of bewilderment. If Paula had been pregnant and didn't confide in her sister, what did that say about the nature of their relationship at the time of Paula's death? Robert echoed this sentiment: "To this day I can't understand why she didn't come to me. I would have taken her to the hospital, you know?"

It did seem difficult to believe that, were Paula in such dire straits, she wouldn't have reached out to her family, maybe not to her mother but to her sister with whom she had been close all her life. But perhaps this fails to factor in the enormity of the panic some girls felt at the prospect of being pregnant. Or, said another way, perhaps it doesn't take into account the effectiveness of the threat of shaming.

"If there's anything to the abortion story, Paula would not have come and told me," said Carol. "She would have gone to [Lynn]. Unless she didn't want to hurt [her]. I think sometimes in my heart of hearts I feel that little Paula Jean felt like maybe she was a disappointment to her family."

● ● ●

Not long before my son was born, I wrote an essay about my grandmother—this was my mother's mother, the one who'd run away from an abusive home when she was sixteen, the one who'd been beautiful. She was the one who had been unable to leave my grandfather who yelled and hit their daughter, the one who, once widowed, had chosen never to marry again. Her presence in my young life had been foundational. From age ten to about fifteen, I spent summers with her in Chicago. She took me downtown on the Rock Island express, then to lunch in the Walnut Room at Marshall Field's. She brought me to see *The King and I* at a dinner theater where we ate and watched Anna and the King in the round. We walked to the library where we checked out stacks of books and then read together in wicker chairs on her brick front porch. She sipped iced tea and read bodice rippers; me, lemonade and Nancy Drew. On rainy days we played hand after hand of cards, Uno at first, and later, as I aged, pinochle. I worshipped her, but she was complicated.

I watched her snap at waiters, huff out of stores, dismiss anyone who disagreed with her. When I was young, I saw her pique as evidence of her strength—she had chutzpah—but as I grew older, I realized that her irritation equated to a sort of generalized anger that applied to everyone and perhaps even to the fact of life. When I was in college, I learned that she had secrets, and as they slowly unfolded, my perception of her transformed, the new information creating a different whole.

My mother told me the first version of what I'd come to understand as my grandmother's story. After my grandmother ran away from home, she found work serving hors d'oeuvres and collecting empty stemware at cocktail parties hosted by Chicago's elite. While she was working one such party, she attracted the attention of a man. Do I need to say that she attracted his attention because she was beautiful? He was in law school or he was a lawyer, the story has been told to me both ways; regardless, he was certainly of higher privilege, economically, socially, than she. He lavished attention on her, took her out, but when, at some point not long into their relationship, she told him that she was pregnant with his child, he disappeared. So there was my grandmother, seventeen years old, in a big city she barely knew, without the support of her parents, and pregnant. Nothing her beauty could do for her now.

Lost and alone, she turned to a friend who suggested she

visit a doctor downtown rumored to have helped girls who were in trouble. This was 1939. The first time she told me this story, my mother said that at my grandmother's appointment, the doctor refused to give her the abortion she was considering. Instead, he handed her the number of a local agency helmed by a flap of nuns. They would take her in, feed and care for her until she gave birth, at which point she would give up her baby. This was what my grandmother chose to do.

The essay I wrote before my son was born included the fact of my grandmother's unwanted pregnancy and that she might have considered an abortion but that she wasn't able to obtain one or had decided not to. It included her lonely time at the agency while she waited to give birth. And it included the aftermath: the baby winding up with my grandmother's brother who cared for her when she was a newborn, the doctor wooing my grandmother (do I need to say he wooed her because she was beautiful?), then marrying her and becoming my grandfather despite their twenty-year age difference. My essay described their wedding followed by his enlistment as a physician and a surgeon in World War II, thus leaving my grandmother to start her married life alone. It included their decision, after my grandfather returned from the war three years later, to reclaim my grandmother's daughter, age four by then, from her uncle and the myriad difficulties that followed from there—my grandfather's never being able to accept this daughter, the child of another man; the girl, my aunt, following in her mother's footsteps by running away from home again and again as a teenager, until one time she simply never returned, just as my grandmother had never returned to her childhood home.

For me, the essay was an attempt to understand this woman who had meant so much to me. I wanted to know how my grandmother had found herself at the end of her life so pickled with anger and regret. I wanted to know what forces had acted on her, how she and I were the same and how we were different. I wanted to think about the ways in which women's lives were limited and expanded by their surroundings. I was proud of the essay, and I found a literary magazine that wanted to publish it.

When I received news of the magazine's interest, I sent a draft of my essay to my mother. I had shared with her versions of the same story in the past, though never this particular piece. I emailed her on a weeknight. She called me the next morning as I was on my way into a work meeting. I knew by the sound of her voice that she was upset. She wanted to know how I could share my grandmother's secrets. My grandmother had entrusted my mother; how could I betray that trust? I tried to explain that I thought my grandmother's story was illustrative, that society had trapped her, abandoned her, judged her, failed her. I told my mother that writing about my grandmother was meant to be liberating and that maybe it would help spark another woman's liberation as well. But my mother wasn't hearing it. She hung up on me that morning.

I relayed the incident to a friend. I told her that my grandmother was in her eighties. That she had dementia. That the literary magazine that wanted to publish the piece had a minuscule readership, less than one thousand people across the whole country. That the likelihood my grandmother would ever see the essay was zero. That the probability that any of her friends or even anyone who had known her would see it was zero. That there was almost no way she would ever encounter the piece, so why shouldn't I publish it? My friend sided with my mother: I was a betrayer.

I pulled the essay from the magazine. I didn't want to, but I also didn't know how not to. I love my mother. I loved my grandmother. My goal had never been to hurt anyone. It took me a long time to realize that my mother's discomfort about my essay wasn't about trying to control my work, but an extremely complex response that had little to do with me. There was my mother's own shame for having betrayed my grandmother's trust, my mother who from her youngest years had served as my grandmother's protector (against my grandfather, against my grandmother's traumatic past and her constant feeling of being disappointed by the world). There was the murky truth; in subsequent retellings of my grandmother's story, my mother said that my grandmother "rescinded" the notion that she had considered an abortion, and then my mother said maybe my grandmother had never said this at all, maybe my mother had just *assumed* abortion would have been an option on the table. My grandmother had been a committed Catholic—she volunteered at the church, at my mother's Catholic school— even considering abortion would have been sacrilege. And, my mother pointed out, if she had wanted one, why didn't she just find a doctor in a back alley?

There was the inherited shame that comes from secret keeping. And of course my grandmother's own shame, which had imprisoned her for her entire life. Shame for becoming pregnant before marriage, shame for attempting to give her daughter away, shame for having an "illegitimate" child. Shame and its resultant isolation, shame and the constant fear of being judged—inadequate, bad, wrong—shame and the terrifying possibility of that judgment's potential truth (what if I really am bad?). These were the forces that kept my grandmother from ever telling anyone about her past. Shame silenced her. Shame kept her forever in her place.

Meanwhile, I felt no shame over my grandmother's actions. They made complete sense to me.

She was a teenager, a girl who'd been beaten by her mother, who'd been neglected by her parents (my mother tells me that as a child a neighbor noticed my grandmother's abscessed tooth, took her to a dentist, and paid to have it extracted). She was alone in the world, barely able to care for herself, dependent on the generosity of the Catholic Church. She was underemployed. She had almost nothing to give a child. This was no failing of hers. She had been abused by the people who were supposed to love her, to care for her.

I knew that society (the Catholic Church, the coffee klatch) then, and possibly now, would say she was at fault for having intercourse in the first place. It would call her weak, or deviant, or sinful. But we are animals. Our bodies were built for sex, wanting it, having it. And asking a woman to reject innate desire in theory and in reality are two wildly different things. Plus, the man who impregnated her also had intercourse, and he was able to walk away with no consequences at all. My grandmother was lonely, she was still a child, and she was impoverished. This man was a professional student; he had financial security. Abandoning her was his choice. The choice available to someone with means, with agency, with options, and without a baby gestating in his belly. My grandmother never had one.

What got me was not just my grandmother's shame but that this sense of disgrace was so powerful that it had moved through generations. Keeping the secret was ultimately more burdensome than the act itself, its grip so tight that even in 2006, my mother worried about the potential embarrassment of my grandmother, a woman who had trouble remembering my mother's name.

Not long after my college graduation my mother said off-handedly that it was such a relief for her to finally be able to relax; I had made it through high school and college without getting pregnant. I thought it was a weird thing to say. I'd just completed a degree program. She'd gotten me educated. Wasn't that the win? That was what was on *my* mind. Considering it now, I realize that her comment spoke to the sheer terror many people still feel at the possibility of a daughter getting pregnant. As if getting pregnant before marriage were the worst thing that could happen to a girl. To be clear, I also was glad that I did not get pregnant before I did. But if I had, I like to think that it would not have haunted me in the same way it did my grandmother. I would have made a difficult choice (both legal and safe) about whether or not to keep the child and then I'd be writing about it here. I would hope that I would not carry any shame for my actions, that were I judged, it would not change my opinion of myself.

At one point during Lynn's interview with Susan, she became fixated on the detail of the dress Paula had worn that night. She said the police "always" called it a nightgown and the Oberbroecklings had to argue that, no, it wasn't a nightgown, it was a dress, a dress Lynn had worn herself. She described it, elastic straps, *not* spaghetti straps, empire waist, built-in-bra, matching panties, like a sundress, *not* something you'd sleep in. When I considered how important this detail seemed to be to her, it felt out of course from what had happened. Her sister was dead. Who cared what she had been wearing? Except maybe Lynn had for decades heard the tacit opinion that the way Paula had been dressed had had something to do with her death. And it dawned on me that Paula had been dead more than forty-five years and it seemed like Lynn was still trying to protect her reputation. Perhaps she was still worried about the shame attendant in premarital sex. In the idea that Paula had been "asking for it" by dressing or behaving in a certain way. And again, my heart broke. Not only did Lynn have to suffer the loss of her sister and her best friend, but perhaps she was still feeling the pain of all the judgment that had been laid at Paula's feet more than four decades ago.

Paula went out in a scanty dress. So what? That means nothing more than she went out in a scanty dress. Paula had sex before marriage. So what? So did I. So do most women and so did most women *at the time*. It wasn't that unmarried women were celibate—65 percent of those who turned fifteen between 1964 and 1973 had premarital sex before they reached the age of twenty—it was that those who became pregnant were the only ones who got caught.

I had sex with many men before I met my husband when I was twenty-nine. I had four relationships that lasted longer than a year with men I had no intention of marrying. I had sex with my husband before we married when I was thirty—of course! Right? There were times when I wasn't on the pill. There were times when I forewent using condoms. These weren't smart decisions, but I think they were human ones, common ones, ones that occurred in the heat of the moment when it seemed nothing more existed beyond myself and my partner, the heat and that room. There was no reason beyond sheer luck (by which I mean timing, where I was in my menstrual cycle, which is a fact of a woman's body I would learn only when I was ready to become pregnant, but was oblivious of before) that I *didn't* get pregnant before I got married. I know women who got pregnant *despite* using protection. Said another way, I deserved to get pregnant. I'll add that I knew better. I had sex education in school. My mother talked to me about intercourse. This wasn't the '30s when my grandmother became pregnant or the '70s when Paula might have.

"My mom never talked to me about sex. But also [my friends and I] didn't talk about sex amongst one another. We really didn't," said Kathy McHugh. "We were curious. . . . But we were pretty naive. I was. And good girls 'didn't.'"

Yeah, sure, except sometimes good girls *did*, because you were only a bad girl if you got caught, and you only got caught if you got pregnant. These women—my grandmother, Paula, and women who were like them—were trapped. They were told that they needed to be beautiful in order to be valued. This beauty would allow them to fulfill a man's desire. But they were given no education regarding their bodies—what they were used for, how to keep from getting pregnant—and so acting on that potential, satisfying that man's desire, their implied job, was to risk pregnancy. At which point they were ostracized, abandoned, shamed. There was no winning. They were damned if they did and damned if they didn't. Here was the double bind.

Paula had at least two friends from high school who became pregnant: one had a daughter and the other a son. I didn't know the circumstances surrounding the second friend's pregnancy and birth, but I did know that the first, Delilah Greene, nee Nollge, was married at sixteen, had her baby at seventeen, and became a widow that same year when her husband died in a car accident in September of 1969. With the insurance money she received from his death, Delilah offered to bring Paula and the other friend to Fort Lauderdale, Florida, for spring break. "Paula had never been anywhere or done anything," Delilah told Susan. So, a couple months before graduation, the two mothers left their children with Delilah's brother and all three girls headed out into the world.

Paula had been afraid of flying, so they drove the twenty-two hours it took to get from Cedar Rapids to Fort Lauderdale by car. What was discussed during all that empty time as the girls sped south on the open highway? Did they talk about what it was like to be married? To have a baby grow inside their body for nine long months? To labor in order to let that baby out and then to care for it all day and all night forever and ever, amen? I'll never know. What I do know was that that trip was not the only exposure to teen pregnancy and parenting that Paula had, nor was it even the closest at hand. In fact, Paula also watched Lynn, her own sister, get married and take a pregnancy to term that year at the age of nineteen.

At the time of her engagement, Lynn worked at a bank. Her fiancé attended community college and was employed by Quaker Oats. After their wedding, the couple moved in with Carol in order to save money on rent and food and to have laundry close by; Carol considered this a prudent choice. Lynn's husband had enlisted in the navy. He left for boot camp in May of 1970. Lynn was due to have the baby in less than three months.

In the days leading up to the birth of her niece, Paula stopped by the house on G Avenue often to check on Lynn, their expanding family serving to draw the sisters together. Paula was at the house with Lonnie Bell the day Lynn went into labor. Eager to meet the baby, she hastened Lynn along, "Come on, Lynn, hurry, hurry, hurry!" as if she knew that her time with the baby was limited. Her niece was born on July 1, 1970. Ten days before Paula disappeared.

According to Lonnie's police statement given after the discovery of Paula's body, Paula had missed two periods by July, when her niece was born. If he was correct, then there, directly in front of her, was the stark reality of new motherhood—with its incessant feeding and soothing and diapering, with its isolation and swift rerouting of every other plan, with its unbelievable responsibility and burden, so much for a girl to bear alone. Lynn's daughter didn't sleep, so Paula likely witnessed the effects of sleep deprivation in addition. One of the last conversations Lynn and Paula ever had was about Lynn's stomach post-labor. "Can I see it?" Paula had asked. When Lynn lifted her shirt, revealing her stretched-out stomach, marshmallowy and shapeless, Paula recoiled. "Ew," she said. "I would not like that at all."

On the night Paula disappeared, Lynn said that she had gone to bed about 10:30 or 11 after the evening news. At some point, from her bed, she heard a car horn honking outside. She said that for a moment she thought it was Paula and Debbie driving by, goofing around, trying to get her attention. She already had the lights out; she didn't get up to go look.

"I can honestly say that I . . . I'm just . . . I had so much regret because I kept thinking . . . for years . . . even to this day . . . if that was the car that was honking honking, and the lights were off . . . if . . . Did she want me? Was she trying to come over, just to say, 'I need you to go with me?'" said Lynn.

Lynn would have been well into her third trimester when Paula was struggling with the potential of her own pregnancy. If Paula were pregnant, perhaps she didn't confide in her sister because she didn't want to burden her. Lynn, facing new motherhood with her husband in the navy, had much to contend with already. Or maybe she didn't want to tarnish the excitement of Lynn's new baby with her own dilemma. Or perhaps she kept quiet because she worried that Lynn would encourage her to get married and have the baby.

When I thought about it this way, Paula's silence seemed reasonable. Throw in the threat of shame by her community, the fact that her family was Catholic, that her mother would, as Debbie Kellogg put it to me, "kill her" if she were pregnant with Robert's baby, and it seemed logical if not inevitable. The way I saw it, all of these factors came together to ensure that Paula faced this crucial decision all by herself.

• • •

One morning as I was pawing through material, my desktop covered in loose paper, two pieces of information that I'd seen dozens of times before ended up side by side and suddenly I saw them differently. There was Carol's obituary published in the *Gazette*. Next to it was the statement Lynn gave the police in which she volunteered her birth date. The *Gazette* said that Jim and Carol had been married in July of 1950. Lynn was born six months later in January of 1951. Meaning, Carol was likely pregnant when she got married.

When this became apparent, I gasped. It felt so meaningful, this connection between mother and daughter. If Paula were pregnant when she died, eighteen and unmarried, then she was following the path her mother had traveled before her. Here was a literal handing down of course, a legacy of circular event. What's unfortunate was that she likely had no idea. Shame had kept all of these women quiet. Perhaps nothing would have changed had she confided in her family. Perhaps her course would have remained the same. But maybe she would have died feeling that much less alone.

Chapter 13

Her Options

ONE NIGHT BACK WHEN WE WERE STILL IN CEDAR RAP-ids and over a glass of wine, Susan told me that in 1970 when she was nineteen and unmarried she became pregnant and had an abortion. We were sitting under the yellow light of a chandelier at the wooden table in her father's kitchen, the rest of the house dark and quiet. Early on in our investigation, Susan had said something to me about the difference between her and Paula, Susan being the type of girl who "came from a good family that taught her to keep her legs closed." But she hadn't. She also had premarital sex (like Paula, like me, like many of us) and had wound up pregnant.

However, this wasn't what surprised me. What surprised me was that she hadn't told me this before now. It seemed so relevant. It seemed like a clear link between her and Paula. It seemed the obvious reason for Susan's years-long obsession with this case. If Paula had been pregnant, then the two women had been weighing their options at virtually the same time, and yet there Susan was, alive, a mother of two grown men and a grandmother of three. For Susan, I imagined Paula's tragedy was a sort of "there but for the grace of God go I."

I was so stunned by her admission that I barely asked any questions that night, and Susan offered little more than the fact of the matter. But I couldn't stop thinking about it after I'd returned to New York, so I asked her if she would tell me the story. She agreed.

One night, late, after putting my son to sleep, I called Susan from my bed, my legs under the covers, my computer open on my lap, headphones in, tape recorder on, nightstand lamp low. Susan, two hours behind in Colorado, had just finished dinner. She sounded nervous when she answered the phone, not fearful nerves, more excited, ready, like someone who had prepared to speak to a group of people and found herself suddenly before them. "I've given this a lot of thought," she said. "There are things you need to know in order to understand."

Apparently, while Paula was preparing to graduate high school, moving out of her mother's house, working at the mall, Susan was all but flunking out of her first year of college. She'd started at the University of Chicago after graduating from boarding school but spent her freshman year sidetracked by drugs and a blossoming politicization. That spring of 1970, the student protests against the United States' invasion of Cambodia had culminated in the massacre at Kent State. In response, student demonstrations swarmed college campuses, including the University of Chicago; some protests were so large that classes had to be halted. Susan hung out with the Weathermen. She talked revolution and dropped acid. She did not go to class or study. When her father came to pick her up for summer vacation, he informed her that she wouldn't be coming back.

At home with nothing to do, Susan's boyfriend persuaded her to move with him to San Francisco. He had been accepted by the California College of Arts and Crafts in Oakland. The two got an apartment above a strip club on Telegraph Avenue. He went to school. She sold tickets to the circus from a booth downtown. They both happily practiced their respective arts: him sculpture and collage, her writing. Before Susan left for California, her mother brought her to a gynecologist who fitted her with a diaphragm. But he didn't teach her how to use it correctly, so she didn't. The joke at the time, she said wryly, was: If you want to get pregnant, use a diaphragm. Within a few months, she had missed two periods.

Desperate, she turned to an older acquaintance of her sister's, who drove her to Planned Parenthood to verify the pregnancy. This they did. Though *Roe v. Wade* was still three years off, there were states where abortion was legal in varying degrees. In 1967, California followed Colorado and North Carolina in liberalizing its abortion laws. The procedure was made available to women whose pregnancy was the result of rape or incest, as well as to women whose mental or physical health would be jeopardized by carrying a pregnancy to term.* Ten other states followed this lead, loosening restrictions in similar ways before the passage of *Roe.* In 1970, Alaska, Hawaii, New York, and Washington repealed their antiabortion statutes altogether.

Planned Parenthood agreed to give Susan an abortion. It would cost her $200. Taking inflation into account, that would be more than $1,300 today. With no money to speak of, Susan phoned her parents. She told them that she was pregnant, that

---

* When I asked Susan whether her pregnancy fell under one of these conditions, she told me that it didn't. All she knew, she said, was that she got a legal abortion in California in 1970. I have to assume this was further evidence of privilege. Women like Susan (white, upper middle class) were able to find their way to Planned Parenthood and to doctors who would liberally interpret the laws, not even feeling the need to tell their clients they were doing so.

she was going to have an abortion, and that she needed $200. They agreed to send half of the money—insisting that her boyfriend pay the other half. In return, they said, Susan must keep the pregnancy, the abortion, all of it, a secret.

"My mother said, 'You will never tell anyone about this, ever. This is our private business, and it is only for us to know,'" Susan said, and then after a moment of thought, "They didn't want their friends to know."

Susan's father was an actuary. A professional who socialized with other professionals and their stay-at-home wives. He and her mother hosted parties where everyone drank too much and people passed out on the floor. They belonged to the country club. Susan said they weren't rich, but they acted like they were. Neither a pregnant single daughter nor an abortion fit with the image they were trying to convey.

Within days Susan received a check from her parents, around which was wrapped a letter from her mother. Susan had saved the letter. She read it to me over the phone. It was perfunctory; it detailed her parents' travel plans for the coming season; it mentioned her sisters' whereabouts and goings-on; and it instructed her to be cautious, to take her boyfriend with her when she went for the abortion (though that word was never used), to insist on anesthesia and to promise that the procedure would be done in a hospital. It also reiterated the one condition her mother had insisted on over the phone. Written at the bottom of the letter were the words: You Must Never Tell. Each was capitalized and underlined three times.

Susan took her parents' money, and she got the abortion she wanted and never looked back. "I was so relieved," she told me. "My life would have been ruined. I had a friend with a baby, and I knew I could never have been who I wanted to be—a writer, an artist—with a child at nineteen. I was free."

Still, she feels her abortion changed her relationship with her father, whom she'd spent her entire life trying to impress. The youngest of his three girls with her mother, Susan was supposed to have been a boy. As his son, she would have followed in his footsteps, become an actuary too. ("A woman was not capable of such a thing," she said.) She went to the University of Chicago because he did, and then failed at that too. "My mom would tell me, 'He likes you best,'" she said. But she was still a girl, not the boy he had wanted, and her pregnancy and abortion only served to put an exclamation point on her gender.

Aside from confiding in her two sisters, Susan kept her abortion a secret just as her mother had insisted. It wasn't until she met her husband, who told her about the abortion *his* old girlfriend had had, that she realized that there were other women who had had abortions too. It was something that, as she put it, "you NEVER told ANYBODY about, EVER."

Susan calls herself extremely lucky: "I didn't die. And I didn't have a baby. I was protected over and over again. I had parents who were educated and smart and had money, and they'd do anything to protect me, and they did."

Perhaps here was where the buck stopped. Not with luck per se, but with access and means and support. Maybe in a slightly different world, under slightly different circumstances—if Susan's parents had been less understanding or had had less money, if Susan had lived in a different state or had gone to a different doctor, one unwilling to interpret California's abortion laws liberally, or if she had become pregnant during a different year. *Or* if Paula had had just one of the privileges that Susan enjoyed, if she had lived in a state where abortion was legal, or had parents with the money to send her away to a maternity home, or access to a trusted doctor, or boyfriends who were "acceptable"—perhaps Paula would have lived and Susan would have died.

"Paula didn't have any money," said Debbie. "Or anyone to help her figure out where she was supposed to go."

Susan and Paula might have faced the same obstacle around the same time, but the experience was completely different; the avenues open to Paula were fewer and riskier. If Paula was pregnant, here was what she faced. In 1970 an unmarried woman with an unintended pregnancy could have her baby, and she could keep it, but that meant risking her reputation and facing social ostracism, not to mention financial hardship.

She could "legitimize" the baby by hastily marrying the father. Which was what Debbie Kellogg did when, not long after Paula died, she got pregnant herself at twenty years old. "[Getting married] was nobody's idea," she said when I asked who had suggested it. "It's just something you did. You got married. Single mothers weren't very likable at the time. They were looked down on. I would have been looked down on." This first marriage of Debbie's lasted two years.

For Paula this solution would likely have included a number of complications. For one, Lonnie's friend told police that while he and Lonnie tooled around town on the night Paula disappeared, Lonnie said that he'd told Paula he didn't want to get married. That said, my hunch was that Paula wouldn't have wanted to marry Lonnie even if he had proposed. And while Robert claimed that he would have happily married Paula had he known she was pregnant, saying that he would have taken care of her and the child with the support of his

mother, marrying Robert would have multiplied the challenges Paula faced, adding judgment and racism—and this
not just from Cedar Rapids' population generally but courtesy of Paula's own mother. And then of course there was the
fact that Paula might not have been certain whose baby she
was carrying. When the child was born, the biological father
would likely be quite clear. Marrying the wrong man could be
cause for marital problems—jealousy, feelings of betrayal—on
top of everything else. Lastly, and I'd argue most importantly,
from everything I'd heard, Paula didn't sound like she was
ready for marriage, *if* she wanted that type of commitment for
herself at all.

If a woman with an unintended pregnancy had enough
money, she could afford to go to a maternity home° where she
could carry her pregnancy to term in secret, deliver the child,
and then put it up for adoption or enlist a family member to
care for the child, like my grandmother did.† Between 1945
and 1973, 1.5 million babies were given up for nonfamily or
unrelated adoptions. This was a lonely, painful option that
involved isolation, shame, coercion, and oftentimes the devastation wrought from having to hand over a baby gestated in
one's own body, something few girls were prepared for when
it actually happened. This, often forced, relinquishment of

° This option included the cost of travel to and from the home, room and board,
and the various hospital and delivery fees. "With an average maternity home stay
of seventy-eight days, the total bill could easily exceed six hundred dollars," writes
Rickie Solinger (*Wake Up Little Susie*, 115). This is $4,133.14 in 2020 dollars. Poor
families could apply for welfare to help with costs, but this necessitated being
able to navigate the welfare system, which likely would have been difficult for an
eighteen-year-old girl.

† Since my grandmother had no money, I can only guess that the uncle who cared
for my aunt after she was born also paid for the maternity home for my grandmother.

(mostly)* white babies set many women up for a lifetime of depression and regret. They struggled under extreme amounts of guilt—for being "deviant," for disappointing their families, for whatever became of their children—and the resultant sadness. Not long before she died, my grandmother, reflecting on the way her life had unfolded, said to my mother, "I could have been somebody." She was crying.

Susan told me that during the summer between boarding school and college, a close friend of hers from childhood admitted to her that she had become pregnant. They were sitting on a hill overlooking the pool at the country club where they'd spent so much time together as girls. Her friend was crying, and Susan said all she could think was, "Oh my God, I'm so glad this isn't me." Her friend confided that her plan was to go and live with a relative until she had the baby, at which point she planned to give it up for adoption. She told Susan that this was a secret and asked her not to breathe a word. But it turned out not to matter. Everyone, Susan said, knew that this friend had "gone away" to hide a pregnancy. It was only later that Susan learned that in fact there was no relative, and her friend had actually been sent to a maternity home. Her friend's shame, it would seem, didn't even allow her complete honesty with Susan.

Federally sanctioned legal abortion was still three years off. Occasionally, doctors took pity on young women, but this required knowing the right doctor and having the money to pay for a D&C (dilation and curettage). Women with means often went abroad, to Mexico or Europe, where there were

---

* According to Solinger, during the postwar era, Black adoption was usually dissuaded. This was another reason African American girls weren't incentivized to take advantage of such homes. Which presents another complication. If Paula's baby had been Robert's, it's possible the maternity home wouldn't have wanted it.

more people willing to perform abortions. But, again, few women could afford the trip, which included airfare, hotel stay, and the cost of the procedure itself. The levels of risk varied.*

A woman with an unwanted pregnancy could find someone willing to perform an illegal abortion, also expensive, oftentimes life-threatening. The number of illegal abortions performed during the 1950s and '60s is estimated to range between 200,000 and 1.2 million per year. In the best case, this meant persuading the woman's own doctor (or any doctor) to perform the procedure; in the worst case, it meant finding someone like the chiropractor in Cedar Rapids. When abortions aren't legal, women don't have them less often, they just have them less safely.

If she couldn't find someone or couldn't afford to pay someone, she could try to perform an abortion on herself—douche with Lysol, Clorox, or turpentine; throw herself down the stairs; get someone to punch her in the stomach; drink hemlock (a well-known poison), quinine, pennyroyal, ergot, lead, mercury, or strychnine; insert a knitting needle, screwdriver, hat pin, umbrella rib, or coat hanger into her vagina.

● ● ●

On January 22, 1968, nearly three years before Susan had her abortion and two and a half years before Paula went missing,

---

* While nonfiction editor at *Guernica*, I edited an essay called "Lucky Girl" by the writer Bridget Potter. The piece was about Potter's resorting to travel to Puerto Rico in 1962 in order to obtain an abortion when she was nineteen. She had been referred to a hospital there, but when she arrived they sent her away because she was too young; she needed to be at least twenty-one to get the procedure. A man at the hospital took pity on her, handing her a slip of paper on which he'd written a name and an address. She followed it to a small house off a dirt road outside of San Juan. There was a wooden table, no anesthesia, and a newspaper-lined bucket.

Sharon Wright, a thirty-two-year-old married woman from Waterloo, Iowa, was found dead in the parking lot behind the Me Too supermarket in Cedar Rapids. Her husband told police that they had traveled an hour to Cedar Rapids for a "medical appointment." When she failed to meet him afterward as they had planned, he began calling local hospitals. He found her at Mercy where her body had been taken by ambulance. The initial coverage of Sharon Wright's death in the *Gazette* listed the above details, including that a preliminary autopsy failed to reveal the cause of death and ended with this sentence: "There is no reason to suspect foul play." She was discovered dead behind a supermarket.

When I first came across Sharon Wright's name and began to look into what had happened to her, I was simultaneously stunned and enraged by every turn in her case. It revealed so succinctly the trap in which many women found themselves, the risks associated with their limited options, and perhaps most importantly the broken system of culpability and the imbalance of power.

Within one month of Wright's death, Merle Meyers, a forty-three-year-old sometime insurance salesman, was arrested and charged with administering illegal abortions. The FBI uncovered an attaché case filled with catheter tubing in Meyers's garage. It matched two pieces of cut tubing that Austin Wright, Sharon Wright's husband, produced as evidence, saying his wife had removed them from her body during a previous unsuccessful attempt at ending a pregnancy. Two other men, Donald Geater, a thirty-six-year-old truck driver who served as a nurse, and Joseph Abodeely, a thirty-seven-year-old businessman who owned the Unique Motel and the Tender Trap nightclub and who expedited the abortions, were charged as well. I should add that Joe Abodeely and Thomas

Sturgeon, the chiropractor Steinbeck identified in his abortion scenario, were related through marriage. Ramza, Sturgeon's wife, was an Abodeely.

To testify on behalf of the state, the prosecution found a twenty-four-year-old divorced woman (in the nearly two years of trial coverage in the *Gazette*, her marital status, "divorcee," was included every single time she was referenced). The state's witness had gotten pregnant by her soon-to-be ex-husband. When she told her divorce attorney she was with child, he warned her that if the judge presiding over the dissolution of her marriage were to learn of her pregnancy, she would likely lose custody of the child she already had with her husband. In other words, she wanted to end her current pregnancy so that the state would not take away her child, something *her lawyer* told her was a likelihood.

During the trial, her doctor testified that when the woman came to him seeking an abortion, she was two months pregnant. He informed the court that, in his opinion, the woman's life had not been in danger, which was why he refused her the abortion she sought. This was when she turned to Joseph Abodeely, her former employer at the Tender Trap, and the man who led her to Meyers, who, she said, gave her an abortion the summer before. Happenstance and shadow networks were often the ways women, pre-*Roe*, found those people willing to give them the medical care they needed.

The *Gazette* did a thorough job of covering each advancement in the story of the Meyers/Geater/Abodeely abortion trials. The coverage spanned years, magnifying the injustices. There was the trap in which the twenty-four-year-old woman had found herself, her pregnancy's potential to jeopardize her custody of her child—which we can assume was not the case for the husband, who was an equal participant in the act that got her pregnant in the first place. There was the way the medical community willfully ignored the life-threatening danger that faced many women. A second "divorcee," whose doctor also had refused her an abortion, told the court that she'd confided in him that she'd already tried to perform an abortion on herself. He warned her that she was "likely to hurt herself by such attempts." There was the defense attorney, who, perhaps predictably, did his best to smear the women who testified on behalf of the state (there were at least eighteen witnesses, six of whom claimed to have received abortions from Meyers). He told jurors to "scrutinize" their testimony to determine whether they were under "mental stress." He tried to turn the tables on one witness by asking if she was "guilty" of attempting to produce an abortion on herself. And there was the *Gazette* with its consistent use of "divorcee" as an identifier and its description of one woman as an "ADC mother," meaning Aid to Dependent Children or welfare. How, exactly, was that relevant? And perhaps most disappointing of all were the words of the county attorney, who was supposed to be on the side of the women, or so one would think, but who continually reminded the jury that these women were not on trial "no matter their transgressions or moral faults." It was impossible not to see that we were here yet again. Another double bind. Castigated on both sides. The state needed these women to testify in order to put these lawbreaking men away, but it would not change the state's judgment of them: immoral, transgressor, bad girl.

Abodeely tried to argue that he was only trying to provide a service for women. Abortion was illegal; he offered a procedure women needed. There was truth to this. But there was also a lot of gray. During the trial, several of the state's witnesses said that they had suffered infections after the insertion of the catheter. One said that the "doctor" had been clumsy, that he'd dropped equipment and then failed to sterilize it after picking it up off the floor. Many said that the procedure had to be done more than once because it failed to work the first time. Sharon Wright, for one, underwent two unsuccessful attempts at abortion prior to the procedure on January 22, the day she died. Austin Wright said that his wife's uterus was tipped, a biological irregularity that can make it difficult to induce miscarriage. But Austin reported that he had "trusted" that his wife was in good hands because he had been told that the person who was to perform the abortion was a doctor. *A doctor.* In fact, of course, Meyers was an out-of-work insurance salesman. His nurse *drove a truck for a living.* These men lied. They recklessly, selfishly convinced desperate women to put their lives in their hands despite their complete lack of qualification to preserve those lives. And they did this for money. Because they certainly were not giving abortions away for free.

During the trial, the six witnesses said they paid from $100 up to $600 for the procedure. Taking inflation into account, this is like paying anywhere from $723 to $4,338 today. Austin Wright testified that his wife paid $450 to Joe Abodeely. Abodeely, during his trial, tried to convince the court that he had never accepted money to put a woman in touch with Meyers. But Geater, who before his own trial turned state's witness against Abodeely, testified that in fact Abodeely once haggled over the price of an abortion, threatening Geater that if Meyers wouldn't agree to perform the procedure for the price Abodeely was willing to pay him—likely much less than he had been given to expedite it in the first place—he'd find someone else who would. This was not about women's health care. It was not about trying to help women. It was about making money by taking advantage of women who had nowhere else to turn.

Meyers was found guilty. He received five years in prison and a $1,000 fine. Geater received the same. Abodeely pleaded guilty and also received five years; he got a $100 fine. Donald Geater's sentence was ultimately suspended. Meyers went to prison in July 1969. An article in the *Gazette* dated September 1970 mentioned that he had already been paroled. Meaning that, of his sentence, the most Meyers served was a year and change. Abodeely fought his punishment, as he'd fought the entire experience.

The lengths Joe Abodeely went to first delay his trial and then to evade his punishment would be comical if they weren't maddening. Leading up to his trial, Abodeely filed motions to attain a change of venue, claiming slanted media coverage. During the trial, his brother testified that if Joe went to prison, their mother, who had a heart condition, would "probably die as a result," and Father Alexander George of the St. John's Eastern Orthodox Church served as a character witness, petitioning the court for leniency and telling the judge that Abodeely was a churchgoing man. (At Abodeely's sentencing, Father George, clearly upset, pushed a TV cameraman to the floor and began to kick him as he was leaving the courtroom.) Then, after Abodeely pleaded guilty, he delayed his incarceration by appealing all the way up to the U.S. Supreme Court (not one single jurisdiction agreed to hear his case), on the claim that his lawyers hadn't adequately explained to him what a guilty plea meant. When this failed, he delayed his imprisonment by asking for extensions in order to get his business affairs in order. And when that failed, he delayed his imprisonment, ultimately, by absconding. The man fled the state of Iowa in order to evade his sentence. In the end he was able to avoid prison for two and a half years.

When the police finally caught up with Abodeely, he served six months in jail before he was paroled. The parole board stated that they'd released him because his business was failing and he needed to tend to it, because his parents were aging and he needed to care for them, and because as a musician Joe Abodeely needed to be able to practice in order to maintain his livelihood. This bears repeating: He was released from prison because he needed to practice his music.

All of this—the motions, the stays, the filings—cost money. Money that, unlike Sharon Wright, unlike Paula Oberbroeckling, Abodeely had. This was the privilege of being male and well-off. Detective Jelinek said of Joe Abodeely: "He was the kind of guy that if he could make ten dollars by being honest, he'd take five and do it crooked." And *this* man was given more leeway, more attention, time, and consideration, more ink and time on television, more community support than any of the women involved.

At the risk of getting too far off track, there is another story that seems relevant. J.D. Smith, one of the cold-case detectives who joined the CRPD after Paula died, told me that Joe Abodeely had been running prostitutes out of the Unique Motel, which he owned. I'd read this in the police file, but it was what Smith said next that interested me. He and a few (female!) officers had operated a sting at the Unique, ultimately confiscating all manner of property from the hotel (air conditioners, silverware, etc.). By law, this property was supposed to be sold at auction. Instead, Smith said, the county attorney sold all of it back to Abodeely for $5,000. And if that isn't enough to suggest their chumminess, Smith also said that the men whose names appeared in Joe Abodeely's registrar at the Unique were powerful men—Smith mentioned a state senator and others. On the mornings after, these men would show up at the precinct and make Alford pleas. An Alford plea is a guilty plea without admission of a criminal act. Meaning a man who'd been arrested with a prostitute could pay his fine and appease the police department without admitting fault. Pretty cozy.

As in Paula's case, no one was ever charged with Sharon Wright's death. The Cedar Rapids medical examiner, Percy Harris, wrote on Wright's death certificate that an abortion had been attempted on her, but he did not specify that she had "died as the result of a wrongful act." Because of this there were no grounds. She hadn't, in the eyes of the state, been murdered at all. This, even though she had been dumped behind a supermarket an hour after she went, by way of Joe Abodeely, to Merle Meyers, a convicted abortionist, to obtain an abortion.

I could not understand this massive failure to track. On the one hand, there was a culture built on secret keeping and shame, on pretending that things were not as they were. Take the refusal to educate girls about sex and their bodies. Take Susan's mother's insistence that she keep her pregnancy and her abortion a secret. Take the cloistering of teenage girls to carry their pregnancies to term in hiding. Ann Fessler, who wrote *The Girls Who Went Away: The Hidden History of Women Who Surrendered Children for Adoption in the Decades Before Roe v. Wade*, describes pregnant girls who were made to duck down while riding in cars with their families too ashamed to even be seen with them. She relays anecdotes about groups of girls who were made to wear wedding bands in order to leave maternity homes, to go to the movies, to go to the grocery store. As if anyone who saw a group of pregnant teenage girls wearing wedding rings believed that they were just some newlyweds out for a bit of fun. No. They knew the truth. Young people were having sex. Girls were getting pregnant. But no one would speak of it. Fine. But *how* can you deny a dead body?

A dead body should say, *This will not be ignored!* And yet the crime that ended up standing trial was not the selfish criminal negligence of the men who risked the lives of the desperate women who trusted them, not the crime of keeping women ignorant of their own bodies and the ways in which those bodies worked, not the crime of forcing them to carry the results of said ignorance to term regardless of whether they had emotional or financial support or any wish to do so. What stood trial were the women themselves. William Faches, the Linn County attorney who tried the case, said that the crime had been "hideous" for "destroying the life of an unborn child and endangering the life of a woman." But, remember, Sharon Wright died.

In the late '60s, abortion wasn't the polarizing political issue it is today. A 1972 Gallup poll found that 68 percent of Republicans (known for being proponents of individual rights) thought the decision to abort was best made by a woman with her doctor. In the Iowa state legislature, abortion reform had been gathering bipartisan support since being introduced in 1967 by Democratic senator John Ely. (Senator Ely, as mentioned, was Butch Hudson's foster parent when Paula disappeared; Butch was Robert's alibi.)

Ely's measure didn't pass, but it did garner enough media attention in Iowa to bring the question to the fore. And for the next six years, until the passage of *Roe*, Iowa Republican W. Charlene Conklin took up Ely's mantle. She successfully rallied support in *both* political parties, the medical community, women's liberation groups, and the electorate at large. But this still wasn't enough to get the measure passed, for where she lacked support was with the Catholic Church, and the Catholic Church had enough money and influence and mouthpieces (whole congregations were encouraged to engage in letter-writing campaigns) to keep the proposition at bay. No, abortion wasn't a political issue, it was a religious one, wherein the church shamed women into believing that if they opted out of their pregnancies, they were failing to fulfill their life's purpose—to create and carry babies. *Roe*'s reform in 1973 would affect this debate, but not in time to save Sharon Wright's life.

It wasn't until the 1980s that it occurred to Republicans that they could lock in the religious vote by attaching themselves to the anti-choice movement. They abandoned the argument that abortion was an individual right and reframed the debate as one of the protection of fetal rights. The culture already treated women like vessels whose life purpose was the creation and carriage of babies. By prioritizing the welfare of fetuses, Republicans had turned women into second-class citizens and expendable ones at that.

• • •

In the summer of 2000, when I was twenty-three, new to New York and to taking care of myself in the world, I fell in love with a man who did not love me back. He was unemployed and wanted nothing more than a friendship with me, but I was so enamored with him that I pursued him in every way I knew how. We had sex one summer afternoon in my tiny unair-conditioned apartment, and the condom broke. As we sat there, the broken prophylactic between us, he told me that he had been raised as a Catholic, and that if I were pregnant, he would marry me.

Even in my haze of love for him, this was unthinkable. Aside from the fact that I knew he didn't love me, I was six months into my first real job after college. I lived with a roommate in a 600-square-foot apartment that I emptied my bank account each month to pay for. I could barely take care of myself—unwashed dishes moldered in the sink, the refrigerator was more likely to have a half gallon of spoiled milk and fuzzy fruit than anything anyone could eat—there was no way I was equipped to care for a child. Nor was this man, unemployed as he was and with no prospects on the horizon.

When I suggested that, rather than marry, we get the morning-after pill, he agreed, which told me all I needed to know about his vow of marriage. The next afternoon he and I took the 6 train uptown to the closest Planned Parenthood clinic. There I was prescribed what was then called "emergency contraception." I swallowed the first dose in the small sunlit office and then woke myself up twelve hours later in the middle of the night to take the second dose as instructed. I have no way of knowing whether or not I would have become pregnant had I not taken those pills, though the nurse who evaluated me pointed out that I was about ten days into my cycle, which is when most women ovulate. This was news to me at the time.

The ease with which I rectified this misstep, righted my course, was not lost on me. I took one day off work. Spent about $60. And never once looked back. A few weeks later, that man I thought I loved took a Greyhound bus back to Texas where he was from. In some ways, it was as if the whole thing had never happened.

When I think back to that time in my life when I so easily procured emergency contraception, I can barely recognize myself. I was so young. I knew so little. By which I mean about the world, but even more so, about myself. I was brand-new to New York and ran around with people I'd known from college who also wound up in Manhattan. I hung out with them because they were there, not because we had anything in common. These were people who spent their weekend nights waiting in long lines outside of nightclubs and, once inside, letting the sweating men there grind up against them under technicolor strobe lights. I love to dance. I love men! But I hate clubs, and I hated the men who went to them, and I hated both then, but I didn't yet know myself well enough to know that. It took that and everything that came after, years of floundering, before I slowly discovered the things that fit me.

Had I gotten pregnant when that condom broke and then had that child, I would not be the person I am today. I would be me. But I would be another me. A me who hightailed it back to Kansas perhaps, not being able to afford her apartment and childcare in New York. A me not married to my now husband, maybe never married at all, or divorced from the Texan who didn't love me. A me who perhaps never became a writer, writing being low-paying and with fewer opportunities in the Midwest. A me who, under the extreme time commitment of childcare and child-rearing, was never able to mature into someone interested in national politics and gardening and cooking and books by and about women. And gut-wrenchingly, a me who never had my child, the child I now have, my boy, the love of my life.

Chapter 14

The Phone Call

WHILE DRESSING MY SON ONE MORNING, I MISSED A telephone call. Susan had forwarded me a voicemail she'd received on her landline in Colorado. As I listened to the woman's voice, steady as a guy-wire, my whole body went tingly with the realization that something important was happening. "Hello. My name is Shermalayne. I ended up in the hands of Doctor Thomas Sturgeon. If you would like, I will tell you about it."

As soon as I put my son down for his afternoon nap, I made a beeline for my desk and listened to the message again. The woman said that she was sixty-two years old and had somehow found herself on the fringes of a "dark part of the culture that lives in Cedar Rapids." She said that she had heard things and that she would share them with Susan if she was interested. I jotted down her phone number, opened a word file I labeled "Shermalayne," dialed Susan and, while she waited on hold, dialed Shermalayne. Shermalayne answered with the same calm voice I'd heard on the voicemail, the same even tone she would maintain during our entire, nearly hour-long conversa-

tion. Susan introduced herself, and then she introduced me
and handed over the call.

I didn't need to say much. Shermalayne launched easily into
her reasons for reaching out. She said that she'd been under the
impression that Paula's killing had been solved. She said that,
though she had been a year behind Paula in school, she knew
Paula for the same reasons everyone did, because Paula had
been so beautiful. When, after our call, I looked up Shermalayne in the Washington High School yearbook, I saw that she
had also been beautiful: a slender brunette with flawless skin
and shiny straight hair, which she had parted just off center.

Shermalayne said that her parents had rented their home
from the Greek Orthodox Church, which "the Abodeelys
practically ran." Then she said that she had gone to Thomas
Sturgeon for an abortion in December of 1970, five months
after Paula disappeared.

I wanted to mirror her unruffled demeanor, but it was difficult. If she was telling the truth, she would be the first person
to substantiate the rumors that Sturgeon had been performing abortions at all. While her experience wouldn't prove what
happened to Paula, it would go a long way toward verifying
that the going theory was within the realm of possibility.

I resisted the urge to let fly a raft of questions: Who put
you in touch with Sturgeon? What did you know about him?
Where did he bring you to perform the abortion? How did
he execute the procedure? Who else was present? I knew I
needed to allow room for Shermalayne to tell her story in her
own way.

Her family had been poor, she said. As a child, Shermalayne received no dental care, no medical care. She remembered a penicillin shot as the extent of her experience with
doctors. Her mother, who had psychological challenges that

resulted in her being committed for a short period of time, was prone to buying into what would evolve into New Age science—things like hypnosis and regression into past lives. Thomas Sturgeon was also interested in these types of pursuits, and this commonality had brought him and Shermalayne's family together.

Not long after she entered high school at Washington, Shermalayne sustained an injury during a gymnastics unit in phys ed, after which her left arm fell asleep whenever she practiced her viola. When Shermalayne's arm didn't get better on its own, her parents brought her to see Sturgeon, the only doctor they knew. Sturgeon evaluated Shermalayne's arm. He said the injury was severe and that Shermalayne would need chiropractic adjustments three times a week in order for it to heal. Her parents, whom Shermalayne described as destitute, scrounged up the money to pay for these appointments. And so every few days Shermalayne walked to Sturgeon's office, checked in with his receptionist, and after being ushered into the examining room, lay back on Sturgeon's table while he slathered his naked hand with K-Y Jelly in preparation for the vaginal exam that began every appointment.

When she said this, as coolly as she'd said everything else, I gasped.

"I just thought that was what doctors did. I never questioned it," Shermalayne said. "I don't know why I was so naive."

"You trusted him," I whispered, gutted by her admission and by the prospect that she blamed herself for what clearly was an ongoing sexual assault. "And you were a child."

Shermalayne never said a word to her parents about the pelvic exams—it was too embarrassing, she told me. Eventually her arm healed. The visits to Sturgeon's office ended. Still he remained a part of the family's life. He made house calls when Shermalayne was sick. He hypnotized her and her mother in their living room. "It was a weird relationship," Shermalayne admitted, and she "knew him quite well."

There was more. One weekend in the fall of her senior year in high school, Shermalayne's boyfriend, who attended college at Iowa State University in Ames, invited her to accompany him to a fraternity party. Shermalayne took a bus to Ames, and stayed the weekend. She had never been to a gynecologist, which among other things, meant that she wasn't on the pill and didn't have a diaphragm. She believed, like many young people, that she couldn't get pregnant.

"That was the weekend I conceived," she said.

That December when her boyfriend came home for winter break, Shermalayne told him that she thought she was pregnant. He informed her that she couldn't be. He said that he was in college, that his parents were already providing child support for a two-year-old that he had fathered out of wedlock, and that he had come home early for winter break because his fifteen-year-old sister was pregnant herself. He told Shermalayne that he feared his parents would disown him. At the very least, he suspected they would stop funding his education. The risk for him was too great. She would have to deal with this alone.

At-home pregnancy tests were still seven years away. In 1970 a woman who suspected she might be pregnant had to go to the hospital or make an appointment with a doctor and then wait two weeks in order to confirm her suspicion. While still on break, Shermalayne's boyfriend drove her to St. Luke's Hospital so that she could verify the pregnancy with a blood test. He dropped her off at the front door and said he would return to pick her up afterward. He never showed. It would be years before Shermalayne saw this boy again.

Once the pregnancy was confirmed, Shermalayne was left alone to determine her course of action. She considered having the baby. She confided in her mother, who suggested she go to her aunt's house to give birth. Her mother said that after Shermalayne returned, she would help care for the baby. But Shermalayne didn't want her mother to raise her child. She heard that a woman could obtain a legal abortion in New York or in Puerto Rico, but when she explored that possibility she found that it would be cost prohibitive. It was then that she turned to her doctor, Thomas Sturgeon.

Shermalayne told Sturgeon she was pregnant. He immediately offered to give her an abortion. He instructed her to come to his office on a Sunday. It was located in the same edifice as his apartment and his wife's hair salon. When Shermalayne arrived, Sturgeon led her downstairs into the basement of the building. There, in the dark, a chair was set up among his wife's hairdressing equipment. Shermalayne climbed onto it and once again lay back in the lithotomy position for Doc Sturgeon.

After flushing a watering can with hot water, Sturgeon made a solution of tap water and Betadine, an antiseptic and disinfectant. He dilated her cervix using a catheter or some other long object, which Shermalayne couldn't recall, then he filled her with the solution. Here, I gasped again. This was not the first time I'd encountered this method.

I'd interviewed Fred Dumbaugh, one of the lawyers who represented Joe Abodeely during his abortion trial. Dumbaugh also represented Richard Zacek, the man who confessed to the murder of Jean Halverson. And his was the name that appeared in Paula's police file as the attorney Lonnie Bell contacted during the investigation into Paula's death—but as I mentioned, Dumbaugh said he had no recollection of that.

In addition to representing many of the lowlifes in Cedar Rapids during the 1970s and '80s, Dumbaugh was convicted of embezzlement and disbarred in 1989.

Sitting across from me in the screened-in back porch of the modest house he shared with his wife in Cedar Rapids, the cicadas buzzing in the background, Dumbaugh had elucidated the way in which Abodeely's associate, Merle Meyers, administered an abortion. He described the insertion of a catheter-like object into the woman's cervix and then her vagina being stuffed with gauze.

I asked Shermalayne whether there had been gauze.

"I was stuffed with gauze, now that you say something," said Shermalayne. "And that would be another way for infection to occur."

Sturgeon was giving illegal abortions in the same way Abodeely's cohort had. Had Joe Abodeely taught Tom Sturgeon, his relation by marriage, how to perform an abortion? Had he handed over the "business" after his conviction?

Shermalayne told me that the procedure had been painful, "but it was my only way out." Afterward, Sturgeon called her a cab, sending her home to bleed. There was no follow-up care, no instructions for what might signify a problem or for what to do if something went wrong. Just the car ride home and then what she called a "very crampy period."

Years later, Shermalayne went on to become a labor and delivery nurse and a professor in nursing school. When I asked whether there was a connection between this formative experience and her choice of profession, she brushed it aside. She was squarely focused on her own luck. When she read about Paula's case on Susan's website, how the investigation had been abandoned and the rumors surrounding Paula's death, she said she thought, "'Oh my gosh, I kind of got away with my life.'"

Her words, and the way they implied luck, recalled so much at this point—my "luck" that high school boy opted not to rape me; Susan's luck that she'd lived in a state where she could obtain an abortion when she needed one, and her luck that her parents agreed to pay for it when she could not; the writer Bridget Potter's luck in finding her way to the shack outside San Juan after she'd been turned away from the hospital in Puerto Rico; and now Shermalayne's luck that the abortion she received from Sturgeon didn't kill her. The word—"luck"— was so damning. When I peered underneath it, I found privilege and money and access, but that wasn't all. When I thought about it, what the use of that word "luck" really suggested was that these experiences were likely to have or were expected to have, really *should* have, gone another way. Which speaks to how deep-seated the expectation of peril is to many women. We accept that our lives are so littered with land mines (unintended pregnancy, violence, abandonment, inadequate medical care, economic insecurity, the list goes on) that when we survive one we count ourselves lucky, because we know that things could have gone, indeed *do go*, another way for many many *many* women.

Shermalayne grew quiet. I stared out the window in a state of overwhelm. I wanted to say the right thing but wasn't certain what that was. I was shattered by her story. The sexual abuse alone must have been devastating and then to be left at the hospital, a fetus growing inside of her, her last year of high school looming, with no support and no money to speak of? It was too much. And that she came forward to talk about it now. For Paula. For other women.

"I'm so grateful you reached out," I said.

"I'm willing to admit that I had a criminal abortion when I was seventeen. I'm a little old lady with five grandkids, but I've always thought I should write this story. Because I became a part of a Christian community and they were very anti-abortion, and I got calls all the time wanting to . . . pro-life kind of stuff, and I just . . . I know what a criminal abortion is, and I know the consequences, and I cannot . . . People get desperate, and I just can't get on board with . . . I am pro-life, but I also think that people should have safe abortions."

I sensed that all the false starts in Shermalayne's attempt to elucidate her position on legalized abortion were indicative of her conflict. Hers was a generation that was told that a woman who had an abortion was shirking her life's purpose: to marry and to bear (that word!) children. But the phrasing she landed on—*I am pro-life, but I also think that people should have safe abortions*—called out to me, a woman who is firmly pro-choice. No one *wants* to have an abortion. Not women who are anti-abortion and not women who are pro-choice. But when circumstances force a woman into a corner, when there is a lack of resources or support or desire to have children, safe medical abortions are by far the better alternative to the types of abortions that kill women.

When I hung up the phone, I could barely breathe. I had put aside my quest to solve Paula's killing, and now suddenly I felt I had never been closer. I'd recently encountered the work of Gillian A. Frank, a postdoctoral research associate in the American Studies Program at the University of Virginia, who was writing a book about clergy who helped women procure abortions pre–*Roe v. Wade*. When I reached out to him, I learned, among other things, that the fact that Paula had left in the middle of the night *didn't* contradict the abortion theory as I'd initially assumed, but supported it instead. According to

Frank, it was common in the years leading up to *Roe v. Wade* for illegal providers to work in the middle of the night, often giving women only a moment's notice before expecting them to arrive. The reasons for this were twofold. First, most people who were giving illegal abortions had day jobs to work around. And, second, they wanted to keep their activities under wraps. The dark of night provided excellent cover.

With the timing possible, and now proof that Thomas Chester Sturgeon *had* been performing illegal abortions in his wife's hair salon within walking distance of the place where Debbie's car had been abandoned, where did that leave us?

According to Paula's police file, the detectives never interviewed Tom Sturgeon in reference to Paula's death. They never searched his office—down the hill and west of the nurse's apartment—nor Ramza's hair salon below it. They never entered his home, never spoke with his secretary or his nurse or with Ramza herself.

"His name's out there all over town, and the police didn't question him? Well, now you go talk to that detective. You tell him that upsets me greatly. That's pitiful," Lynn said to Susan when Sturgeon's name was raised during her interview. "Did they think [Paula] wasn't worth anything? Was he some big shot? Did he have power?"

Lynn's incredulity echoed my own. The line from the CRPD was that the police didn't have grounds on which to approach Sturgeon. "Well, you got to have probable cause," said Detective Jelinek. "I mean, if you can ask a guy to come down voluntarily, and he comes down, fine. But Doc Sturgeon wasn't that kind of guy."

There was a level of truth to this. By all accounts, Sturgeon

214 • WHAT HAPPENED TO PAULA

was a man who considered himself above the law. He was intelligent—a regular in local chess tournaments as well as the president of the Iowa State Chess Association—and industrious. In addition to near-constant advertisements for his chiropractic business, in the years leading up to Paula's death he purchased ads in the *Gazette* shilling all sorts of services— self-defense classes, karate instruction, Swedish massage therapy, yoga practice, weight-loss clinics, and life-science study. Shermalayne told me that on top of the office appointments that Sturgeon insisted on to treat her arm, Sturgeon put her on a regimen of supplements that she was to ingest at breakfast, lunch, and dinner. Supplements her family purchased, no surprise, from Sturgeon himself.

In the *Gazette*, I read about a handful of minor skirmishes Sturgeon had with the law. In 1968, he was booked for discharging a firearm within city limits. And there had been two major fires at properties that were owned by him—the first in 534 10th Street SE in 1966 where he lived above his chiropractic offices and Ramza's hair salon, and the second two years later in the house next door, where his father was living at the time and where he was remodeling with the intention of relocating the hair salon and his office. In the second fire, the city charged Sturgeon with violating gas regulations. In the Paula file, one of the people who came forward with information about Sturgeon claimed that he had set the second blaze himself in order to collect the insurance money. I read in the paper that within a year of the fire, Sturgeon turned around and sued the gas company for just over $35,000. He lost.

It seemed Doc Sturgeon was forever in search of a way to make a dollar. This would turn out to be a literal pursuit. In January 1973, just over two years after Paula's body was discovered, the U.S. Secret Service obtained a warrant to enter Sturgeon's home in the middle of the night. There they caught Sturgeon and an accomplice printing counterfeit money on a small press. Both men were arrested and charged. After a lengthy trial in which Sturgeon represented himself before the court, he was convicted by a federal grand jury and sentenced to ten years in prison.

Shermalayne's story seemed incriminating, but there was something that had given me pause. She had her abortion in December of 1970. This would have been five months after Paula disappeared and one month *or less* after her body was found. What kind of person would *continue* performing illegal abortions even *after* he'd watched someone die on his table? At the least I would expect that, if he was responsible for Paula's death, he'd want to keep a low profile during the investigation. All of which made me question him as a suspect. When I'd posed this to Shermalayne, she seemed to shrug on the other end of the line: "He was doing me a favor. I was in trouble."

But in light of Sturgeon's public record—his wielding guns and potentially committing arson (twice!), his counterfeiting money and representing himself on federal charges in a court of law, his hands in *so* many pies, his arrogance laid bare— he recalled every philandering politician who initiated affairs confident that *he* would be the one to evade consequence. Sturgeon displayed the type of superciliousness present in people who believe they are beyond reproach. Perhaps this kind of guy simply didn't care that a woman had died and didn't worry about getting caught.

"He definitely was a guy in a cheap suit. He wanted to be a big operator. He was into one financial scrape after another," said Detective Steinbeck. "He was a bright guy, but the problem was he thought he was brighter than he really was."

Which brought me back to the police. This might all have been true. But the argument that, because Sturgeon wasn't "the type of guy to voluntarily come down to the police station for an interview," he was somehow irreproachable regarding the Paula Oberbroeckling case was specious. The police knocked on all sorts of doors in Cedar Rapids during the course of their investigation into Paula's homicide—why not Sturgeon's? Wasn't showing up at Sturgeon's door their very job? Sure, he might have resisted, he might have refused to answer any questions, he might have told the police there was no way he'd come down to the station of his own accord, slammed his door in their faces. But how could the police possibly have known without knocking in the first place?

When I spoke to Steinbeck most recently, he claimed to remember that the Cedar Rapids Police Department *did* question Sturgeon about Paula's death. He said he hadn't conducted the interview nor had he been at the station at the time, but someone had told him about it. "[Sturgeon] admitted to nothing. . . . He had an airtight story," he said.

This interview is not in the case file. Nor is it *referenced* in the case file. I wondered if it could have been accidentally filed with Sturgeon's counterfeit investigation or another of his crimes—Thomas Sturgeon would have many run-ins with the law before his death in 1999, including an arrest made in 1990 that led to a charge of two counts of sexual abuse and sexual assault, one of a thirteen-year-old boy, on whom police claimed Sturgeon had performed a sex act while on his chiropractic table, and the other of a fourteen-year-old girl whom he'd fondled after hypnotizing. But when I employed the Freedom of Information Act in an attempt to obtain the counterfeit file from the Secret Service,* the federal department that handles counterfeit infractions, I received a letter in response that claimed the department had conducted a "reasonable search" and turned up nothing. Further, the current CRPD cold-case team assured me that an interview Sturgeon submitted to during the Paula investigation would never have been moved from one file to another. At the very most, the police might have made a copy of the interview and included it in *both* files. But reports were not to be removed. This was protocol.

Detectives Millsap and Jelinek both claimed that county attorney William Faches said that, despite the department's firm belief in Sturgeon as a suspect, there wasn't enough evidence to prosecute him for Paula's death. Jelinek and Detective Steinbeck said that for this reason, they were unable to obtain a warrant from a judge to search the premises of Sturgeon's residence. But my question was why? Wasn't it reasonable to suspect Tom Sturgeon of wrongdoing? His name appears in Paula's police file 73 times, spoken by six different sources, all of whom told one version or another of the exact same abortion story. When I asked Steinbeck what circumstances might have allowed them to go after Sturgeon, he pointed to Shermalayne, whom I'd told him about. If we'd had someone like that, he said. Then.

The account that led Steinbeck to believe the abortion theory came from a man who had himself just been arrested for murder. The shooting death of Ernie Jordan, a pimp and local

---

* Before going to the Secret Service, I tried the Cedar Rapids county clerk, who told me she wasn't able to locate anything on Sturgeon.

gangster known as Big Man for his 300 pounds, occurred during a poker game three months after Paula's body was discovered. There was no question who was responsible; Perry Harris shot Ernie Jordan in front of a room full of witnesses.

After his arrest, Harris sat down with Detective Millsap and told him this story: Jordan had been blackmailing Doc Sturgeon. For what, Harris claimed not to know, but whatever Jordan had over Sturgeon was potent enough that he could squeeze Sturgeon for a few hundred dollars at will. Doc Sturgeon carried a lot of money when he played poker. Knowing this, Harris and Jordan concocted a scheme to relieve him of that cash. They would stage a fight over a card game. Harris would run out and come back with a gun with which to threaten Jordan, who would beg Sturgeon to cover his debt. Then the two men would escape to Des Moines where they planned to take over a house of prostitution. Point being, the gun was never supposed to go off. But it did, killing Harris's friend and accomplice.

The report that documents Millsap's tête-à-tête with Harris, which he placed in Paula's file, ends with a short account of a call that had come from a "confidential informant." Millsap said that the informant had already indicated that Ernie Jordan and Doc Sturgeon were involved in Paula Oberbroeckling's homicide. Now the informant was claiming that the abortion had taken place in the basement of a house Jordan and Harris owned together.

The police searched the basement of the house. There they recovered a woman's blue headscarf and a bunch of cording similar to the rope that bound Paula's wrists. (The CRPD sent the cording to the FBI to see if it matched the rope that had been found at the scene of the crime. The FBI determined that it did not.) In the trunk of Jordan's car they found a champagne headscarf and a pair of sandals. Carol Oberbroeckling was unable to identify any of the effects as belonging to Paula. But she did say that Paula owned headscarves in both colors and, though Paula rarely wore sandals, the shoes were her size.

In the days and weeks that followed Millsap's interview with Harris, other versions of the same story bubbled up. The shooting wasn't an accident. Harris shot Jordan because Jordan owed him money for the disposal of Paula Oberbroeckling's body, something they had been commissioned to handle together after Paula received an abortion by a doctor from Iowa City. Or: The information Jordan had over Sturgeon was Sturgeon's involvement in Paula's death. And Harris shot Jordan because Doc Sturgeon put him up to it.

Paula's file ends with a report wherein a "fairly reliable informant" delineates a version of the above in which Paula had been to Sturgeon for an abortion prior to the night she disappeared. On that Friday she began to bleed and reached out to Sturgeon, who told her to meet a nurse in the Eagle parking lot. But the nurse was unable to help her, and Paula died. Sturgeon then employed Harris and Jordan to dispose of her body.

Steinbeck said that, though he believed Harris's interview, the problem was that Harris was compromised, a bad seed, in trouble with the law himself and thus unreliable. Everything he'd said would remain hearsay because he would never put the scenario in writing.

Weeks after my conversation with Steinbeck, I reread Detective Jelinek's interview with Susan, and something popped into focus. Susan had asked Jelinek about Millsap's conversation with Harris. She wanted to know why the police couldn't use the story Harris had told in order to go after Sturgeon. Rather than claiming a problem of reliability as Steinbeck had, Jelinek said that the reason Harris's statement to the police was worthless was that the police hadn't Mirandized him.*

"[The conversation was a] product of him shooting off his mouth," said Jelinek. "We weren't gonna say anything about that stuff. We didn't question him about it. We were just talking to him one day and that was what came up. And you just . . . we didn't realize he was gonna say anything about it. And so therefore you're done. Because as soon as you go to the court, they'll say, 'Did you Mirandize him?' 'Well, no.' 'Well, then, get the hell outta here.' That's about what it amounts to."

Detective Jelinek is dead, so I couldn't return to him, but what this led me to believe was that the police were so chummy with the criminal element (so removed from the victims) that this man, who had already admitted to killing his friend, was able to give police information that led to a scenario that they feel (or felt) was credible, and they bungled it. Oops. Now what? Oh, let's just forget about it.

---

* When I went back to the police file to examine the entry where Millsap talks to Harris, I saw that the first thing Millsap had written in the report was: "On Sunday morning, 2-14-71, I brought Perry Harris to the Detective Bureau from his cell where I advised him of his constitutional rights and he read a Rights Waiver and said that he understood it and would talk to me but did not wish to sign the waiver." Two paragraphs after that, Millsap wrote that later in the day he advised Harris of his rights *again* and Harris *again* agreed to talk but would not "sign anything." The report was dated 2-15-71, meaning it was written a day *after* the interview took place. I'd note that in the whole of Paula's file, this was the only time an officer mentions constitutional rights.

In 1979, nine years after Paula's death, an eighteen-year-old who attended nearby Kennedy High School was found stabbed to death in her car, which had been parked in the lot of Cedar Rapids' Westdale shopping mall. Michelle Martinko's murder also remained unsolved nearly forty years after the fact. In Iowa, I'd met a man who had been possessed by Michelle's death in the same way that I had been possessed by Paula's. This man had theories and suspects and frustrations, just as I did. But I couldn't help envying him; his case was so much more hopeful.

In 2006, the detectives working on Michelle's case were able to procure DNA from evidence that had been taken from her car. Eleven years later, advancements in technology allowed the CRPD, in conjunction with a crime lab, to use that DNA to create a physical profile of Michelle Martinko's killer. It revealed the killer's hair color, eye color, probable weight and build. The crime lab created computer-generated images that illustrated how the culprit likely appeared in 1979 when Michelle was murdered and how he might look today. The police also ran the DNA profile through the FBI's Combined DNA Index System (CODIS). The test didn't return any results, but there was still the potential that the police could cross-reference the DNA with that of genetic material collected by a personal genomics company such as 23andMe where people send saliva samples in order to gain information about their ancestry and biological proclivities.* This was how the Golden

---

* Detective Steinbeck is intimately familiar with the potential of DNA testing. In 1990, his eight-year-old niece, Jennifer Schuett, was kidnapped from her home, raped, and left to die in a field, her throat slashed. Miraculously, she survived and was discovered within twelve hours of the attack. Police took a DNA sample at the

State Killer, a man who committed more than twelve murders and fifty rapes in California between the years 1974 and 1986, was identified and arrested thirty-two years after the fact. At the very least, with this profile of Michelle's murderer, the police have been able to narrow their suspect pool.

The common refrain among the detectives assigned to Paula's case is that had they access to modern technology they would have been able to make an arrest. That might be true. Unfortunately, as I understood it, all the material evidence the police recovered at Otis Road—the ligatures, Paula's dress—has been so contaminated by river water from the flood of 2008 as to make it unusable. And because the police failed to collect fingerprints—or search for blood or hair or fingernails—from Debbie's car on the day it was located, less than twenty-four hours after Paula disappeared, they missed an opportunity to rule out anyone already in the criminal database.

From the police report: "At about 7 PM this date Debbie Kellogg brought her black Chevy Nova, 1962 model to the station and consented to let me look through it. At that time I removed the rear seat and checked the entire interior of the car, but found nothing of any consequence. Debbie stated her car has been cleaned a number of times since July 11, 1970."

"This date" refers to December 3, 1970. Five months after Paula disappeared. Yes, I would have expected that Debbie's car would be clear of anything "of consequence" five months afterward.

In addition to the material evidence, it appeared that all

---

time, but the technology wasn't yet sophisticated enough to return a result. Then in 2009, nineteen years and many advancements in crime-scene technology later, police retested that same sample and came up with a match. The man was a welder who had been living with his wife and children. Once arrested, he confessed. However, he killed himself in jail before he could stand trial.

the trial records and case files for all the criminal cases touching on Paula's (Sturgeon's counterfeit case; the state's case against Perry Harris for the murder of Ernie Jordan) either washed away in the flood or are buried so deeply in the criminal justice system that not even their keepers can find them. Thomas Sturgeon is dead. Ben Carroll is dead. Percy Harris is dead. Carol and Jim and William Faches, the Linn County attorney, and most of the detectives, Jelinek, Millsap, all dead. Robert Williams died not long before the completion of this book. The nurse did too. There is an excellent chance that the answer has already been buried with the last person who knew it. Which means that, barring someone coming forward and confessing to the killing of Paula Oberbroeckling, the grim reality is that there is little probability that her homicide will ever be solved. And no one will be held accountable for it.

When I first heard about Sturgeon's counterfeit conviction and how soon after Paula's death it occurred, I wondered whether the Secret Service had already begun investigating Sturgeon when Paula died and whether those federal charges trumped the charges that might have been brought against him in Paula's case. According to the *Gazette*—indeed, the only information I had, as no one seemed to be able to locate the file—the Secret Service began their investigation six weeks before Sturgeon's arrest. Which would have been nine months after the last entry in Paula's file, which made my theory less likely. Though when this was posed to Steinbeck, it seemed reasonable to him.

"They just didn't have enough to nail Sturgeon with the case with Paula. But the counterfeiting case had federal charges and was more equal to it or exceeding anything they could've done relevant to the botched abortion with Paula. Even though you could probably justify, not a premeditated murder, not murder one, but probably could justify a second-degree murder or a reckless homicide," said Steinbeck.

Boil this down and what I understood was that, according to the law, Sturgeon's printing counterfeit twenties in his office was a crime greater than the potential that he had been so careless with the life of a young woman as to kill her. Which brought me back to Lynn's question. "Did they think she wasn't worth anything?" My guess was that, no, they (the police, the lawmakers, the media, the powers that be) did not.

Chapter 15

The True Crime

THE *GAZETTE* IGNORED PAULA'S DISAPPEARANCE COM-
pletely and then printed just those three stories about the
discovery of her body. The CRPD's investigation went cold
despite the fact that there were still leads to follow. When
Susan sent me the police file, it struck me, a layperson with
no frame of reference, as long at 150 pages. But recently I
listened to a podcast about a thirty-five-year-old cold case in
Manitoba, Canada, where the police file consists of *45 bank-
ers boxes* worth of material. There are more than 14,000 documents; 2,500 people are listed. This might represent the other
extreme, but still. It seemed few were committed to finding
out what happened to Paula, to holding accountable whoever
was responsible for her death.

"What I can't wrap my head around is, you have two girls
in roughly the same year or the same couple of years that
died under horrible circumstances. One of them you never
hear a thing about—nothing. And one of them, for so many
years on her anniversary, it was in every single newspaper
on every single television station," Lynn said to Susan. "Is
it because they think if what happened to [Paula] . . . if it's

the Dr. Sturgeon thing, that's hush-hush, and you can't talk about that? I don't get it."

For the record, here Lynn was confused. Michelle Martinko was the woman whose murder Lynn felt the media paid inordinate attention. But Michelle died nine years after Paula did. Jean Halverson was the girl from Paula's class who had also been killed; her case had been solved almost immediately. Her murderer was the man who'd been able to reduce his sentence by thirty-five years because of police misconduct. Lynn can be forgiven for mixing them up, though. There are a lot of dead girls in this story. Plus, her question is salient: the powers that be failed Paula; did they do so because they felt her death was her fault?

I raised this question with Steinbeck, asking him about the attitude of the police department toward a teenage girl. A girl who had two boyfriends, one of whom was Black. A girl who might or might not have been pregnant. Might or might not have gone for an abortion. He told me that, sure, most of the department was racist (to illustrate, he used an anecdote from when he was a rookie cop. During a lecture on the use of the baton, the assistant chief told his recruits that if the person happened to be Black you'd want to "give them a few extra raps") and sure, most of the department was sexist. They probably "thought she was a bad girl and looked down their noses at that type of activity."* But he was confident that these biases

---

* Having read *Down Girl: The Logic of Misogyny* by Kate Manne, I understand the term "sexism" as different from the way Steinbeck employs it. Manne defines sexism as the belief that women are inherently less capable than men. Believing that Susan couldn't become an actuary because she is a woman is sexist. Misogyny on the other hand is a tool of social control used by the powerful to enforce gender norms

didn't affect the treatment Paula received from the CRPD. "Once that girl becomes a dead person, and it's a matter of a homicide investigation, none of that would have an effect on that case. I really feel comfortable about that."

I believe that Steinbeck believes this to be true. And maybe it's true of him. But, in 1970, there were only a couple of women on the CRPD, all relegated to office work, and no African Americans. So my question is, was it true of the all-white, overwhelmingly male Cedar Rapids police department?

Some context: On July 4, 1970, one week before Paula disappeared, the *Gazette* reported that there had been a "near riot" in front of a bar in Oak Hill. According to the story, an altercation between two men, which had begun outside one lounge and moved to another, had grown to include more than one hundred people, most of them Black. In order to contain the conflict, the CRPD called in all of its backup, "most of the night staff of the police department, Linn sheriff's deputies and the highway patrol." Arrests were made. People wound up in the hospital. After the chaos subsided, fifty African Americans showed up at the police station, demanding to be heard.

The *Gazette* painted the event as a melee, a sort of piling on in frustration. But while reading oral histories given by African Americans to the African American Museum of Iowa, I found that more than one interviewee referenced the event. Their tellings painted the night differently than the *Gazette* had. They claimed that the catalyst hadn't been a fight between two men but the police's decision to pull over a

---

that benefit this hierarchy. "Misogyny ought to be understood as the system that operates within a patriarchal social order to police and enforce women's subordination and to uphold male dominance" (*Down Girl*, 33). What Steinbeck describes, shaming women for their actions, is not sexism but misogyny. Its purpose is to keep women in their place.

drunk Black motorist in front of the Brown Derby, a bar. The police heckled and physically intimidated this man and the crowd that gathered did so in support of him.

I can't know what transpired that night, but what I do know is that *one week, seven days* before Paula disappeared— Paula, who had flouted cultural norms by dating an African American—a cultural clash took place in Cedar Rapids leaving the relationship between the CRPD and the Black community strained if not outwardly aggressive. Did this affect the lens through which the CRPD viewed her case?

• • •

I returned to Cedar Rapids in the summer. The night before I arrived a man who had been acquainted with Paula during high school argued with Susan about who or what was to blame for Paula's death. He eventually said that Paula had deserved what happened to her. She had premarital sex with more than one partner; she moved out of her mother's house; she was scantily clad; she knowingly entered a "bad" part of town in the middle of the night; she might or might not have tried to procure an abortion. As Susan relayed the conversation to me on the way back from picking me up at the airport, I could feel myself heating up. He was the problem.

Placing the onus on Paula for whatever befell her was a logic so twisted it boggled my mind. The implication that whoever killed Paula did so in response to a choice that *she* made (because she was pregnant; because she was independent; because of her appearance; because of her mere presence in a given place at a given time) rather than of his own volition turned the perpetrator into the victim, the person powerless before an outside force. This reasoning robbed Paula of her victimhood and granted it to whoever killed her.

———

Carol Kean's sister, Julia Benning (Carol called her Julie), was murdered 75 miles from Cedar Rapids in Waverly, Iowa, in 1975, five years after Paula died. Carol's home lay off a country road, down a long, narrow drive flanked with wildflowers. In her living room, as her own teenage daughter puttered about—in and out of the kitchen, the front and back of the house—Carol candidly told me about her sister and the many parallels between her death and Paula's.

Like Paula, Julie Benning had been eighteen when she disappeared, had also been discovered missing when she failed to report for work. And just like in Paula's case, the police refused, despite Julie's pleading family, to take immediate action, convinced as they were that Julie would turn out to be a runaway. Not quite four months after she went missing, Julie's body was found stuffed into a culvert (that word, culvert, another echo of Paula's story). And also like Paula, Julie's murder has never been solved.

At the time of her death, Julie was employed at a local nightclub called the Sir Lounge where women danced without clothes. According to Carol Kean, the sisters' father had refused to send Julie to college after she graduated from high school, insisting that she get a job instead. Though Julie applied to positions all over town, the only offer she received was from the Sir. She was hired as a waitress rather than a dancer—not that it should have mattered in either case—still, it was implied that her decision to work at the Sir was the catalyst that led to her death. (Not, say, the actions of the person who killed her.)

"Here's the thing, all these people who condemn [her working at the Sir]? Who do they think went to the Sir? The police went there, and the lawyers and the doctors and everybody's husband and boyfriend and brother and son were there. [The men, though] they get the free pass," said Carol. She then referred to a scene in the movie *Schindler's List*, when a Nazi who coveted his Jewish maid turned around after their sexual encounter and beat her for tempting him. "Even if [the man's] guilt comes out, it's always the woman."

Blaming the victim is convenient. It relieves perpetrators from taking responsibility for their actions. It alleviates society from having to examine its own failure to legislate, to protect, and to apprehend, excusing all the ways violence is allowed to go unchecked.

Victim blaming is also an excellent way to control women. The message sent to women in Paula's day was: *You must behave in exactly this manner (marry young, have children, focus on the house, aim low at work, if you work at all, don't provoke the men in your life, be content, be compliant, be quiet). If you don't, you will be responsible for any violence inflicted on you.*

My conversation with Susan in the car was not the first time I'd heard someone blame Paula (overtly or not) for her own death. There was some version of this allusion in many of the police interviews. Here's Steinbeck: "She was such a pretty girl, and her conduct seemed so twisted. Not because she dated interracially but because of the conditions that went with those that she ran with, the socioeconomic issues, the filth, the abuse, the drugs, conditions she didn't need to put up with. She could have elevated herself to better ways and conditions, regardless of who she was racially attracted to."

Though this warped system of culpability was most certainly created by men and by the great wheels of society, if I was to be fair, it was perpetuated at least in part by women.

Because it wasn't only men whom I heard tacitly blaming women for their own deaths. According to Carol Kean, Julie Benning's aunt and grandmother both called Julie a "Jezebel" for working at the Sir Lounge. Julie's mother admitted to Carol that after Julie's death she'd ripped two pages out of Julie's diary—on the first Julie had written that she'd gotten an IUD and "it hurt like holy hell," and on the second she'd confessed to losing her virginity. Carol Kean didn't say it, but I presumed Julie's mom was trying to both protect Julie's reputation from those who would judge her for being sexually active and erase any evidence that indicated for those who were into victim blaming that Julie had a role in whatever horror had befallen her.

As for Paula, consider the nurse. When I brought up the possibility that whoever killed Paula had actually been trying to help her by giving her the abortion she might have needed, her words were: "I'm all for choice but it doesn't mean you have to run out and do it." Her fate, her fault.

So men blame women, and women blame women. But it doesn't even stop there; women, at least in my own experience, also blame themselves.

One winter day, when my son was nine months old, I took him on the subway. It was bitter cold, and I had him strapped to my chest facing outward. I'd covered us both in a fleece with two neck holes, one for me and one for him. The coat made me look like a kangaroo, my son, the joey peeking out from my pouch.

As we descended the subway steps, another train traveling in the opposite direction was unloading across the platform. When I reached the bottom of the staircase, I inadvertently made eye contact with a man sitting in the window of the train. The man held my gaze and then raised his first two fingers to his mouth and stuck his tongue between them. Feeling the rush and spark of anger, I instinctively raised my middle finger and held it low by my side where it was visible only to him. In a flash, the man disappeared from the window, out of his seat, and through the doors just before they closed and the train pulled out of the station.

My heart thrummed with fear. Having just missed my own train, the platform was virtually empty. There were a couple of men seated on opposite ends of a wooden bench near the terminus. I walked steadily toward them and chose a seat between them, my son's pudgy legs pressing into my thighs. Only then did I dare glance to my left. There I saw the man from the window of the train rushing toward me. When he reached the bench, he stood over me and in a deep voice, the growl of a big dog, yelled, "Bitch, you need to watch out who you fuck with. I'm going to hurt you." The men on either side of me did not move or speak or even glance over. It was as if nothing were happening at all. I sat mute, paralyzed, my son's cold-reddened cheeks a foot and a half from the spittle arcing out of this man's mouth. The man yelled other things, but I don't remember them. The blood was so loud in my ears that I thought I might faint. Then, as quickly as he came, he turned and left.

Shaking, I clutched my son to my chest, willed the tears to stay in my eyes. And then here was what happened: I did not blame this man for his obscene gesture. I did not fault him for jumping off the train and chasing me down. I did not hate him for threatening and yelling in my infant son's face. Instead, I hated *myself*. For being so brazen, for thinking that I might gain the upper hand with my silly raised finger, for putting my son, the most important thing in my life, in danger, for exposing him to the ugliness of this man. *All my fault. All my fault. All my fault.* So much so that, before now, I have never told this story to anyone, so convinced was I that it proved me to be a horrible mother. Because it wasn't like I didn't know what I risked when I flipped this guy the bird; in fact, I had been warned.

My mother has a story about driving to her second-shift med-tech job at dusk one night in Omaha sometime before 1980. From out of the highway's falling dark, a pickup truck materialized beside her, keeping pace with her station wagon until she looked over. The man in the truck met her glance with a series of crude gestures and honking. In response, my mother stuck out her tongue. Here, her innocence and sweetness killed me. I raised my middle finger; she retorted with all the bite of a kid on an elementary school playground. Her tongue! How benign! But not to this man. He became enraged and proceeded to try to run my mother off the road. For five or more terrifying minutes, he pulled in front of her, slowing down so much that she was forced to go around him, at which point he sped up beside her and swerved toward her car as if to sideswipe her. When she slowed down to avoid being hit, he repeated the intimidation. At some point, she was able to exit the highway and leave him behind.

She told me this story when I was a teenager. Though she didn't say it outright, what I heard was: *Learn from my mistake. Don't fight back.* I understood from this that it was best to let these things go. "These things" being obscene gestures like the ones made by the guy in the truck and the man on the train, but also comments made by men about my appearance, about what they thought when they looked at me, about what I should and shouldn't do or say. They included instances of touching or grabbing. My mom had stories about these too—

the guy who reached through the space between the window and my mother's seat on a New Orleans trolley and grabbed her left breast; the floor manager at her first job at Henry C. Lytton in Chicago who came up behind her and placed his hands on the cash register in front of her, trapping her between his forearms. He then asked her out as his wedding ring winked up at her. She was nineteen.

Let them go, and then get away.

Because here was the sad truth: in most cases, confidence and control were illusions, a man was almost always capable of overpowering a woman should he want to. There is rarely physical equality between men and women. In this way a woman would nearly always be at a disadvantage.

When I questioned this presumption—There were strong women! There were weak men!—what stopped me was this: Occasionally, when my husband was roughhousing with my son, no longer an infant—the two of them rolling around on our king-sized bed on a Saturday morning—my husband and son would gang up on me. My husband would pin me to the bed so that my son could force his tiny fingers into my armpits or just under my ribs to tickle me. My husband, who is not a big man nor meant me real harm, was unfailingly able to render me immobile no matter how hard I fought back. The experience sometimes put me into fight-or-flight, and I had to resist biting my husband or kneeing him in the groin in defense, the only moves I felt I had. I knew this was a game, but I never won. I told him that this feeling of being incapacitated bothered me in a deep way that I didn't fully understand. He was considerate of that, and we didn't play like this often. More frequently, my son and I tried to pin my husband, to tickle him, work our fingers into the sensitive place between his thigh and his hamstring, but we *never, ever* could. He was too big. He was too strong. He moved too fast. And somehow this play, which was supposed to be fun, felt like a giant metaphor for my physical power in the world. My weakness relative to his strength was a truism that I loathed and also that I respected.

But that morning with my infant son on the subway I had forgotten my place and I had forgotten my mother's warning, so here was this man to remind me: It was his right to make crude gestures at me. I needed to accept them or I would be hurt. And that, I'd been taught, was on me. (Look even at how I've written this: "I needed to accept them or I would be hurt," rather than "or he would hurt me." I've been brainwashed to believe that I am in control of my safety, when clearly I am not.) So my mother informed me of my place. And when I didn't listen, this man reminded me. And then my own shame over my actions kept me from commiserating with all the other women who had experienced similar intimidations. In this way, I too was complicit. When I thought hard about my own culpability, it got worse.

In the years before I began this book, when I was working at the literary magazine and in my third trimester of pregnancy, one of the essays I acquired was a frank account of domestic abuse. It was a piece that I had taken on for its lyricism, its complexity, its truth. But, also, it made me squeamish. At its heart, it was a small story about a woman who was physically abused by her husband. It focused on the complicated reasons she stayed as long as she did and how she gradually stoked the courage to leave. I worried that the piece would be thought of as maudlin. That, despite its many beautiful moments, its revealing of humanity and the complications implicit in relationships, it wouldn't be considered literary or even relevant.

At that time, I had been teaching nonfiction to continuing-ed students for more than a few years, and the number of essays or short memoirs my students had submitted that contained violence against women was staggering—women raped in their dorm rooms, in the entryways of their apartment buildings, in the bathrooms of bars; by boyfriends, acquaintances, uncles; women beaten by their fathers, by the guys they'd just begun dating, and by the men they'd been dating for years; wives abused by husbands, girls by fathers, one in which a girl watched her father shoot her mother and then shoot himself. So much so that I'd begun to think of violence against women as a sort of cliché. (An essay written by another writer included in an anthology I'd contributed to had been titled "Cliché Rape Story"!) "Well-trod territory" was how I described such topics to writers when rejecting their work. The stories seemed small, microcosm as opposed to macrocosm, effectively about two people, one of them very dysfunctional. I was wrong, of course, but I didn't know it even after I'd accepted this particular piece.

Once the essay about the woman who left her abuser was published, the magazine was inundated with emails, as was the writer. Women from all over the country said that the piece had spoken to them, that the writer's experience had mirrored their own. One man admitted sorrowfully to his own proclivity for violence; another said that the essay had been "hard to read . . . but probably necessary." The piece proved one of our most popular ever. It was included in *Best American Essays*. From its publication, the writer secured a six-figure book deal. This was a piece that I had worried would seem clichéd.

Yes, as an editor it was my job to look for fresh stories, but this story *was* fresh. It was a look at domestic violence through the lens of complexity. This woman had been beaten by her husband, but she had also loved him and he loved her. The writer did not demonize her abuser but humanized him instead. This was novel. However, because my internal cliché censor lumped together all stories about domestic violence, I questioned my own attraction to the story even as I felt it.

My tin ear came from a lifetime of observing the minimization of women's experiences, the characterization of them as unimportant and uninteresting, this compounded by the simultaneous assumption that experiences of this type—by which I mean on the whole spectrum of the violence scale, from harassment to abuse to rape—were inherent to female experience. In other words, what else was new?

And I am white. The media vastly overrepresents victims who are white (and female) as opposed to those who are Black. This, despite the fact that Black women are the victims of intimate partner violence at rates higher than white women. And Black women are murdered by males at more than two times the rate of white women. Meaning that if I have spent my life thinking stories that feature women like me are uninteresting and unimportant, how much worse is this phenomenon in the Black community?

Alongside Kathy McHugh's continued astonishment that not one but *two* girls from her high school class had been murdered was an attempt to reconcile Paula's and Jean Halverson's deaths by defining the type of woman each had been while she was alive. Kathy described Jean Halverson, the girl Richard Zacek shot point-blank in the woods, as a goody-two-shoes, follow-the-rules, Camp Fire–type girl, while Paula was this "dangerous, cool woman." As if the fact of their being polar opposites should have protected at least one of them.

But they weren't opposites. They were the same. They were *both* women.

The fact is, a woman can take self-defense classes and cover her body head to toe. She can be careful not to consume too much alcohol, avoid eye contact with strange men, forgo walking alone at night, and hold her keys out like a weapon when she does. She can avoid wearing headphones and meandering in dark or desolate places. She can refuse to open her door to strangers, put a man's voice on her answering machine (as my mother did after my father moved out). But none of this will solve the problem, which is that she cannot control the actions of another person. Nor can it change the fact that she is a woman, which is the very thing that places her in danger.

Winding up in a ditch has less to do with making sure your skirt comes down to your knees (look at Jean Halverson) or being employed by a respectable business (look at Paula) or coming from a well-off family (look at Stephanie Schmidt) or being married (look at Sharon Wright) or being innocent (look at Jennifer Schuett) and much more to do with being a woman. How many men, after all, wind up in ditches? Or stuffed into culverts? Or raped or assaulted or, or, or . . . ?*

Susan was no goody-two-shoes, no Camp Fire girl, but she had been safeguarded in ways that Paula had not—with her

---

* Yes, men are murdered in the United States in much higher numbers than women—nearly four to one in 2017, according to the National Vital Statistics Report. But men tend to be killed by strangers during disputes over drugs, turf, property. And they are killed on the street. Women are more often sexually brutalized and murdered in their homes by their boyfriends, their husbands, their dates, people who purport to love them. These crimes are personal. The perpetrators know their victims. They don't want their wallets; they want to hurt their bodies. That said, in both cases the murderers are usually men.

parents' money and unqualified support, with her residence in California where an abortion could be legally obtained, with the support of her boyfriend and of her sister's friend. But while Susan's privilege potentially saved her life by expediting the safe abortion she needed, it was incapable of shielding her from the fundamental trappings of womanhood. From the shame of the experience ("You will never tell anyone," her mother had said to her over the phone and in writing afterward) or from being sexually assaulted by the very doctor who had helped her.

After her abortion, Susan returned to the Planned Parenthood clinic for a follow-up appointment. In the office, she lay back on the examining table and the doctor who administered the initial procedure assessed her recovery. Then he used his hand to bring her to orgasm, after which he cleared her to go.

Susan told me she didn't even know that she'd been assaulted until she confided the experience to the same acquaintance who had suggested she go to the clinic in the first place. "Noooo," Susan remembered the woman saying when she asked her whether her orgasm was part of the procedure.

"He was a doctor," Susan told me. "I thought he was making sure everything still worked."

Her blind trust and subsequent bewilderment recalled Shermalayne's abuse at the hands of Doc Sturgeon. For me, their stories spoke to the ways in which men can wield their power and position in order to take advantage of women and also to the lack of information disseminated to teenage girls at that time and the ways in which this failure stripped them of power. Susan and Shermalayne had been taught to trust (men, doctors, teachers), and no one had ever spoken to them about their bodies and their personal rights, so when they were violated they didn't even know they had been so.

Aside from the acquaintance whom she confided in immediately after her own assault, Susan didn't breathe another word about what happened at that follow-up appointment (because she was ashamed; because she blamed herself) until she told me about her abortion that late night over the phone. When I asked my husband the next day whether he knew his mother had been assaulted, his jaw dropped.

An interview I conducted with Larry Martin, one of Paula's friends, had spun off into what I'd begun to call the spiral of possibilities:

While looking for Paula during those unaccounted-for hours, Lonnie Bell and his friend had found her (maybe at Robert's where she was waiting for him to return, not knowing he would be out all night, perhaps in the "shack" Steinbeck had described in the back. But then Robert's mother, who had been home that night, would have heard an argument. And how would Debbie's car have gotten to the Eagle supermarket?). Or maybe they spotted her driving on Mt. Vernon Road and forced her to pull over (a couple who lived over an upholstery shop just up the block from where Debbie's car was found said they heard a girl scream that night. They also thought they heard her call out "Mommy!" What if it was "Lonnie!"?) and then beat her (for being pregnant with Robert's baby or for being pregnant at all) with or without the intention of killing her.

Or maybe the gears failed on Debbie's car a second time, and while Paula was fixing them (in front of Eagle?) she crossed paths with a stranger who meant to do women harm.

Or maybe she was raped and held hostage in a house in Oak Hill (another rumor that came up more than once in the

police file, except that her body was discovered with a headband she'd worn. It was hard to believe she kept it on for days
and nights during a kidnapping).

Or maybe she bled out from an abortion, not conducted
the night she disappeared but four days earlier. Her time card
from Younkers shows that she was off work on Monday after
the July Fourth holiday and that she called in sick on Tuesday (an abortion takes days to complete, most of the bleeding done at home; maybe she'd called Sturgeon or someone
else on Friday night because the bleeding hadn't stopped or
because the catheter had fallen out and the procedure needed
to be repeated; but then why the dress?). Or maybe she was
never in contact with Sturgeon and she'd asked someone to
beat her up in the hopes of inducing a miscarriage (according
to the autopsy, the police were unable to recover two teeth.
Had someone knocked them out?).

Or, or, or . . .

Once Larry and I had been through all the scenarios,
tested all the theories, each one feeling plausible until we
hit the one fact that refused to fit, leaving us shaking our
heads, he said something that struck me. Something about
the number of plausible scenarios regarding what happened to Paula that night in 1970 equaling the deaths of so
many Paulas. Something clicked. He was right; there were
so many Paulas.

The thing that I'd begun to realize about all these events—
the literary magazine writer's abuse at the hands of her husband, my grandmother being berated by hers, the assaults
of Susan and Shermalayne on the examining tables of doctors, the intimidations of myself and my mother by strange
men on the street, the murders of Stephanie Schmidt and
Julie Benning and Michelle Martinko and Jean Halverson

and Maureen Brubaker Farley and Sharon Wright and Paula Oberbroeckling—was that they were not isolated.

On the one hand, the men who committed these heinous acts were, in the words of a male friend, "crazy outliers." On the other, virtually every woman I know has a story. These so-called outliers aren't working in the shadows. They are operating out in the open. They have been made bold by our culture. They have been protected by the law and continue to be. They flourish as a result of our continued shame.

Maybe in this respect it was a good thing not to have a culprit. Maybe having a culprit was the very thing that allowed us to look away. To blame a violent act on a specific person is to distance ourselves from responsibility, to believe these violations to be exceptions committed by "crazy outliers." But when we have no culprit, we must look at ourselves. For we are the ones who embolden, who create safe environments, who protect aberrant individuals with the law or with our silence or by looking away.

During Donald Ray Gideon's sentencing for Stephanie Schmidt's murder, Jeni told me that he addressed the court: You created me, he said. By which he meant that all the ways the system had forsaken him—his negligent upbringing, the failure of the criminal justice system to keep him behind bars or to rehabilitate him, his inability to get help even though he'd asked for it after his release—had played a part in his becoming.

"[His were] not acceptable choices. He could have done better," said Jeni. "But I realize that there are so many solutions to the problem and that we all contribute to it."

There it is. This is not some spiderweb in a shadowy corner that we can ignore. We are in the web. My sense is that to dismantle it we need to see what it's made of. To identify what holds it up (language, silence, shame, apathy, acceptance of things as they are, the law) and employ those things that can bring it down (renaming, reclaiming, use of our voices, refusals to turn away, to be shamed, to be complacent, to be quiet). But most of all, we need the help of men. Men must own up to their actions; men must speak out against toxic masculinity; men must vow to be the last in their line to rage, to intimidate, to coerce.

The day after Donald Trump was sworn in to be the forty-fifth president of the United States, I got up in the dark of night to catch a bus from New York City to Washington, DC, to take part in the inaugural Women's March. Susan, as always, came with me. Standing in a sea of pussyhats so thick we couldn't move, we chanted, "My body, my choice!" Spontaneously, a chorus of male voices rose up to meet us, "Her body, her choice!" And something about their deep voices showing deference and support made tears spring to my eyes, perhaps at the potential for change, a change that is only possible under unified forces.

Chapter 16

The Paulas

WHEN HER DAUGHTER DIED, CAROL OBERBROECKLING was forty years old, the same age I am as I write this sentence. Fitting, for if I began this project feeling bonded with Paula, I ended it empathizing with Carol. Two months after my August trip to Cedar Rapids, I conceived my second child. And that child would be a girl.

Upon hearing that word, "girl," while lying back on the radiologist's table—the room chilly and dark, the gray static screen before me both familiar and indecipherable—I found myself elated and terrified in equal measure. I had wanted a girl this second time around. One of each, I'd said aloud to my husband, the full experience. I adored my son, but, never having been a boy myself, he would always be something of a mystery to me. But a girl, a girl I had been.

I had always enjoyed being a girl. There were so many things I imagined teaching a daughter, doing with her, showing her. I wanted to read *Beezus and Ramona* aloud to her under lamplight, wrap up the whole set of *Little House on the Prairie* books and give them to her when she turned ten, introduce her to Nancy Drew. I wanted to take her to see *The*

Nutcracker before the holidays like my mother had taken me. I wanted to enroll her in basketball from a young age, as I had been; maybe she would show more talent than I did, or maybe not, who cared!

I wanted to model for her the fine line between attending to one's appearance and not being obsessed by it. I liked my long neck and the feeling of my hair falling around it, the curve of strong hips, butt, thighs. I liked the look of painted nails, slender fingers. I liked changing my appearance with my moods, flouting my femininity as a teenager—baggy ripped jeans and angry black tees, my limp hair in my face, eye shadow like a bandit—and embracing it in my twenties with dresses. Every. Single. Day. As an adult I went back and forth, found my own balance.

I liked that I was the one who built and carried and then fed my son all with the stuff of my self—creator *and* sustainer of life. I was awestruck over my body's capabilities. I found power in exceeding expectation, in surprising people with my opinions. I felt pride and connection when I saw other women succeed. I was inspired by all the creative women around me, how they negotiated their careers, the ways they became active in their communities, how they struck a balance between work and home. I was excited to watch my daughter grow into whatever kind of woman she wanted to be. And I was thrilled to have a lifelong friend. Aside from those fraught teenage years when all we did was yell, my mother and I had always liked each other despite our differences. We could talk for hours and did so over cards or in the car or on walks; there was always something more to say. I envisioned this same closeness for my daughter and me. But here was the thing: Carol had imagined being close to Paula too, and it never came to fruition because Paula died during her teenage years, during her fraught years, during her difficult years. Which brings me to the terror.

In her book *The Red Parts*, about the murder of her aunt, Maggie Nelson describes what she has termed Murder Mind, which was her ability, while writing and researching her book, to passively read through graphic accounts of violence against women during the day only to have them bubble up in gory detail while she slept. Nightmares woke her in the dark hours, and she crept around her shadowy house with her heart racing. She said this experience was a visceral part of the writing of her book. The work was affecting her subconscious; it was seeping into her being. The hard work that went into considering the death of her aunt was changing her. In the years I read about, thought about, obsessed over Paula's case, I never suffered Murder Mind. And for a while I worried about what that said about me, about my ability to stomach all sorts of awfulness, about my capacity for empathy. But I understand it differently now.

When my son was an infant, I read James Ellroy's memoir, *My Dark Places*. The book detailed Ellroy's failed attempt to solve his own mother's nearly forty-year-old murder. While looking for parallels, for clues, Ellroy excavated dozens of accounts of sexual predation. All of which occurred in the vicinity of the ivied roadside in El Monte, California, where his mother's body had been found and during the years surrounding her death. The result equaled page after page filled with incident after incident of violence against women—rapes, attacks, murders, home invasions, women being strangled, shoved into cars, tossed into alleyways, into ditches—every single event occurring during a shockingly short period of time in a shockingly small swath of one single American city. The book was harrowing. But I was able to read it, to turn the pages, to internalize the message without going to pieces. That was, until Ellroy detailed an account of a woman who was murdered in her home while her eighteen-month-old daughter slept in her crib. The child starved to death before she was found, pulling out large tufts of her own hair. And suddenly I was weeping. I had to put the book down on my chest and blink rapidly up at the ceiling to wrest control over my ragged breath, reminding myself that this one horror was just that, one horror. It did not define the world.

My reaction was overly dramatic. Not because the story didn't call for this level of drama and heartbreak, it did, but so did hundreds of thousands of incidents that we come in contact with—in newspapers, on television, walking down the street—every day. But we can't let every suffering we witness affect us at full capacity. If we did, we would break. No, my reaction was overly dramatic because since having my son, I was no longer me. *I* was new. I wasn't the woman wary of a line cook who might offer me a ride home and then pull over and drag me from the car. I was now a woman immobilized by love for my child, one who knew intimately—from watching my son helpless on his back in the middle of the floor, literally unable to move much less to take care of even one of his own needs—how vulnerable, how helpless children are. I never suffered Murder Mind because my biggest fear now was not that someone might hurt me, but that someone might hurt my child.

Susan told me that she thought it was strange when Carol admitted that the first thing she thought upon seeing the Nova abandoned on the street in front of the Eagle supermarket was that when they opened the trunk, they would find Paula inside of it. Why on earth would Carol's first thought be of Paula in the trunk? Paula hadn't even been missing twelve hours. Did Carol know something that everyone else didn't?

But I understood Carol's impulse. My son was two and a half then, and if he slept too late in the morning I was convinced he was dead in his crib. I could not imagine how this terror would manifest with a daughter. When she was old enough to go out by herself at night, when she broke curfew, when I drove away after making up her bed for her in her college dorm.

Carol said Paula wasn't afraid of anything. I want my daughter to be fearless too. But will I be able to teach her the delicate balance between confidence and carelessness? Because she will be sixteen, seventeen, eighteen at some point. She will likely have that same fire and curiosity that I did, that Paula did, that Susan did, that many women do. And while I want that for her, while I know that that fire is what leads to life and living and being, I am simultaneously afraid of what its bright light will attract. It shouldn't be on her to protect herself, and also it is.

Or maybe this is more about how I will respond to her. What will I do when she wants to wear makeup? When she comes downstairs in clothes that reveal her body? What will happen when she disobeys me? Will I be capable of supporting her decisions because they are hers? Or will my own perception of the world's ways blind me into alienating rather than guiding her? I probably will seem old and outdated, but I *do* know some things. I was her. Just as Carol was Paula. And my mother was me, her mother her.

One of the last times Carol saw Paula was on the night of Paula's graduation from Washington. Carol and Lynn and Grandma Vera and a woman whose name I didn't recognize were hanging out at the house on G Avenue drinking wine and feeling light. Paula had stopped by, and Carol said she could remember Paula laughing playfully when she saw them sitting there and saying, "Oh, you guys."

"I can hear her just say, 'Oh, you guys,'" said Carol. "'Oh, you guys.'"

In those three words, I hear a young woman lovingly rolling her eyes at the generations before her, the generations she, having just graduated from high school, is poised to eclipse. She is in possession of all the confidence that comes from being capable and smart and well-liked, even envied. All the anticipation that comes from sitting on the precipice of her whole life, everything still before her. Though she has technically only *been* a woman for less than five months, meaning she is still mostly girl even if she doesn't feel it.

• • •

Susan had come up with the idea to hold a roundtable in Cedar Rapids while we were in town. The purpose would be to explain the work we'd been doing and to share our research with the community in the hopes of reigniting interest in Paula's case and maybe even generating a few leads. An independent bookstore agreed to host us on a Thursday evening.

Just before 6 p.m. when the event was scheduled to begin, Susan and I walked over from across the street where we'd grabbed dinner. The neighborhood, called NewBo in an attempt at hipness (it was short for New Bohemia), had risen in the wake of the flood. What had been submerged under thirteen feet of water in the summer of 2008 now hosted artisans, a gourmet grocer, the bookstore, and more than one microbrewery. Though really no more than a few quiet blocks, NewBo's existence was evidence of optimism and resilience. The area had survived and was better for it. Still, the Cedar

River lazed in the distance, a sort of cheeky reminder that the power dynamic remained the same.

The bookstore was wood-floored and cozy and looked to be capable of holding about thirty people. Susan and I set up around a small table that I imagined usually boasted a display of new books. There were a handful of chairs in front of us and a couch. I'd invited Lynn to the roundtable, telling her that I hoped the event might give Paula some of the attention Lynn was always insisting she was lacking. She told me that she would try to make it, but if she wasn't able to, she hoped I'd fill her in.

I'd finally gotten her on the phone just before leaving New York. She apologized for dodging my calls but told me that she was angry at Susan whom she believed had withheld information from her. I awkwardly apologized on Susan's behalf and then asked if there was any way we could start over from scratch, leave Susan out of it, move forward, just us. Lynn seemed wary, though not completely opposed to the idea. In what I understood to be a test of my loyalty, she told me that Susan had alluded to my call with the nurse but never filled Lynn in on the details; this was one reason she felt betrayed. She asked if I would tell her about the call. Of course, I said. I'd tell her anything she wanted to know.

I explained that we'd gotten the nurse's name from Detective Steinbeck when we spoke with him in late fall and that I'd called her in the winter. I told her that it had taken a while to connect with the woman because she didn't have long-distance phone service. I told her that at first the nurse claimed not to know who Paula was, but once I jogged her memory she easily came forth with a version of the abortion story that she said she'd heard around the neighborhood. I then told Lynn that when I carefully admitted to the nurse that there was at least one theory wherein Paula died in her, the nurse's, home, the woman had yelped and called out in shock to someone on her end of the line in a way that I had believed in the moment.

"So this lady couldn't tell you who dumped her, when she died, how she died?" Lynn asked.

"No, Lynn," I said. "Do you want to know her name?"

"I don't need to know now," she said.

Lynn's disappointment was an anvil.

"Lynn, I just want to meet you," I said in an attempt to begin again. I told her I was coming to Cedar Rapids, and that I'd love to buy her dinner or just a beer. "We don't even have to talk about Paula. I just want to see your face, and I want you to see my face."

"It's a very old face," she responded, chuckling and sounding amenable. But when I arrived, Lynn began avoiding my calls once again.

So I didn't really expect her to show up that night at the bookstore, but as people trickled in, I kept one eye on the door just in case.

We had a small turnout, maybe eight people, most of whom were white men in their sixties who knew Susan in addition to having known Paula. After waiting a few minutes for stragglers, I cleared my throat and introduced myself, explaining my background and how I came to be interested in Paula's case. I briefly detailed the gist of some of the interviews we'd conducted since arriving in Cedar Rapids earlier in the week. I told them about Julie Benning's sister. I talked about a visit I made to the local Planned Parenthood, and how street construction had made it so I could drive past the building but could not turn into the parking lot, no matter what direction I came from. How I ended up abandoning my rental car a few blocks away and simply walking, and how this felt like an apt metaphor for access to women's health care in this country. The construction had done nothing to dissuade an older white man from holding a sign with the picture of a fetus on it while standing some required distance away. He had scowled at me as I walked past. The director of the facility told me that the man never missed a day. She wondered what good he might do if all that energy was spent helping educate young women on birth control instead of glaring at girls who were just leading their lives. When no one bit, I opened the floor up to questions.

One man said something about how he'd gone to school with Paula and how she was so great because "she'd engage you; she'd actually talk to you." Another concurred. And suddenly everyone was nodding in agreement over Paula's kindness and her confidence.

One man asked whether Debbie Kellogg had gotten her keys back after her car was found. Another person wondered whether there were records of women turning up with septic abortions in Cedar Rapids during the years surrounding Paula's death. I made a note to follow up on both questions. One man speculated about where Paula might have been heading. And another pointed out a conflict and made another guess. The conversation was beginning to devolve into that spiral of possibilities I recognized. As the voices crashed over one another it dawned on me: Maybe this is it. Maybe this is the truth.

Maybe the truth was all of it. It was that the facts were irreconcilable, and that Paula wasn't dressed for an abortion and that her car was left in a place that made no sense. The truth was that the hypothesizing and the "what ifs" *could* go on forever. I would always be able to tell someone about Paula and then we could spend an hour going back over everything we thought we understood, winding up nowhere. And maybe this was the thing that Lynn also knew. This was the reason she didn't need or want to show up to the roundtable. Because it was no longer about finding the truth, if it ever had been; she already knew the truth. The truth was that Paula died and that we didn't know how.

I received an email from Lynn after the roundtable explaining that she needed to tend to a family member and wouldn't be able to see me this trip after all. She told me to let her know if I made any progress. I felt deflated, but not surprised. The way I understood it, if I had news, she wanted to hear it, otherwise, please leave her alone.

I didn't know it then, but it was time for me to move on too. I would soon have my own chance at a new beginning. With a new baby, a new life. Figuring out how to move forward with the knowledge that we send our daughters into a world tilted against them, reconciling our own roles in making this so, and keeping our eyes open to the dangers that lurk as well as to the many wonders and opportunities for change; these would be my challenges now.

Afterword

MY DAUGHTER SCREAMED INTO EXISTENCE TEN MONTHS after the roundtable at the bookstore. She surprised me by showing up early in a cyclonic, two-hours-from-first-contraction-to-baby labor that nearly broke me. And then she surprised me again by being a perfectly content, joyful baby. My mother was the one who pointed out that my daughter had been born on my grandmother's birthday, ninety-four years to the day.

My grandmother had died two years before, living the rest of her life as she vowed to, and as Carol had, alone. She chose to stay in her house with the brick porch on the south side of Chicago rather than moving downtown as she'd purported to want when she was younger. She never held a job. Instead, she spent her time volunteering at Christ the King, reading her romances, playing bridge with the same group of women she'd played with for fifty years.

Sharing a birth date was where the similarities between my daughter and my grandmother began. I wondered where they would diverge and end, fold in on themselves, linked but somehow different, particular to person, time, and place. For if I'd learned anything over the course of my journey with Paula, it was that the experience of womanhood shared many

qualities. That the decisions women faced—to marry or to
remain single, to stay or to leave, to have children or to not,
to work in the home or out of it, to raise our voices or to keep
them quiet—appeared generation after generation. The turning points in the lives of the women in my family, the women
in Paula's, in Susan's, revealing layers of cyclical event and
mirroring, a merry-go-round and round—my grandmother
running away from her abusive mother at sixteen followed
by her daughter's running away a generation later. Paula's rift
with Carol, Susan's with her father, me with my mother. My
conflict over working versus parenting and my mother's belief
that she couldn't work in the way she wanted and Carol's having to work so many jobs. And when to have children and how
and the effect on our lives. Dizzying. I suppose it will take my
daughter's whole life to really know which threads will repeat,
and by then I will be gone.

What I do know is that my daughter is smart and strong.
She keeps up with her older brother easily. She is physically
capable in ways I am not. By eighteen months she could con-
fidently ride a scooter; at two and a half she could do a som-
mersault, climb anything you put in her way. The instructor of
her tumbling class moved her into the older group before she
officially aged into it because she was "ready." She has ideas
and opinions and also she is unbelievably sweet. "My mama,"
she says when I pick her up. She places her cool hands on my
cheeks and marvels as if I've done something right.

I stopped reporting while my daughter was brand-new, tiny and
pink. She and I found our rhythms—took long walks through
the park followed by long naps curled together like kittens on
top of the covers; in late afternoon we'd wait on the corner for

her brother's school bus, do dinner and bedtime and then meet again in the wee hours for long nursing sessions while my husband and son breathed heavily. Still, Paula was never far from my mind. While my daughter slept on the porch in her bassinet, I read back issues of the *Gazette*. And, as always, so much of the zeitgeist seemed to underscore Paula's relevance—there was Harvey Weinstein and the Trump presidency, and so much of what I was reading, nonfiction and fiction alike. Paula was everywhere; I recognized her in everything. Then, not long after my daughter turned three, just before she started preschool, I found my way back to Cedar Rapids.

The CRPD had just had a major win. In 2018, thirty-nine years after Michelle Martinko was found stabbed to death in the parking lot of the Westdale mall, the detectives were able to make use of the DNA they'd taken from her car when the crime was committed. The crime lab that created the profile of Michelle's killer in 2017 uploaded the DNA to a public database created to expedite genealogical research, and up popped a person who showed shared genetic material. Using this link, the lab built a family tree, drawing out the potential suspects. The police employed covertly collected DNA to narrow the pool to three brothers. Ultimately, employing some true gumshoeing, they surreptitiously took DNA off a drinking straw used by one Jerry Burns while he was dining at a pizza restaurant. The DNA matched. They arrested Burns immediately.

In the wake of the arrest, the city was awash in congratulations and pats on the back—there were pieces in the *Gazette*, a podcast conducted with one of the cold-case detectives, Facebook groups breathlessly rehashing every turn in the story. I wanted to know how this success would affect Paula's case.

Ever the faithful companion (or perhaps just powerless to resist digging in yet again), Susan came with me. We considered renting another Soul, but didn't, winding up with a Subaru instead. As we drove into the city, I saw a heavy-haul truck carrying a wind-turbine blade in the opposite direction. Iowa has wind farms all over the state; it's third in the nation in terms of wind-power capacity. To see the turbines in the distance is like sci-fi, but up close, this single blade was otherworldly. It was shockingly big, the wing of an airplane, but so much longer, sleeker. Its presence on the flat road beside me felt like hope, a sign of good things to come.

Since the flood, the city built a new central library, a new fire station. When I landed, I found that the airport was being modernized. Everything felt like rebirth. But, as with anything, it was more complex than it seemed. There was an eight-acre plot that the city had reclaimed with a casino in mind. Those plans never flew, and now the area sat in limbo, a giant piece of fallow land, physical evidence of indecision and competing interests. Time Check, the working-class neighborhood that had seen a large share of the flooding, looked like it had been clear-cut. More than five hundred houses had been condemned, purchased by the city and then razed and planted over with grass.

"But where are the foundations?" I said stupidly to Susan as we drove past. It seemed impossible that whole blocks of homes, a whole community, could just be erased. But as far as I could see there was no evidence of what had been, only grassland and geese.

The Cedar Rapids Police Department rested squarely in the flood zone. It had taken in seven feet of water, damaging files, evidence, equipment, firearms. In the interim, the facility had been fully restored and when Susan and I visited, it presented as unaffected.

The Cedar Rapids cold-case team is made up of three (white) men: Matt Denlinger, the son of Harvey Denlinger, a detective who was on the force when Michelle Martinko was murdered; and two retired detectives, J.D. Smith, who had been an agent for the Iowa Division of Criminal Investigation, and Ken Washburn, who wasn't able to make our meeting. Detective Denlinger met Susan and me in the lobby of the station and escorted us to a stark white room where we arranged ourselves around a conference table.

Smith and Denlinger were straight out of central casting, a study in opposites. Both men were bald and freckled, but Smith was short and round, the older of the two, warm and affable, while Denlinger was tall and leggy, younger, inscrutable, his cards held tight to his chest. I started by congratulating them on their progress in the Martinko case. Denlinger smiled, revealing dimples and pride. The case had been a legacy for him. His father had tried to solve it, and now, decades later, Denlinger was close to finishing what his dad had begun.*

When I asked what the Martinko arrest did for Paula's case, Denlinger shook his head and used euphemisms like "evidentiary stumbling blocks" and "solvability." He admitted that he hadn't spent much time with Paula's file. (J.D. Smith, whom I'd spoken with a couple times over the years, had a greater familiarity with Paula's case, having read the report more than once.) Denlinger said the fact of the matter was, *if* there was anything left in the evidence room from the inves-

---

* In fact he would complete his father's pursuit. Six months after our meeting, a jury in Scott County, Iowa—where the trial had been moved in an attempt to avoid publicity going back decades—convicted Jerry Burns for the murder of Michelle Martinko. In August of 2020 he was sentenced to life in prison without parole.

tigation into Paula's death, it had likely been so contaminated by floodwater as to render it unusable. "Public enemy number one to DNA is humidity," he said. And without DNA, "solvability" in a decades-old crime was low.

He explained that even the Martinko case, with its positive genetic match, was far from open-and-shut. It was rare to employ DNA evidence during a murder trial in the United States. When I expressed shock at this (they use DNA in the movies all the time!), Denlinger explained that the defendants in these cases often pleaded, meaning they never made it into a courtroom. At the time of our conversation, even the case of the Golden State Killer, one of the most famous for the employment of DNA, was still in the future, scheduled to begin preliminary hearings a few months after the case against Jerry Burns started in February 2020. Point being, there was next to no precedent for how to explain genetic genealogy to a jury in a way that made it sound believable.

Denlinger and his team were working with limited time, on a limited budget. With no DNA, no fingerprints, no physical evidence, it simply wasn't worth spending those resources on Paula when there were other cold cases, Maureen Brubaker Farley's for one, that were more promising, that possessed more "solvability."

This didn't prevent Denlinger from engaging Susan and me on some of the ins and outs of Paula's case. He even asked at one point, if we were to recommend that the police circle back to any of the people from the file, who would they be? (We suggested Sturgeon's accomplice in his counterfeit scheme and the kid who'd ridden around with Lonnie Bell on the night Paula disappeared.) But when I look back on the overall tone of the conversation, I'm pretty sure those interviews fall at the end of Denlinger's list of things to do. I expected this, and it was disappointing.

Off the highway on the west side of the river, Susan and I saw mountains of earth being moved by diggers and backhoes.

"The levee," she said, when I asked.

Progress, I had thought. But when I looked into it later, I found that the city was a long way from finishing its flood-safety measures. A *Gazette* story published on the ten-year anniversary of the flood projected 2035 for completion. Until then the city was still at risk. Even after, as long as the levees went untested, no one could know whether they would hold.

Beth DeBoom, a Cedar Rapidian who had lived through the flood and had dedicated much of her time to advocating for historic preservation after it, told me about this very real fear. While visiting New Orleans, a bellhop had said to her: Rain is never just rain anymore. "That's how we feel. It could happen again," she told me. Beth was devoted to protesting the demolition of water-damaged houses. She'd even saved a couple herself by moving them, literally, across the city and then rehabilitating them from the studs.* Both her brother's and her father's houses had flooded. Family collections of books had been waterlogged. Both men chose to rebuild their homes rather than sell out to the city, but they lost her grandmother's house completely. For her it was an erasing of

---

* One, in NewBo, functions as Little House Artifacts, an architectural salvage shop, over which is an Airbnb named the Heart House. The other is the White Elephant, originally constructed in the 1870s and which was flooded with twelve feet of water.

history. And, as everything I encountered seemed to do in those days, this too felt like a metaphor for Paula.

DeBoom and I met for lunch on a clear blue afternoon at an historic Czech tavern in NewBo called Little Bohemia. I admitted that the city's interest in razing buildings was counterintuitive to me.

"It's a mindset here, to tear down," she said. But if we tear down, she continued, "the communities, the neighborhoods, our maps of the past are forever lost."

A weathered sign above the bar to my left read: "Sorry we are closed due to flooding." Below the typeface, the flood line was drawn in red nearly ten and a half feet above the floor. The date was Friday, June 13, 2008. I'd seen this sort of thing all over the city. Businesses pointing out high-water marks, signage from condemned buildings. More than ten years on, the flood is still everywhere in Cedar Rapids. To me, mementos like the sign above the bar said: *We were here, and we have survived. We came through this, and we will not forget it. We have learned from the flood. It has made us stronger.*

In 1991, the man Beth DeBoom's mother had been having an affair with shot and killed her during an argument the two were having in a parked car in downtown Cedar Rapids. The man had been tried and convicted, sentenced to life in prison, where he died on the same day that Beth led a protest to save a Cedar Rapids bar that had been devastated by the flood, though to no avail. ("I was in the paper twice that day," she said ruefully.) When discussing the flood, she had said, "It's not ten degrees of separation between flood victims in Cedar Rapids, it's like three. Everybody knows someone." But she could just as easily have been talking about women affected by violence. When I agreed to meet with her, I had no idea her mother had been murdered.

Before she'd thrown herself into her restoration projects, Beth herself had spent a long time writing about her mother's death; it was one way she processed what had happened, one way she made meaning, to hold it up, to make it known. The same work of that sign above the bar.

● ● ●

Before leaving Cedar Rapids, I returned to Mt. Calvary Cemetery. What was white and barren before was now green and lush. Our landmark trees were covered with leaves winking in the breeze. The rectangles of grass were in various stages of growth—some thick as shag carpet, others thin and brand-new baby green.

I walked up and down the rows scanning the headstones, the heat on me like a wet blanket. Susan, just down the slope from me, was doing the same so that we were systematically working our way toward each other. And then I found her. Etched into the granite were the words: "Paula Jean Oberbroeckling Feb. 25, 1952 / July 11, 1970." Encroaching crabgrass made the edges soft as a tattered business card.

I felt my throat tighten, called out to Susan who was close now. I must have appeared upset because she looked at my face and then walked away as if to give me space. In my hand I held three sunflowers, which I'd purchased at a flower shop a couple blocks outside the cemetery. I chose yellow for friendship, for sun and warmth, for joy, for Paula.

I wondered whether Paula would have been surprised to hear that more than four decades after her death, a woman who'd never met her, who was from another place, another time, would become so consumed by what had happened to her that, despite having a young family to attend to, she would find her way to Cedar Rapids not once but three times to try to find her. Because the truth was, I could still lose the better part of a day following a Paula lead. Like Susan I will never be able to resist a tip, I will always answer a call, always consider a new angle. Paula will always be a question I ask.

I leaned over and laid the flowers at an angle above Paula's name, hoping that had she known about me and my quest, she would have understood that I came as a friend and that I was on her side. That what happened to her matters. Her story matters.

One night, not long after that last trip, I was lying in my son's bed listening to him sound out words in an early reader. I was trying to encourage him while simultaneously entertain my daughter. She had a toy veterinary kit, which came with Velcro bandages, a plastic thermometer, and a play tube of ointment. She squeezed it into her hand and asked me to close my eyes. I did and felt her fingers ladybug their way over my forehead, my temples, my cheekbones. "I'm putting on your sunscreen, Mama," she whispered in my ear so as not to interrupt her brother. Then, "Would you like a snack?" I told her I would, and she reached down into the bag to find something to pretend was food.

As she handed me a banana, which was really the plastic thermometer, she looked into my eyes and, nodding, said, "You are the baby. And I am the mama."

"OK," I said.

"Now let me give you a kiss."

When I offered her my cheek, she became annoyed. "No, like this," she said, and pulled my head down to her height, where she pretended to push back bangs I did not have in order to put her lips on my forehead, the same thing I do to her every night when I tuck her in. She wasn't being just any mama; she was being me.

I recently heard a report on the news about a woman who, while jogging, was flashed not once, but twice by some crazy outlier (my words). Rather than flee, the woman chased the man down, tackling him to the ground and shouting out to passersby to phone the police. None did, and the woman lost her grip on the man when she reached for her own phone, allowing him to get away. But still. This story. The woman is a former Israeli soldier, so she has trained for speed and strength. But it took more than that for her to decide she would not tolerate this aggression. It took self-assurance, self-reliance, the capability of being incensed.

The newscasters framed the story as one about a man who'd messed with the wrong woman, implying that there was a *right* woman to harass, a weak one I assume, maybe compliant. So the messaging is wrong. But still, I can't imagine this man having it in him to ever flash another woman again. "You should have seen his face," the woman said into the camera in the clip I found online. "He was terrified." Maybe my daughter will do this, if not literally then metaphorically; or at least she will pick up her phone and call the police in order to help another woman who has tackled some crazy outlier; or she will pick up her pen and write about it as I have.

Acknowledgments

THE CIRCUMSTANCES SURROUNDING PAULA'S LIFE and death have consumed me for more than six years. During this time virtually everyone I know has played some role in support of my pursuit—acting as sounding board or engaged listener, lending knowledge or time, and, most important, demonstrating over and over that you didn't have to know Paula to be incensed by what happened to her.

I am forever indebted to Susan Taylor Chehak—for bringing this project to me, for not taking "no" for an answer, for serving as my indefatigable researcher and sidekick, for answering every call, text, and email, for making me think deeply about my own womanhood, and especially for showing such confidence in me. Without you, this book would not exist.

Thank you to the Oberbroecklings for trusting Susan with your story and for speaking to us both over the years. And further to everyone who sat for interviews with Susan and with me. The topics were charged and emotional, and I'm so grateful for your willingness to trust me with your stories and with your hearts. I hope I have done your experiences justice.

Thank you to my agent, Duvall Osteen, who knew long before I did that Paula's story was worthy of a book. Your careful guidance and encouragement have opened worlds for me. Thank you to my acquiring editor, Ashley Patrick, for your belief in this project, and to the editor who saw me through my revisions, Melanie Tortoroli. Working with you, Melanie, has always felt like sparkling. Your thoughtful approach and inspired feedback have added so much complexity and depth to this book. Thank you too to Mo Crist, Erin Lovett, Meredith McGinnis, Nancy Palmquist, Rebecca Munro, and the rest of the team at Norton.

Thank you to those who helped with valuable background, sitting for long interviews, particularly Stephanie Coontz, Rosana Klajner, Gillian Frank, and Sara Sedlacek.

I'm so appreciative to those in Cedar Rapids who ushered me through my trips, providing guidance or background information or directions or a place to stay: Mary Susan Taylor, Jared Taylor, Allen Taylor, and Robert Riley.

Thank you to all my early readers—Meakin Armstrong, Erika Anderson, Helen Wan, Carol Clouse, Megan Feeney, Quintan Ana Wikswo, Abby Sher, Brian Schwartz, Suzanne Cope, Elizabeth Isadora Gold, Lisa Selin Davis, Aimee Molloy, and Laura Allen. And to the reader who has seen this book more than any other—from a two-paragraph idea to an essay, through the proposal and nearly every major draft after—John Fischer. I am so grateful for your brain, your heart, and your unflagging support of my work.

Thank you to Hope Edelman and Nancy Rawlinson and Carrie Lamanna, editorial shapers and coaches extraordinaire. Each of you helped me at crucial turning points during my journey. Thank you too to my fact checker, Ewa Beaujon, whose attention to detail and consideration of nuance was key to getting as close as possible to some semblance of truth.

Thank you to my mentors and teachers: Susanna Sonnenberg, Robert Polito, Phillip Lopate, Eric Adler, Linda Breche-isen, Andy Wang, and Michael Archer. And to Lacy Crawford for your strength and conviction, which came at just the moment I needed it.

Thank you to Muhammad, Gloria, and Chris for lending your expertise. Thank you to Leila, Jenny, and the Harvard Mommas for your steadfast support and for being strong women. I look up to you always. And thank you especially to Ashley Muse, who has never failed to live up to her name. Even with the whole country between us, you've served as a constant inspiration for this book. Your words echoed in my head as I wrote and do still.

Thank you to my father for all the ways you help take care of my family and for teaching me that the world is big and that there are no wrong choices, only different paths. And the biggest thank you to my mother for being the very best role model and the very best friend. You demonstrate every single day the vast potential of personhood. I am the woman I am today because of you.

Thank you to my husband, Parker, for never letting me turn away from this project even when it was difficult, even when I thought I might fail. Your love and encouragement have helped me become the writer and woman I always wanted to be. And thank you to my children for whom this book became a mission. I want a better world for you more than I want anything.

Notes

THIS BOOK BEGAN AS AN INVESTIGATION INTO A TRUE CRIME and evolved into a braided work of narrative nonfiction including research, investigation, memory, speculation, association, history, and memoir. During the more than six years that I worked on the project, its themes became for me a metaphor for everything.

For the sections based in my own past and history, I've relied on my memory, checking family stories, dates, and names with my parents. For the sections about Susan's past, I used both hours of formal recorded interviews as well as our untold time spent together reporting on the case. I took three trips to Cedar Rapids explicitly for this book. Susan has taken many.

Susan obtained a court order to procure Paula's police file and witness statements in 1999. In 2008, she recorded interviews with Lynn, Tim, and Carol Oberbroeckling, Debbie Kellogg, Robert Williams, and Detectives Jelinek and Millsap. She interviewed Paula's friends George Steinke, Steve Scheib, Delilah Greene, and Rick Williams, as well as medical examiner Dr. Percy Harris. She also interviewed Art Pennington, a Negro Leagues baseball player who hosted poker games in Oak Hill in Paula's day, and Perry Harris, the man who shot Ernie Jordan.

In the years that followed, I was able to conduct my own interviews with Debbie Kellogg, Tim Oberbroeckling, and Detective Steinbeck. Unfortunately, by the time I came on board, Carol Oberbroeckling, Detectives Millsap and Jelinek, and Percy Harris were all deceased. I was able to expand Susan's research by speaking with the nurse mentioned by Steinbeck, Shermalayne (the woman who was given an abortion by Tom Sturgeon), Fred Dumbaugh, Larry Martin, J.D. Smith, Matt Denlinger, and Lonnie Bell, as well as numerous other people not directly related to Paula's case, including Lovie Bassett, Kathy McHugh, Carol Kean, Jeni Schmidt, Beth DeBoom, Gillian Frank, and Stephanie Coontz.

Where it isn't clear in the text exactly where a fact came from, I've tried to point to my process in the following notes.

Chapter 1: The Crime

In order to reconstruct the sequence of events that took place on the night Paula disappeared, I've relied on multiple sources, corroborating information wherever I could. The details come mainly from the reports made by detectives in the police file and the statements taken from witnesses by investigators after Paula's body was found—specifically from Ben Carroll, Lonnie Bell, Robert Williams, Carol Oberbroeckling, Lynn Oberbroeckling, and Debbie Kellogg. I also used the interviews Susan conducted with Carol and Lynn Oberbroeckling and Robert Williams in 2008 and my own interviews with Debbie Kellogg conducted in 2019. When statements conflicted, I did my best to double-source information or to choose what seemed to fit with whatever was understood at the time, choosing to complicate those events with inconsistencies later. For example, Robert's alibi on the night that Paula disappeared continues to puzzle me. As far as I can tell, the police never asked him directly where he was that night, and his supposed whereabouts only came up during Ben Carroll's lie-detector test. In this first chapter I go with the accepted narrative: Robert was at Butch Hudson's all-night party. Then I raise and question this premise in Chapter 7, "The Detective."

 2 **The evening had been:** This is according to Ben Carroll's police statement.
 3 **one of whom was Debbie Kellogg:** In almost all cases when speaking of women who knew Paula, I've chosen to use their maiden names—that is, the names they used at the time. For

other women included in the book who never knew Paula, I've used married names where applicable.

4 **Around 1 a.m.:** Pinning down exactly when Paula left her house in the early hours of July 11th has been difficult. In her police statement, Debbie said that Paula left at 2 a.m. However, the merchant policeman said he helped Paula with her car sometime between 1 and 2 a.m., and the two girls who corroborated his story said that they saw Paula stopped in front of the old post office at 1:15. Paula's house was about fifteen minutes, maybe less, from the post office, so I've gone with 1 a.m., knowing that I could be off by as much as 45 minutes.

4 **Between 9 and 9:30:** This is according to the statement Ben gave to police after Paula's body was found. Debbie corroborates this timing.

5 **Paula was probably:** The quoted material comes from Carol's interview with Susan.

7 **She was friendly with Joe Hladky:** The account of Carol's conversations with Hladky comes from Carol.

Chapter 2: An Inheritance

The details surrounding the murder of Stephanie Schmidt come from conversations I had with her sister Jeni Schmidt, from my own memory, and from coverage in the *Kansas City Star* following her death in 1993.

15 **But Stephanie didn't know that:** https://law.justia.com/cases/kansas/supreme-court/1995/71-412-3.html.

21 **Ray Rice, a running back:** Ken Belson, "After Punch Is Seen, Rice Is Out," *New York Times*, September 9, 2014, sec. A.

21 **female bloggers were threatened:** Nick Wingfield, "Feminist Critics of Video Games Facing Threats," *New York Times*, October 16, 2014, sec. A.

21 **more than fifty women:** Bill Carter, Graham Bowley, and Lorne Manly, "Comeback by Cosby Unravels as Accounts of Rape Converge," *New York Times*, November 20, 2014, sec. A.

22 **states across the country:** Elizabeth Nash et al., "Laws Affecting Reproductive Health and Rights: 2015 State Policy Review," Guttmacher Institute, accessed November 27, 2019, www.guttmacher.org.

Chapter 3: The Girl

Nearly all of the details about Paula's young life that appear in this and in the following chapters come from the interviews Susan conducted with Lynn and Carol Oberbroeckling in person, in their homes in Cedar Rapids, Iowa, in 2008.

29 **In a portrait photograph:** I spent nearly six years believing the photo referenced here was Paula's senior high school yearbook picture. It could be at a glance—in the photo that actually ran in the 1970 Washington Monument yearbook, Paula is wearing the same shirt, her hair is parted in the same way, the camera's perspective is the same—but it is not. The look on Paula's face is night and day. The photo that ran in her yearbook is missing all the fire and confidence of this other photo, which, it turns out, was published on the front page of the *Gazette* alongside the paper's coverage of the identification of Paula's body. I can only guess that it was an outtake from her senior photo shoot.

44 **In *The Beauty Myth*:** Naomi Wolf, *The Beauty Myth: How Images of Beauty Are Used Against Women* (New York: William Morrow, 1991), 31.

45 **Naomi Wolf identifies:** Wolf, *The Beauty Myth*, 284.

Chapter 4: Her Birthright

For a window into Carol's young life, I spent an afternoon at the Cedar Rapids branch of the Genealogical Society of Linn County, located in the basement of the Iowa Masonic Library and Museum, a gorgeous historic building with Art Deco interiors in marble and brass. A kind woman there helped me to locate both Carol and Jim's yearbooks from the mid-1940s as well as family trees on both sides and public records from the couple's divorce. Carol was stunning in every single photograph I found of her. Jim not as much, goofy with big ears when he was young. But as Susan said, "He grew into his face."

50 **indeed, a third of the marriages:** Stephanie Coontz, *Marriage, a History: From Obedience to Intimacy, or How Love Conquered Marriage* (New York: Viking, 2005), 252.

50 **African American marriages:** R. Richard Banks and Su Jin Gatlin, "African American Intimacy: The Racial Gap in Marriage," *Michigan Journal of Race and Law* 11 (2005): 120.

50 **Divorced Catholics were forbidden:** Michael Paulson, "As Vatican Revisits Divorce, Faithful Long for Acceptance," *New York Times*, January 25, 2015, sec. A.

51 **Until October 1974:** *United States Code, 2011 Edition*, U.S. Government Publishing Office, Title 15: Commerce and Trade, Chapter 41, Subchapter 4, https://www.govinfo.gov /content/pkg/USCODE-2011-title15/html/USCODE-2011 -title15-chap41-subchapIV.htm.

51 **A man's financial outlook:** Karen C. Holden and Pamela J. Smock, "The Economic Costs of Marital Dissolution: Why Do Women Bear a Disproportionate Cost?" *Annual Review of Sociology* 17 (August 1991): 51.

51 **African American women:** Holden and Smock, "The Economic Costs of Marital Dissolution," 56.

57 **The median age of marriage:** "Estimated Median Age at First Marriage, by Sex: 1890 to Present," U.S. Census Bureau, September 15, 2004.

Chapter 5: Her Coming of Age

65 **While IQ tests are fraught:** I shared Paula's results with a child psychologist. She compared the Henmon-Nelson test, which is no longer administered, to the WISC (Wechsler Intelligence Scale for Children), the most common IQ test for kids up to age sixteen. The psychologist found studies that said there is a significant equivalence between the tests (in the range of .7 to .9). Meaning Paula's score of 118 on the Henmon-Nelson

has a 70 to 90 percent chance of being equivalent to a "high average" score on the WISC IQ test.

68 **Historian and author Stephanie Coontz describes:** Stephanie Coontz, *A Strange Stirring: The Feminine Mystique and American Women at the Dawn of the 1960s* (New York: Basic Books, 2011), 176. Coontz cites Barbara J. Risman and Elizabeth Seale, "Betwixt and Be Tween: Gender Contradictions Among Middle Schoolers," in *Families as They Really Are*, ed. Barbara J. Risman (New York: W. W. Norton, 2010).

68 **Homicides, globally:** United Nations Office on Drugs and Crime, "Homicide and Gender" (2015), https://www.heuni.fi /material/attachments/heuni/projects/wd2vDSKcZ/Homicide _and_Gender.pdf.

71 **"one of those wheelie":** The quoted material from this and the next sentence comes from Carol's interview with Susan.

74 **There were no popular television shows:** Ann Fessler, *The Girls Who Went Away: The Hidden History of Women Who Surrendered Children for Adoption in the Decades Before Roe v. Wade* (New York: Penguin, 2006), 116.

75 **Children of divorce:** I conducted an interview with historian Stephanie Coontz, who discussed the judgment and social isolation attendant in being a child of divorce in the decades after the war.

Chapter 6: The Black Boyfriend

The evolution of Robert and Paula's relationship and the reactions of Paula's family and friends to it come from interviews with Robert Williams conducted by Susan in 2008 (Robert has since died) as well as information from the police file and the interviews Susan conducted with Carol and Lynn Oberbroeckling and with Paula's friends and acquaintances, including Rick Williams, Debbie Kellogg, and George Steinke, and those I conducted with Debbie Kellogg, Larry Martin, and Kathy McHugh. The background about the effect of the civil rights movement on Cedar Rapids and more specifically on Washington High School comes from interviews with Rick Williams and Lovie Bassett, from articles published at the time in the *Gazette* (note: the paper changed its name from the *Cedar*

Rapids Gazette to the *Gazette* in 1979), and from two collections of local oral histories—together totaling more than a dozen interviews and hundreds of pages. The first, about the civil rights movement in Linn County, was organized by the African American Museum of Iowa and shared with me by the curator, Felicite Wolfe. And a second, more general series, put together by the Linn County Historical Society, in which a number of members of the Black community were included. The story of Albert Carr and Warren McCray comes from coverage of the altercation in the *Gazette* as well as from Susan's interview with Rick Williams. The story of Carol calling the police to fetch Paula from Robert's house comes from Detective James Steinbeck, who told it in a number of ways to both Susan and me.

81 **In 1954, the U.S. Supreme Court:** *Brown v. Board of Education*, 347 U.S. 483 (1954).

82 **The population of the city:** 1970 United States Census.

82 **There was an uproar:** In 1999, Percy Harris donated the taped debate over whether to sell his family the land (among other effects) to the University of Iowa. Dick Hogan, "Harrises Donate Documents, Tape of Lot Sale Debate," *Gazette*, February 19, 1999, 1.

86 **Carol was aware that Paula:** The story of the state basketball tournament and Carol's discovery of Robert's race comes from Lynn's interview.

90 **Fifty years seems not so long:** *Loving v. Virginia*, 388 U.S. 1 (1967).

90 **Secretary of State Dean Rusk:** Margaret Talbot, "Wedding Bells," *The New Yorker*, May 21, 2012.

92 **Though the *Gazette*'s coverage:** "Charge Will Be Filed in School Fight," *Cedar Rapids Gazette*, January 10, 1963, 1.

Chapter 7: The Detective

Much of this chapter is constructed out of the interviews with Detective James Steinbeck conducted in 2014 by Susan and in 2019 by me. I was able to verify Steinbeck's accounts of the scandals within the CRPD during the years leading up to and after Paula's death using the *Gazette*'s extensive coverage of the events at the time. The phone call I had with the nurse occurred in 2014, not long after Steinbeck found Susan and posted on her website. The nurse has since died. Also employed were interviews with CRPD detectives Kenneth Millsap and Charles Jelinek conducted by Susan before I came on board. Both men are now deceased. (Wally Johnson, the police captain at the time of Paula's death, declined to speak with Susan when she approached him. He has also died in the interim.) I refer to portions of the police file and witness statements in order to complicate the "accepted" narrative.

98 **In 1968, the University of:** Rachel Benson Gold, "Lessons from Before *Roe*: Will Past Be Prologue?" *Guttmacher Policy Review* 6, no. 1 (2003).

98 **Renal failure, for example:** Patricia G. Miller, *The Worst of Times: Illegal Abortion—Survivors, Practitioners, Coroners, Cops, and Children of Women Who Died Talk About Its Horrors* (New York: Harper Perennial, 1993), 327–28.

99 **a front-page story in the *Gazette*:** Dale Kueter, "C.R. Police Department Dissension Explored," *Cedar Rapids Gazette*, July 8, 1973, 1.

101 **Zacek's lawyers heard about it:** *Zacek v. Brewer*, 241 N.W.2d 41 (1976). https://law.justia.com/cases/iowa/supreme -court/1976/58039-0.html.

102 **It's been forty-nine years:** Juliet Muir, "Family of Maureen Brubaker Farley Looking Answers on 47th Anniversary of Her Murder," September 14, 2018, accessed September 3, 2020, https://www.nbcnews.com/feature/cold-case-spotlight/family -maureen-brubaker-farley-looking-answers-47th-anniversary -her-murder-n909851.

102 **And *Escobedo v. Illinois*:** http://www.mirandawarning.org/ historyofmirandawarning.html.

108 **humans depend on the construction:** David Aaronovitch, *Voodoo Histories: The Role of Conspiracy Theory in Modern History* (New York: Riverhead, 2010), 369.

113 **He pleaded guilty:** *State v. Gideon*, 257 Kan. 591 (1995). https://law.justia.com/cases/kansas/supreme-court/1995/71 -412-3.html.

115 **The Oberbroecklings, the Farleys:** Martin Kaste, "Open Cases: Why One-Third of Murders in America Go Unresolved," NPR, *Morning Edition*, March 30, 2015.

Chapter 8: The City

The descriptions of Cedar Rapids in the 1960s when Paula was alive and the city's history prior to that come from *Tales of the Town: Little-known Anecdotes of Life in Cedar Rapids* by Ralph Clements and *Cedar Rapids: The Magnificent Century* by Harold F. Ewoldt.

119 **Kansas City proper has:** fact-finder.com.

120 **With a population of about:** http://worldpopulationreview .com/us-cities/.

122 **The decades that followed:** Harold F. Ewoldt, *Cedar Rapids: The Magnificent Century* (Chatsworth, CA: Windsor Publications, 1988); Ralph Clements, *Tales of the Town: Little-known Anecdotes of Life in Cedar Rapids* (Cedar Rapids: Stamats, 1967).

Chapter 9: The White Boyfriend

This section comes from interviews I conducted with Debbie Kellogg and Larry Martin, and from interviews Susan conducted with Robert, Lynn, and Carol Oberbroeckling. I also used portions of the police file and witness statements to re-create the sequence of events regarding Paula's relationships with Lonnie and with Robert.

125 **but she was considering:** A friend told the police this. It is recorded in the case file.

128 **In 1962, Gloria Steinem wrote:** Gloria Steinem, "The Moral Disarmament of Betty Coed," *Esquire*, September 1, 1962, 97.

129 **There were laws in several states:** Elaine Tyler May, *America and the Pill: A History of Promise, Peril, and Liberation* (New York: Basic Books, 2010), 72.

129 **they were also getting unintentionally pregnant:** May, *America and the Pill*, 83.

129 **only 15.2 percent of women:** National Center for Education

Statistics, "120 Years of American Education: A Statistical Portrait," Figure 2: Percent of 20- to 24-year-olds and 25- to 34-year-olds enrolled in school, by sex: 1940 to 1991, p. 7, accessed December 3, 2019, https://nces.ed.gov/pubs93/93442.pdf.

130 **The fear was that educating:** Fessler, *Girls Who Went Away*, 8.

130 **one that painted unmarried Black:** Rickie Solinger, *Wake Up Little Susie: Single Pregnancy and Race Before Roe V. Wade* (New York: Routledge, 1992), 85.

133 **" 'The periods of violent behavior' ":** "Psychiatry: The Wife Beater & His Wife," *Time*, September 25, 1964.

137 **If the woman in question:** Jeani Chang et al., "Homicide: A Leading Cause of Injury Deaths Among Pregnant and Postpartum Women in the United States, 1991–1999," *American Journal of Public Health* 95, no. 3 (March 2005): 471–77.

137 **Even without a pregnancy:** Emiko Petrosky et al., "Racial and Ethnic Differences in Homicides of Adult Women and the Role of Intimate Partner Violence—United States, 2003–2014," *Morbidity and Mortality Weekly Report* 66 (July 21, 2017): 741–46, https://www.cdc.gov/mmwr/volumes/66/wr/mm6628a1.htm.

137 **Victimizations are at their highest:** Jacquelyn C. Campbell et al., "Risk Factors for Femicide in Abusive Relationships: Results from a Multisite Case Control Study," *American Journal of Public Health* 93, no. 7 (July 2003), https://www.ncbi.nlm.nih.gov/pmc/articles/PMC1447915/.

Chapter 10: The Timeline

The timelines for the night Paula disappeared were constructed by piecing together statements given to the police after Paula's body was found as well as interviews conducted by the police at the time. I did my best to corroborate stories where I could and, if I couldn't, then I tried to point out the inconsistencies. At the same time I didn't want to bog the reader down with needless detail. For example, the police interviewed Angie Nejdl and her roommate as well as both Ben and Lonnie, so there were four accounts of Lonnie and

Ben's hangout at Angie's house. They all differ slightly, but they had commonalities, and for the most part I went with the consensus and also what seemed reasonable.

148 **A couple summers before:** "Charges Follow Arrest of Eight in Narcotic Raid," *Cedar Rapids Gazette*, July 15, 1968, 2.

149 **Lonnie and his buddy:** "2 Arrested Following Disturbance," *Gazette*, October 17, 1979, 8c.

Chapter 11: The Flood

The descriptions of the flood of 2008 and Cedar Rapids' response to it came from my experience of being in the city at the time as well as from talking to many residents who lived through the disaster: people who lost homes, who had to clean out businesses.

155 **Seven years before that morning:** Cedar Rapids: City of Five Seasons, "Flood of 2008 Facts & Statistics," accessed December 1, 2019, http://www.cedar-rapids.org/discover_cedar_rapids /flood_of_2008/2008_flood_facts.php.

157 **"When the traumatic events":** Judith Herman, *Trauma and Recovery: The Aftermath of Violence—From Domestic Abuse to Political Terror* (New York: Basic Books, 1992), 7.

159 **Who will support us:** According to Judith Herman, "The core experiences of psychological trauma are disempowerment and disconnection from others. Recovery, therefore, is based upon the empowerment of the survivor and the creation of new connections." Herman, *Trauma and Recovery*, 133.

160 **in advanced cases of scurvy:** Rebecca P. Sinkler, Review of *Hoosh: Roast Penguin, Scurvy Day, and Other Stories of Antarctic Cuisine* by Jason C. Anthony, *New York Times*, December 2, 2012, Sunday Book Review, 16.

160 **old wounds will literally reopen:** Alexander J. Michels, "Vitamin C and Skin Health," Linus Pauling Institute, Oregon State University (2011–2020), accessed August 4, 2020, https:// lpi.oregonstate.edu/mic/health-disease/skin-health/vitamin -C#reference31.

160 **"the imprints of trauma on body":** Bessel van der Kolk, *The Body Keeps the Score: Brain, Mind, and Body in the Healing of Trauma* (New York: Penguin, 2014), 205.

162 **of women who'd been raped:** Herman, *Trauma and Recovery*, 73.

164 **"We really feel that we are":** Susan Saulny, "Flooded Iowa City Rebuilding and Feeling Just a Bit Ignored," *New York Times*, August 27, 2009, sec. A.

165 **in 2017 alone:** Federal Bureau of Intelligence, "Murder Victims: by Race, Ethnicity, and Sex, 2017," Crime in the United States 2017, accessed December 3, 2019, https://ucr.fbi.gov/crime-in -the-u.s/2017/crime-in-the-u.s.-2017/tables/expanded-homicide -data-table-1.xls.

165 **"Remembering and telling the truth":** Herman, *Trauma and Recovery*, 1.

Chapter 12: The Double Bind

Rickie Solinger's excellent *Wake Up Little Susie: Single Pregnancy and Race Before Roe V. Wade* provided essential background in my understanding of what young women, both Black and white, faced if they became pregnant in the years leading up to 1973. The story of Paula's trip to Florida came from information in the police file as well as Susan's interview with Delilah Greene.

171 **Or Debbie could have told Lynn:** Today, Debbie claims not to remember whether or not she told the Oberbroecklings that Paula thought herself pregnant. But Debbie does admit that it's a possibility.

171 **Single mothers were stigmatized:** "In explaining society's response to the single pregnant female after the war, Sara Edlin, the director of a large maternity home in New York wrote, '[Society] regards illegitimacy as an inroad on the family's stability and permanency, and repels it by ostracizing the unwed mother.'" Solinger, *Wake Up Little Susie*, 22.

171 **Under the law, pregnant girls:** Solinger, *Wake Up Little Susie*, 4.

171 **They could be fired:** U.S. Equal Employment Opportunity Commission, "The Pregnancy Discrimination Act of 1978," https://www.eeoc.gov/laws/statutes/pregnancy.cfm.

172 **Black women, on the other hand:** Solinger, *Wake Up Little Susie*, 17.

180 **65 percent of those:** Lawrence B. Finer, "Trends in Premarital Sex in the United States, 1954–2003," *Guttmacher Institute: Public Health Reports* 122 (2007): 76.

Chapter 13: Her Options

I reconstructed the sequence of events surrounding Sharon Wright's journey to Cedar Rapids, the discovery of her body behind a dumpster, the apprehension of Meyers, Geater, and Abodeely, and the legal case against them using the extensive coverage of the matter in the *Gazette*. The *Gazette* followed each advancement in the story. Combined, these stories are an excellent piece of journalism and public record.

187 **Ten other states followed this lead:** Gold, "Lessons from Before *Roe*."

191 **Between 1945 and 1973:** Fessler, *Girls Who Went Away*, 8. As cited in Kathy S. Stolley, "Statistics on Adoption in the United States," *The Future of Children* 3, no. 1, Center for the Future of Children, David and Lucile Packard Foundation (Spring 1993): 30, figure 2, citing P. Maza, "Adoption Trends: 1944–1975," *Child Welfare Research Notes*, no. 9, Administration for Children, Youth, and Families, Washington, D.C. (1984).

193 **The number of illegal abortions:** Gold, "Lessons from Before *Roe*."

193 **douche with Lysol:** Miller, *Worst of Times*, 323–25.

201 **A 1972 Gallup poll found:** Linda Greenhouse and Reva B. Siegel, "Before (and After) *Roe v. Wade*: New Questions About Backlash," *Yale Law Journal* 120, no. 8 (June 2011): 2028–87.

202 **But this still wasn't enough:** James C. Mohr, "Iowa's Abortion Battles of the Late 1960s and Early 1970s: Long-Term Perspectives and Short-Term Analysis," *Annals of Iowa* 50, no. 1 (Summer 1989): 63–89.

Chapter 14: The Phone Call

The material in this section comes from my phone conversation with Shermalayne in 2015. The background on Thomas Sturgeon's comings and goings and doings comes from the *Gazette*'s thorough coverage of his activities as well as from the dozens of advertisements for his businesses that he placed in the paper himself.

208 **At-home pregnancy tests:** Office of National Institutes of Health History, "A Timeline of Pregnancy Testing," accessed December 3, 2019, https://history.nih.gov/exhibits/thinblueline/timeline.html.

208 **In 1970 a woman who:** Erin Blakemore, "This Is What the First Home Pregnancy Test Looked Like," Smithsonianmag.com, June 2, 2015, accessed December 2, 2019, https://www.smithsonianmag.com/smart-news/what-first-home-pregnancy-test-looked-180955478/.

210 **Dumbaugh was convicted:** "Court Fund Pays $150,230 to Victims of Dishonest Lawyers," *Gazette*, April 11, 1990, 7a.

212 **I'd recently encountered:** https://gillianafrank.wordpress.com/.

217 **The shooting death of Ernie:** Roland Krekeler, "C.R. Man Shot to Death: Alleged Assailant Arrested," *Cedar Rapids Gazette*, February 14, 1971, 1.

221 **In 1979, nine years after:** Kurt Rogahn, "C.R. Student, 18, Slain," *Gazette*, December 20, 1979, 1.

221 **This was how the Golden State:** Thomas Fuller, "Genealogy Site Led to the Suspect's Front Door," *New York Times*, April 27, 2018, sec. A.

223 **Robert Williams:** Robert Williams died in Cedar Rapids on August 21, 2020, at the age of seventy.

Chapter 15: The True Crime

In an attempt to figure out why the *Gazette* barely covered Paula's death, I reached out to Mike Deupree, who covered city hall for the *Gazette* starting in 1973. He put me in touch with the police beat reporter who was on staff in 1970. Gary Peterson had written the front-page story about the identification of Paula's body. He had a vague recollection of Paula being killed, but could remember little else.

225 **There are more than 14,000:** *Someone Knows Something*, season 5, episode 2, minute 12:36.

227 **On July 4, 1970:** "Mob Invades Police Station After Fight," *Cedar Rapids Gazette*, July 4, 1970, 1.

236 **Once the essay about the woman:** Kelly Sundberg, "It Will Look Like a Sunset," *Guernica*, April 1, 2014, accessed December 2, 2019, https://www.guernicamag.com/it-will-look -like-a-sunset/.

236 **From its publication:** Kelly Sundberg, *Goodbye, Sweet Girl: A Story of Domestic Violence and Survival* (New York: HarperCollins, 2018).

237 **The media vastly overrepresents:** Zach Sommers, "Missing White Woman Syndrome: An Empirical Analysis of Race and Gender Disparities in Online News Coverage of Missing Persons," *Journal of Criminal Law and Criminology* 106, no. 2 (Spring 2016): 274.

237 **This, despite the fact that Black:** Shannan Catalano et al., "Female Victims of Violence," *Bureau of Justice Statistics*, U.S. Department of Justice, October 23, 2009.

237 **And Black women are murdered:** "When Men Murder Women: An Analysis of 2017 Homicide Data," Violence Policy Center, September 2018, www.vpc.org.

242 **They have been protected:** The Violence Against Women Act, which sought to improve criminal justice and community-based responses to all manner of violence directed at women, expired in 2018, received a temporary extension, and then expired again in February 2019. As of this writing, though it has passed the House, it's been held up in the Senate because of partisan disagreements around provisions including firearms and civil rights protections.

The Equal Rights Amendment, guaranteeing equal protections for men and women under the Constitution, passed in 1972 but has been waiting for ratification for *48 years*. In January 2020, Virginia became the thirty-eighth state to ratify the ERA, which satisfied the threshold for ratification. However, the deadline for states' ratification passed in 1982 (after an initial extension from 1979), which means the passage of the amendment depends on Congress agreeing to another extension. Further complicating matters, there are five states that want to rescind their ratification.

Selected Readings

IN GRADUATE SCHOOL, I LEARNED FROM THE GREAT PHILLIP Lopate that the root of the word "essay" comes from the French *essai*, meaning to try. Thus essays are attempts, stabs at understanding. They make a run at, endeavor to, work toward and sometimes away, not always finding their footing, many times circling but always with the best of intentions, with the goal of reaching some sort of truth. In many ways I consider this work a book-length essay, an attempt at understanding how the death of a woman could go unsolved and then be largely forgotten. The associative nature of the essay lends itself to finding inspiration in all sorts of texts, and that was the case for me. Once I began looking, I found Paula all over the place, in researched nonfiction on the situation of women, in true-crime narratives, in memoirs about the experience of being a woman, and in novels with women at their centers. While this list is not comprehensive, I hope it will serve as a launching pad for anyone interested in any of the topics I've broached in this book.

Critical Studies and Nonfiction

Aaronovitch, David. *Voodoo Histories: The Role of the Conspiracy Theory in Shaping Modern History.* New York: Riverhead Books, 2010.

Berger, John. *Ways of Seeing.* London: British Broadcasting Corporation and Penguin Books, 1972.

Boss, Pauline. *Ambiguous Loss: Learning to Live with Unresolved Grief.* Cambridge, MA: Harvard University Press, 1999.

Coontz, Stephanie. *Marriage, a History: From Obedience to Intimacy, or How Love Conquered Marriage.* New York: Viking, 2005.

———. *A Strange Stirring: The Feminine Mystique and American Women at the Dawn of the 1960s.* New York: Basic Books, 2011.

Fessler, Ann. *The Girls Who Went Away: The Hidden History of Women Who Surrendered Children for Adoption in the Decades Before Roe v. Wade.* New York: Penguin Books, 2006.

Herman, Judith. *Trauma and Recovery: The Aftermath of Violence—From Domestic Abuse to Political Terror.* New York: Basic Books, 1992.

Levine, Peter A. *Trauma and Memory: Brain and Body in a Search for the Living Past.* Berkeley, CA: North Atlantic Books, 2015.

Maloney, Carolyn B. *Rumors of Our Progress Have Been Greatly Exaggerated: Why Women's Lives Aren't Getting Any Easier and How We Can Make Real Progress for Ourselves and Our Daughters.* New York: Modern Times, 2008.

Manne, Kate. *Down Girl: The Logic of Misogyny.* New York: Oxford University Press, 2018.

May, Elaine Tyler. *America and the Pill: A History of Promise, Peril, and Liberation.* New York: Basic Books, 2010.

Miller, Patricia G. *The Worst of Times: Illegal Abortion— Survivors, Practitioners, Coroners, Cops, and Children of Women Who Died Talk About Its Horrors.* New York: Harper Perennial, 1993.

Senior, Jennifer. *All Joy and No Fun: The Paradox of Modern Parenthood.* New York: Ecco, 2014.

Snyder, Rachel Louise. *No Visible Bruises: What We Don't Know About Domestic Violence Can Kill Us.* New York: Bloomsbury, 2019.

Solinger, Rickie. *Wake Up Little Susie: Single Pregnancy and Race Before Roe V. Wade.* New York: Routledge, 1992.

Staal, Stephanie. *Reading Women: How the Great Books of Feminism Changed My Life.* New York: PublicAffairs, 2011.

Taddeo, Lisa. *Three Women.* New York: Avid Reader Press, 2019.

van der Kolk, Bessel A. *The Body Keeps the Score: Brain, Mind, and Body in the Healing of Trauma.* New York: Penguin Books, 2014.

Wolf, Naomi. *The Beauty Myth: How Images of Beauty Are Used Against Women.* New York: William Morrow, 1991.

Essay

Adichie, Chimamanda Ngozi. *Dear Ijeawele, or a Feminist Manifesto in Fifteen Suggestions.* New York: Knopf, 2017.

Beard, Mary. *Women & Power: A Manifesto.* New York: Liveright Publishing, 2017.

Bolin, Alice. *Dead Girls: Essays on Surviving an American Obsession.* New York: William Morrow/HarperCollins, 2018.

Cusk, Rachel. *A Life's Work: On Becoming a Mother.* New York: Picador, 2001.

Daum, Meghan. *The Unspeakable: And Other Subjects of Discussion.* New York: Farrar, Straus and Giroux, 2014.

Enright, Anne. *Making Babies: Stumbling into Motherhood.* New York: W. W. Norton, 2011.

Harrison, Kathryn. *True Crimes: A Family Album.* New York: Random House, 2016.

Johnson, Lacy M. *The Reckonings.* New York: Scribner, 2018.

Luiselli, Valeria. *Tell Me How It Ends: An Essay in Forty Questions.* Minneapolis: Coffee House Press, 2017.

Manguso, Sarah. *Ongoingness: The End of a Diary.* Minneapolis: Graywolf Press, 2015.

Monroe, Rachel. *Savage Appetites: Four True Stories of Women, Crime, and Obsession.* New York: Scribner, 2019.

Nelson, Maggie. *The Red Parts: Autobiography of a Trial.* Minneapolis: Graywolf Press, 2007.

———. *The Argonauts.* Minneapolis: Graywolf Press, 2015.

Rankine, Claudia. *Citizen: An American Lyric.* Minneapolis: Graywolf Press, 2014.

Solnit, Rebecca. *The Mother of All Questions.* Chicago: Haymarket Books, 2017.

Sontag, Susan. *Regarding the Pain of Others.* New York: Picador, 2004.

Fiction

Albert, Elisa. *After Birth*. New York: Mariner Books, 2016.

Didion, Joan. *Play It as It Lays*. New York: Farrar, Straus and Giroux, 1970.

Erens, Pamela. *Eleven Hours*. Portland, OR: Tin House Books, 2016.

Machado, Carmen Maria. *Her Body and Other Parties: Stories*. Minneapolis: Graywolf Press, 2017.

Morrison, Toni. *The Bluest Eye*. New York: Vintage Books, 1970.

Offill, Jenny. *Dept. of Speculation*. New York: Vintage Contemporaries, 2014.

Shulman, Alix Kates. *Memoirs of an Ex-Prom Queen*. New York: Picador, 1972.

Ward, Jesmyn. *Salvage the Bones*. New York: Bloomsbury, 2011.

Memoir

Johnson, Lacy M. *The Other Side: A Memoir*. Portland, OR: Tin House Books, 2014.

Levy, Ariel. *The Rules Do Not Apply: A Memoir*. New York: Random House. 2017.

Mailhot, Terese Marie. *Heart Berries: A Memoir*. Berkeley, CA: Counterpoint Press, 2018.

Mann, Sally. *Hold Still: A Memoir with Photographs*. New York: Back Bay Books, 2015.

O'Connell, Meaghan. *And Now We Have Everything: On Motherhood Before I Was Ready*. New York: Little, Brown, 2018.

Ptacin, Mira. *Poor Your Soul: A Memoir*. New York: Soho Press, 2016.

Valenti, Jessica. *Sex Object: A Memoir*. New York: Dey Street, 2016.

True Crime

Berendt, John. *Midnight in the Garden of Good and Evil*. New York: Vintage Books, 1999.

Capote, Truman. *In Cold Blood*. New York: Vintage International, 1965.

Carroll, Leah. *Down City: A Daughter's Story of Love, Memory, and Murder.* New York: Grand Central Publishing, 2017.

Ellroy, James. *My Dark Places.* New York: Vintage Books, 1997.

Harrison, Kathryn. *While They Slept: An Inquiry into the Murder of a Family.* New York: Ballantine Books, 2009.

Imbrie, Ann E. *Spoken in Darkness: Small-Town Murder and a Friendship Beyond Death.* New York: Plume, 1994.

Kolker, Robert. *Lost Girls: An Unsolved American Mystery.* New York: Harper Perennial, 2014.

Marzano-Lesnevich, Alexandria. *The Fact of a Body: A Murder and a Memoir.* New York: Flatiron Books, 2017.

McNamara, Michelle. *I'll Be Gone in the Dark: One Woman's Obsessive Search for the Golden State Killer.* New York: Harper Perennial, 2018.

Murnick, Carolyn. *The Hot One: A Memoir of Friendship, Sex, and Murder.* New York: Simon & Schuster, 2017.

Nelson, Maggie. *Jane: A Murder.* Berkeley, CA: Soft Skull Press, 2005.